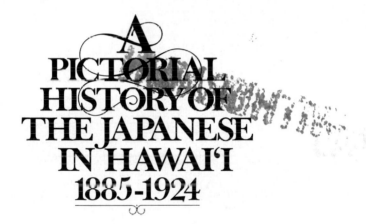

A PICTORIAL HISTORY OF THE JAPANESE IN HAWAI'I 1885-1924

Mother and child, Wainaku village, island of Hawai'i, ca. 1890 (C. Furneaux, photographer).

A PICTORIAL HISTORY OF THE JAPANESE IN HAWAI'I 1885-1924

Franklin Odo

and

Kazuko Sinoto

*Commemorating the Centennial
of the First Arrival
of Government Contracted Japanese Laborers
in Hawai'i*

HAWAI'I IMMIGRANT HERITAGE PRESERVATION CENTER
Department of Anthropology ● Bernice Pauahi Bishop Museum

Bishop Museum Press
Honolulu, Hawai'i
1985

Library of Congress Catalog No. 84-45978

ISBN-0-930897-07-2

First Printing 1985
Second Printing 1985

Bernice Pauahi Bishop Museum
W.D. Duckworth, Director

Editor

Bonnie Tocher Clause

Graphics and Photography

Peter Gilpin

Ben Patnoi

Marc Smith

Design and Layout

Yoshi Hayashi
Associate Creative Director
Ogilvy & Mather Hawaii

Aki Sinoto

Printed in the United States of America
Color Separation: Wy'east Color, Portland, Oregon
Printing: Dynagraphics, Portland, Oregon

CONTENTS

TABLES

GRAPHS

MAPS

ACKNOWLEDGMENTS

This publication of *A Pictorial History of the Japanese in Hawai'i, 1885–1924* was made possible with the generous support and cooperation, understanding and patience of the following institutions and individuals, to whom we express our sincere appreciation.

Funding agencies:
> This project has been executed with a grant from the Commemorative Association for the Japan World Exposition.
> Hawaii Imin Shiryo Hozonkan Association, Honolulu, Hawai'i.

Helping with source materials and photographic loans:
> Diplomatic Record Office, Ministry of Foreign Affairs, Tokyo, Japan;
> Friends of Waipahu Cultural Garden Park; Linda Nakasone Oamilda, Executive Director;
> Hawaii State Archives: Mary Ann Akao, Janet Azama, and Susan Shaner, Librarian Archivists;
> Hawaii Public Television: Christopher R. Conybeare, Producer;
> Hawaiian Sugar Planters' Association; Robert H. Hughes, President, Deborah Ann Saito, Archivist, and Linda K. Menton, Librarian;
> Peabody Museum of Salem, Massachusetts; Gregor Trinkaus-Randall, Librarian, and Kathy Flynn, Photographic Assistant;
> Social Science Research Institute, University of Hawaii at Manoa: Don Topping, Sady Sakai, Marsha Yama, and Nancy Nishioka;
> Taito Co., Nagoya, Japan: Tomohiko Fujimoto;
> Tenri Library in Tenri, Japan, and Honolulu, Hawai'i: Yoshiko Yagi and Hideko Mukuno;
> U.S. Department of Interior, National Park Service, Golden Gate N.R.A.: Irene A. Stachura, Reference Librarian, and John Maounis, Photo Librarian;
> June Arakawa of Hui O Laulima, Honolulu, Hawai'i;
> Takenobu Higa, Honolulu, Hawai'i;
> Arnold Hiura of the *Hawaii Herald*, Honolulu, Hawai'i;
> Hiroshi Kimura of *Chugoku Shimbun*, Yamaguchi Branch, Yamaguchi, Japan;
> Gaylord Kubota, Director of the Alexander and Baldwin Sugar Museum, Pu'unēnē, Maui;
> Hideo Matsunaga of *Sanyu Shimbun*, Tokyo, Japan;
> Kazuo Nakamine, *Pacific Press*;
> Jiro Nakano, Hilo, Hawai'i;
> Kazuyoshi Nakayama of the National Museum of Ethnology, Suita, Japan;
> Takao Nihei, Honolulu Sake Brewery and Ice Co.;
> Kiyoshi Okubo of the *Hilo Times*, Hilo, Hawai'i;
> Michael M. Serikaku, Honolulu, Hawai'i;
> Kiyomi Katsunuma Suzuki, Honolulu, Hawai'i;
> Ryokin Toyohira, Honolulu, Hawai'i;
> Lydia Tsuha, Honolulu, Hawai'i;
> Yoshiko Tsukiyama, Honolulu, Hawai'i;
> Reizo Watanabe and Paul Yempuku of the *Hawaii Hochi*, Honolulu, Hawai'i.

Production Assistance:
  Hawaii Hochi, Honolulu, Hawai'i;
  Innovative Media Inc., Honolulu, Hawai'i;
  Norma Gorst, Honolulu, Hawai'i;
  Ogilvy & Mather Hawaii, Honolulu, Hawai'i;
  Hawaii-Typro, Honolulu, Hawai'i;
  Asa Plans, Tokyo, Japan.

Additonal funding for this publication was received from the following individuals and organizations:
  Clara H. Boyer;
  Takashi Genishi;
  Takenobu Higa;
  Hanako Kimura;
  Miyomatsu Motoyama;
  Joanne Ninomiya;
  Kiyoshi Sasaki;
  Kyohei Tsuji;
  Hui O Laulima;
  Okinawa Nenchosha Club, Lanakila Multi-Purpose Senior Center;
  United Okinawan Association of Hawaii;
  Twenty-One Corporation, Tokyo, Japan.

Apologies are extended to those other contributors whose names could not be included here due to production deadline considerations.

Bishop Museum departments and staff:
  Pat Bacon, Maureen Liu-Brower, Rosemarie S. W. Chang, Bonnie Tocher Clause, Peter Gilpin, Helen H. Leidemann, Aki Sinoto, and Marc Smith of Anthropology;
  Eiko Lynch, Janet Short, and Cynthia Timberlake of the Bishop Museum Library; Robert Benedetto, Business Archives; Clarice Chinen, Debbie Dunn, and Betty Lou Kam of the Photo Collection; Ben Patnoi and Christine Takata of the Photo Lab.; and Lee Motteler of the Pacific Science Information Center; Yoshitami Tasaka, HIHPC field affiliate.
  A special acknowledgment to HIHPC colleagues Dora Jacroux Chang, Acting Manager, and Rhoda Rogers Komuro, Curatorial Assistant, for their assistance in locating and screening thousands of photographs and for their critical contributions and moral support in the preparation of the text and captions.

Franklin Odo
Kazuko Sinoto

PRESERVED ETHNIC HERITAGE
HAWAII IMMIGRANT HERITAGE PRESERVATION CENTER

INTRODUCTION

One hundred years ago, on 8 February 1885, the first group of 944 government-sponsored contract laborers from Japan arrived in Hawai'i aboard the *City of Tokio*. In celebration of this centennial, the Hawai'i Immigrant Heritage Preservation Center (HIHPC) at Bishop Museum has published this pictorial history. Primarily through photographs, this volume shows how the Japanese immigrants met the demand for laborers on the Hawaiian sugar plantations, a need that could not be met by the declining Hawaiian population, and how their labor built much of the sugar economy upon which agribusiness in Hawai'i is based. The book emphasizes the period from the 1885 arrival to 1924, when the United States prohibited Japanese immigration. The immigrants' success is evident in the advances they made and in the many outstanding Hawai'i citizens of Japanese descent, who today include the governor and both United States senators.

The 250 photos presented here are mainly from Bishop Museum collections, with additions from various other sources. The photographs and artifacts from the HIHPC collections document the process of adaptation and cultural change in establishing a new life within the context of a different culture.

The Hawai'i Immigrant Heritage Preservation Center was established at Bishop Museum in November 1976. Its purpose is to preserve the artifacts, documents, and other materials relating to immigrant ethnic groups and to provide for the exhibition and study of these collections. Hawai'i is a land of immigrants, beginning with the first Polynesian settlers. The collections of HIHPC represent not only the Japanese, but also the other groups who came in answer to the call for laborers in the sugar industry: the Chinese, Portuguese, Puerto Ricans, Koreans, Filipinos, and others. All the collected materials help to tell the history of the "common man" and the work that was done to build the Hawai'i of today. At the end of 1983, there were 3,000 artifacts, 3,650 documents, and 1,381 photographs and photo albums curated under the auspices of HIHPC. We are very thankful for the generous donors who have given artifacts, photographs, and documents to the HIHPC collections, and to the charter members who have supported us in various ways.

The HIHPC Japanese collection is based on the planning and efforts of a group of leading Japanese *nisei* (the second generation in Hawai'i) to preserve what they could of the Japanese experience in Hawai'i, including the memories of the hardships and successes. This group, the Yanagi Gori Committee, deserves the thanks of all the researchers who have used the HIHPC materials, as well as of all those to come; with special appreciation to Dr. Baron Goto, Mr. Kiyoshi Okubo, and Mr. Masayuki Tokioka.

While all the immigrant groups to Hawai'i have contributed through labor, culture, and ideas, the 100th anniversary of the arrival of the Japanese contract laborers, sponsored by the Japanese and Hawaiian governments, gives HIHPC a reason to focus this book on the significance of the Japanese in Hawai'i and the early contributions they made.

Dora Jacroux Chang
Acting Manager
HIHPC
January 1985

The family of *gannenmono* Matsugorō Kuwata, ca. 1899.
Matsugorō, a tailor, was nicknamed Umiumi Matsu (Matsu-the-Beard). From left: front, Matsugorō, Seiichi, Meleana with baby Shirō, Lindo; back, Umi, Ome, Kimi.

PROLOGUE

In 1985, Hawai'i celebrates the 100th anniversary of the arrival of the government contract laborers from Japan. This pictorial history is dedicated to the memory of that hardy band of pioneers who braved the unknown to secure better lives. There had been predecessors: it is more than likely that, for centuries, shipwrecked sailors and fishermen had drifted from Japanese waters on the powerful Kuroshio current to Hawaiian shores. There were also the 148 Japanese who had arrived in 1868 as sugar plantation contract laborers, known as the *gannenmono* because they were "People of the First Year" of the Emperor Meiji's reign (1868–1912). But the substance of the story of the Japanese in Hawai'i begins with the arrival on 8 February 1885, of the 944 men, women, and children on board the *City of Tokio*.

By 1924, when Congress prohibited the further immigration of Japanese into the United States and the Territory of Hawai'i, approximately 200,000 Japanese had immigrated, most to work and live on the sugar plantations, which had been rapidly increasing production from the mid-nineteenth century onward. For all of the immigrant groups in Hawai'i, as well as for the native Hawaiians, these first forty years, 1885–1924, were critical in establishing the ethnic, racial, and class boundaries that our present generations are still attempting to understand and transcend. Arriving in such large numbers during a period when Hawai'i was being absorbed into a dynamic America, the Japanese were instrumental in the development of the islands' unique cultural mix.

Historical interpretations often reflect important issues of the period in which they are written. Thus, the topics examined and the perspectives used in this book are distilled from the central concerns of the writers at this point in history, as well as those faced by the subjects during the last 100 years. Two of the most important issues of the latter half of the twentieth century are the extraordinary surge in national, class, racial, ethnic, and women's liberation movements around the world, and the related struggles for redefinition of individual and collective identities. Many of these momentous developments are the legacies of earlier periods of colonialism and imperialism, when indigenous populations and massive numbers of immigrants were caught in historical shifts over which they had no control, and about which few had more than passing comprehension. The Japanese Americans in Hawai'i, like others, are involved in redefining their identities and re-examining their histories. One important aspect of that history involves the background of the first generation of emigrants, the *issei*, and the reasons for their emigration from Japan.

Meiji Emperor, reigned 1867–1912.

After King Kalākaua's visit in 1881, the friendship between the Japanese emperor and the Hawaiian king continued.

King Kalākaua's visit to Japan, 1881.

Left to right, front: Prince Yoshiaki, Lieutenant General; King Kalākaua; Tsunetami Sano, Minister of Finance. Back: Charles H. Judd, Chamberlain; Ryōsuke Tokunō, First Secretary of Finance; William N. Armstrong, Foreign Minister and Head of the Bureau of Immigration of Hawaii.

While the present ʻIolani Palace was under construction, King Kalākaua took a 10-month journey to see the world. His first stop was Yokohama, as the first head of state to visit Japan. Throughout his stay in Tokyo and his tour of the country, he was greeted with the honor accorded royalty.

14

Japan had managed to escape the direct colonial control that involved so many nations and peoples of Asia, Africa, the Americas, and the Pacific. Nevertheless, the threat and fear of interference from western Europe and the United States had a major impact on the direction and speed of Japanese development in the nineteenth century. Government policies, designed to protect national independence and achieve international respect, severely disrupted the lives of millions of Japanese. One result was internal migration from rural areas to towns and cities, as well as from one region to another within Japan. Another result was the great wave of emigration into North and South America, East and Southeast Asia, and the islands of the Pacific, including Hawaiʻi. These population movements were precipitated by a major change in the character of the Japanese government.

Although Japan of the Tokugawa Period (1600–1868) had been remarkably advanced for a feudal state, it was no match for the power of the Western nations. It was this realization that inspired the powerful slogan *fukoku kyōhei* ("rich country, strong military"), which obsessed the Meiji leadership after they took control in 1868. The Tokugawa *shogun* and their major advisers had been fully aware of the power of Western countries because of their close and regular contact with the Chinese and the Dutch in Nagasaki. Thus, by the time Commodore Matthew Perry arrived in 1853 to demand access to Japanese ports, the Japanese had studied the significance of the Opium Wars in China (1839–1842) and the seemingly invincible European movement into Asia. Fundamental disagreements over the appropriate response to this threat eventually led to the overthrow of the Tokugawa and helped to shape the character of the Meiji elite, made up of progressive *samurai* and ambitious businessmen.

The Meiji leaders transformed a weak emperor system into the central pillar of a new political system that drove Japan into the world of modern nation-states. The government introduced reforms to broaden the political base by promoting nationalism, and ended the *samurai* era by conscripting commoners into a modern military. It imposed compulsory education and encouraged widespread adoption of Western cultural practices. The Meiji leaders destroyed the remnants of a village subsistence economy by pushing an extensive series of changes that forced the people and the nation into the modern and industrial era. One effect of these radical changes was the development of a relatively powerful militaristic nation which confronted weaker Asian neighbors in the late nineteenth century. By the early twentieth century, Japan was capable of causing concern among Western imperial powers over potential confrontation in the Pacific. Another result was seen in the millions of *dekasegi* peasants who left their villages to find employment, in a period that demanded increasing reliance on money. When Japan, even with developing industrialization, could not accommodate the masses of *dekaseginin*, the government was forced to concede the wisdom of allowing Japanese to go abroad to work in places like Hawaiʻi.

In the meantime, the Hawaiian Islands were falling under the domination of European and American foreigners, in the very process of colonial domination that the Meiji leaders were working so mightily to avoid. Before Captain James Cook arrived in 1778, an estimated several hundred thousand Hawaiians lived in a complex society in which land was allotted by the chief or chiefs (*aliʻi*), through intermediaries, to commoners (*makaʻāinana*) who produced a wide array of goods from the resources of the forest, cultivated lands, and the sea. The high chiefs and subsidiary groups of lower-ranking chiefs governed large areas (*ahupua'a* and *'ili*) that were parceled out. A degree of luxury, in the form of material goods such as elaborate feather capes and cloaks, and activities such as sports and festivals, was made possible by the expropriation of food and labor from the *maka'āinana*. Nevertheless, there was a strong tradition of common use and sharing, which sustained many of the physical and spiritual needs of the people. In the decades after 1778, however, Hawai'i was caught in the maelstrom of European and American competition that spelled the end of the traditional Hawaiian way of life.

Hawai'i served as a convenient stopping point for traders involved in the China market, and the *ali'i* were quick to use the situation to enrich themselves, using *maka'āinana* labor to harvest sandalwood. The whaling industry, with its ships using Hawai'i as a base for refitting, resources, and recreation, became another source of profit in the early nineteenth century. Thus, by the mid-1800s, there was considerable money available for investment by European and American merchants in Honolulu. With this capital in hand, entrepreneurs in Hawai'i needed to overcome several other obstacles: first, to secure title to the land; second, to secure access to a market; and third, to secure quantities of cheap and controllable labor.

Sugarcane, introduced to Hawai'i by early Polynesian voyagers, was part of the traditional native Hawaiian diet. Small sugar mills had been operated by early Chinese immigrants, but large scale efforts had their direct antecedent in the 1835 establishment of the Koloa Plantation on the island of Kaua'i. Early efforts there helped to convince planters that holding title to the land was crucial. Foreign advisers to the Hawaiian monarchy were instrumental in leading the way — in spite of resistance on the part of the kings and chiefs — to eventual changes in the traditional system of land tenure. In a series of legal acts between 1845 and 1855, land was divided (*māhele*) among the monarchy, the government, and the chiefs, with a small number of claims filed by commoners. The way was cleared for foreigners to acquire and own land.

With money to invest and ready access to large amounts of land, sugar planters needed a reliable market for their product. The dramatic population growth that accompanied the California gold rush of the 1850s provided consumers for Hawaiian agriculture products, including sugar. The American Civil War (1861–1865) disrupted the flow of sugar from the South to the cities of the North, and further increased the demand for Hawaiian sugar. Domestic producers were always seeking protective tariffs against foreign sugar, however, and Hawai'i planters were periodically challenged in their attempts to compete in the American market.

The search for a secure market for their sugar led the planters to negotiations with the United States. The signing of the Reciprocity Treaty of 1876, which lifted the import tax on Hawaiian sugar, did much to speed the eventual overthrow of the Hawaiian monarchy in 1893 and annexation to the United States in 1898. But it was the desperate need for vast amounts of cheap labor that led most directly to the immigration of Japanese to Hawai'i.

The impact of Westerners had taken a severe toll on the sheer numbers of Hawaiians, as well as on their traditional lifestyle, political economy, and autonomy. The imposition of a market economy forced Hawaiians into the labor force in ways similar to the experiences of the *dekaseginin* in Japan. Hawaiians became seamen, worked on plantations and in shops, and, during the gold rush, left for adventure and work on the West Coast. These factors,

Four *gannenmono* in 1922.

From left: Katsusaburō Yoshida, Yoneikichi Sakuma, Sentarō Ishii, and Matsu Aoki.

Table 1
HAWAIIAN SUGAR PRODUCTION, 1837–1928

YEAR	TONS	YEAR	TONS
1837	2	1885	85,695
1840	180	1890	129,899
1845	151	1895	147,627
1850	375	1900	289,544
1855	145	1905	426,428
1860	572	1910	518,127
1865	7,659	1915	646,445
1870	9,392	1920	556,871
1875	12,540	1925	776,072
1880	31,792	1928	904,040

SOURCE: Hawaii Sugar Planters' Association 1929: 96.

The family of *gannenmono* Kintarō Ozawa, Tokyo, 1890.

From left: sitting, Fuji with Matsu, Kenji, Kintarō, and Ume; standing, Itoko, Kenzaburō. Mrs. Ozawa, who had been the only woman among the *gannenmono* to remain in Hawai'i, was deceased.

By 1885, about forty to fifty *gannenmono* remained in Hawai'i, most married to Hawaiians. In 1884, when Iaukea and Irwin were to arrange the conditions for the Japanese immigrants, two *gannenmono*, Tōkichi Miura and Katsusaburō Yoshida, were summoned to tell of their experiences in the previous 17 years in Hawai'i. Itoko Ozawa, the 12-year-old daughter of a *gannenmono*, served as their interpreter.

combined with the decimation of the native Hawaiian population through disease, forced planters to look to foreign sources of labor. Also, in response to the dramatic decline in the number of Hawaiians, from several hundred thousand in pre-Cook days to fewer than sixty thousand in 1866, King David Kalākaua and the court sought immigrant laborers from some ethnic group that might provide "appropriate" partners to increase the part-Hawaiian population.

By 1850, the Masters and Servants Act had laid the legal foundation for control of the plantation labor force, paving the way for a contract-labor system enforceable in the courts. The planters then had the support of the police and judicial power of the state to punish laborers who refused to follow the contract. Shortly thereafter, the Chinese became the first group to be recruited in a systematic and serious way. Until 1883, when the Hawaiian government excluded their laborers, the Chinese were the major immigrant group, although the Portuguese were also recruited beginning in 1878. The Chinese quickly left the plantations for other occupations, however, and the Portuguese were too expensive to import and maintain. All of these considerations combined to make Japan an important potential source of plantation labor.

•   •   •

Relations between the Hawaiian Kingdom and Japan date back to 1860, the latter days of the Tokugawa, when the members of the first Japanese foreign mission stopped briefly in Honolulu on their way to Washington to exchange treaty ratification documents with the United States government. During the 14-day stopover, King Kamehameha IV officially requested the Japanese to consider a Treaty of Friendship. In August 1867, Tokugawa officials finally signed an agreement expressing good will and friendship between Japan and Hawai'i, with the understanding that it was a temporary agreement to begin recruiting sugar plantation laborers. This haphazard recruitment resulted in the 1868 *gannenmono* group, who were shipped out of Yokohama despite the fact that the new Meiji government had refused authorization.

The first group of Japanese laborers was made up of various types, including a few *samurai*, a 13-year-old heavy drinker named Ichigorō, nicknamed Mamushi-no-Ichi or "Ichi the Viper," artists, a hairdresser, cooks, and others hardly prepared to cope with the rigors of sugar plantation work.

Allegations of brutal treatment and expressions of dissatisfaction with the low pay and high prices for daily necessities appeared very quickly, and the Meiji government dispatched an official to investigate conditions in Hawai'i. An agreement was finally reached on 11 January 1870, providing for the return of 40 people to Japan at Meiji government expense. The remaining 108 elected to stay and most were assimilated into the Hawaiian population. The *gannenmono* experience, however, was an unhappy one for the Meiji leaders. It illustrated their relative weakness in the international arena, and made them apprehensive about further emigration of Japanese laborers.

Hawaiian efforts to convince Japan to permit emigration continued with the signing of a Treaty of Commerce and Friendship in August 1871. In 1876, King Kalākaua entertained Captain Ito of the visiting naval vessel, the *Tsukuba*, and asked him to convey the Hawaiian government's continuing interest in Japanese immigration. It was no coincidence that this was the same year in which the Reciprocity Treaty was negotiated. Kalākaua subsequently undertook a trip around the globe and met with Emperor Meiji in March 1881, when he made several important proposals.

First, he proposed a marriage between his niece, the Princess Ka'iulani, and Japan's Prince Komatsu to symbolize friendship between the two island kingdoms. Second, Kalākaua encouraged the Japanese to consider establishing economic colonies in Hawai'i, joining with Hawai'i in a "Union and Federation of Asiatic Nations and Sovereigns" to "maintain their footing against those powerful nations of Europe and America, and to establish their independence and integrity in future." Finally, he suggested that Hawai'i become the first nation to give up extraterritorial rights in Japan (This policy, patterned after the one imposed by Western nations on China, provided for foreign legal jurisdiction over crimes committed by foreigners, even those involving Japanese victims. Japanese courts were powerless to intervene, thus creating a deeply felt sense of national inferiority and humiliation.). All of the proposals were declined by the Japanese, but the expressions of friendship did much to prepare the way for resumption of emigration to Hawai'i.

Attempts to convince the Meiji government to allow Japanese to leave for work on Hawaiian sugar plantations were further intensified in the early 1880s with the appointment of Robert Walker Irwin as, successively, Consul General, Chargé d'Affaires, and Acting Minister of Hawai'i, and the dispatch of John M. Kapena for assistance in the negotiations. In 1883, the Japanese sent a delegation to attend Kalākaua's coronation and to open a consulate in Honolulu. In 1884 Curtis Iaukea, who had been sent to Russia as the Hawaiian government's official representative at the coronation of Alexander III, stopped in Tokyo to help finalize negotiations. He and Irwin returned together to prepare an immigration agreement. Finally, in 1885, the Japanese began arriving in significant numbers, ensuring their substantial role in the subsequent history of Hawai'i.

Prince Yamashina, as a 15-year-old student at the naval school in Tokyo, Japan, 1881.

After a formal meeting with Emperor Meiji, King Kalākaua visited him privately to propose a betrothal between the Japanese prince and Princess Ka'iulani, Kalākaua's niece. The offer was refused through an official letter delivered by a special envoy to Hawai'i in 1882.

The young prince visited Hawai'i as Prince Komatsu on 30 October 1893 when he was a navy lieutenant aboard the Japanese warship *Naniwa*.

Princess Ka'iulani (1875–1899) in *kimono*, Honolulu, 1889.

Miss Riyo Aoki, who had arrived in Hawai'i with the first group of Japanese immigrants in 1885, later worked for the Princess' household after leaving Wainaku plantation.

Japanese farmers harvesting rice, Saitama Prefecture, Japan, ca. 1898.

Street scene, Isezaki-cho, Yokohama, ca. 1898.

18

Table 2
THE POPULATION OF HAWAI'I, 1853–1970: ETHNIC COMPOSITION, DISTRIBUTION, AND RATES OF GROWTH

											CAUCASIANS						
YEARS	TOTAL		HAWAIIANS		PART HAWAIIANS		TOTAL CAUCASIANS		PUERTO RICANS		PORTUGUESE		SPANIARDS		OTHER CAUCASIANS	
	No.	%	No.	%	No.	%	No.	%	No.	%	No.	%	No.	%	No.	%
1853	73,137	100.00	70,036	95.8	983	1.3	1,687	2.3			87	0.1			1,600	2.2
1860	69,800	100.00	65,647	94.1	1,337	1.9	1,900	2.7			85	0.1			1,815	2.6
1866	62,959	100.00	57,125	90.7	1,640	2.6	2,400	3.8			90	0.1			2,310	3.7
1872	56,897	100.00	49,044	86.2	2,487	4.4	2,944	5.2			424	0.7			2,520	4.4
1878	57,985	100.00	44,088	76.0	3,420	5.9	3,748	6.5			486	0.8			3,262	5.6
1884	80,578	100.00	40,014	49.7	4,218	5.2	16,579	20.6			9,967	12.4			6,612	8.2
1890	89,990	100.00	34,436	38.3	6,186	6.9	18,939	21.0			12,719	14.1			6,220	6.9
1896	109,020	100.00	31,019	28.4	8,485	7.8	22,438	20.6			15,191	13.9			7,247	6.7
1900	154,001	100.00	29,799	19.3	7,857	5.1	28,819	18.7			18,272	11.9			10,547	6.8
1910	191,909	100.00	26,041	13.6	12,506	6.5	44,048	23.0	4,890	2.5	22,301	11.7	1,990	1.0	14,867	7.8
1920	255,912	100.00	23,723	9.3	18,027	7.0	54,742	21.4	5,602	2.2	27,002	10.6	2,430	0.9	19,708	7.7
1930	368,336	100.00	22,636	6.1	28,224	7.7	80,373	21.8	6,671	1.8	27,558	7.5	1,219	0.3	44,895	12.2
1940	423,330	100.00	14,375	3.4	49,935	11.8	112,087	26.5	8,296	2.0					103,791	24.5
1950	499,769	100.00	12,245	2.5	73,845	14.8	124,344	24.9	9,551	1.9					114,793	23.0
1960	632,772	100.00	11,294	1.7	91,109	14.4	202,230	32.0							202,230	
1970	768,559	100.00			71,274	9.3	301,429	39.2							301,429	

SOURCE: Nordyke 1977: table 3.

Women plantation workers of various ethnic groups at Kīlauea, Kauaʻi, 1888 (courtesy of Hawaii State Archives).

The Hawaiians were the first plantation workers, followed by the Chinese immigrants in 1852. Other immigrants followed: the Japanese *gannenmono* in 1868; the Portuguese in 1878; Germans and Scandinavians in 1881; the Japanese government contract laborers in 1885; and the Spanish in 1899. Later other groups, such as the Okinawans and Puerto Ricans in 1900, the Koreans in 1903, the Filipinos in 1906, and the Spanish in 1907, were added to the plantation community.

YEARS	CHINESE		JAPANESE		KOREANS		BLACKS		AMERICAN INDIANS		FILIPINOS		OTHERS		YEARS
	No.	%	No.	%	No.	%	No.	%	No.	%	No.	%	No.	%	
1853	364	0.5											67	0.1	1853
1860	816	1.2											100	0.1	1860
1866	1,306	2.1											488	0.8	1866
1872	2,038	3.5											384	0.7	1872
1878	6,045	10.4											684	1.2	1878
1884	18,254	22.7	116	0.1									1,397	1.7	1884
1890	16,752	18.6	12,610	14.0									1,067	1.2	1890
1896	21,616	19.8	24,407	22.4									1,055	1.0	1896
1900	25,767	16.7	61,111	39.7			233	0.2					415	0.3	1900
1910	21,674	11.3	79,675	41.5	4,533	2.4	695	0.4			2,361	1.2	376	0.1	1910
1920	23,507	9.2	109,274	42.7	4,950	1.9	348	0.1			21,031	8.2	310	0.2	1920
1930	27,179	7.4	139,631	37.9	6,461	1.8	563	0.2			63,052	17.1	217	0.1	1930
1940	28,774	6.8	157,905	37.3	6,851	1.6	255	0.1			52,569	12.4	579	0.2	1940
1950	32,376	6.5	184,598	36.9	7,030	1.4	2,651	0.5			61,062	12.2	1,618	0.3	1950
1960	38,197	6.0	203,455	32.2			4,943	0.8	472	0.1	69,070	10.9	12,002	1.9	1960
1970	52,375	6.8	217,669	28.3	9,625	1.3	7,517	1.0	1,216	0.2	95,354	12.4	12,100	1.6	1970

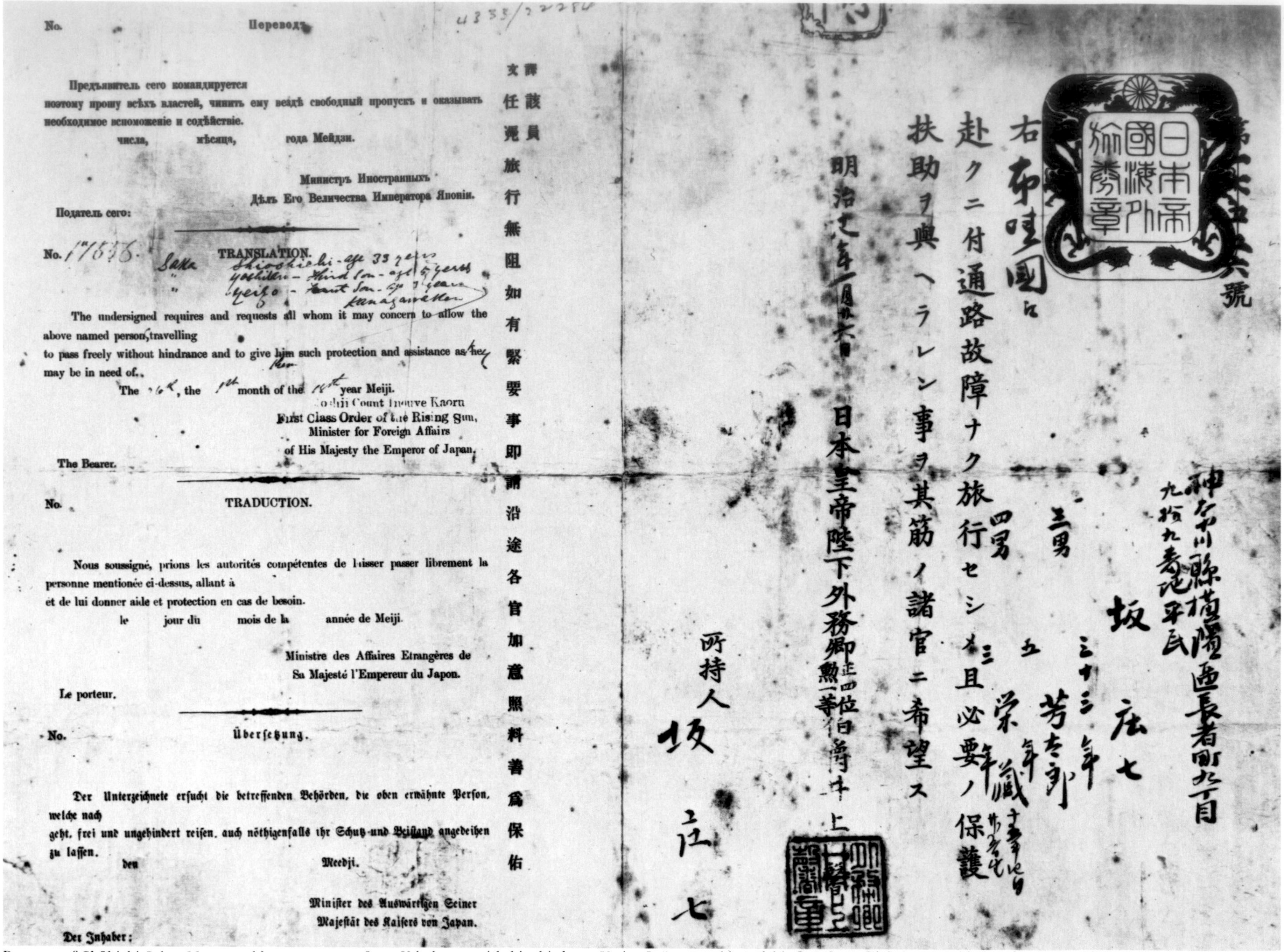

Переводъ.

譯

文

Предъявитель сего командируется поэтому прошу всѣхъ властей, чинитъ ему вездѣ свободный пропускъ и оказывать необходимое вспоможеніе и содѣйствіе.

числа, мѣсяца, года Мейдзи.

Министръ Иностранныхъ Дѣлъ Его Величества Императора Японіи.

Податель сего:

No. 1"856. Saka Shiōhichi – age 33 years
Yoshitarō – Third Son – age 5 years
Yeizo – Fourth Son – age 3 years
kanagawaken

TRANSLATION.

The undersigned requires and requests all whom it may concern to allow the above named person, travelling to pass freely without hindrance and to give him such protection and assistance as they may be in need of.

The 26, the 1st month of the 18th year Meiji.

Count Inouye Kaoru First Class Order of the Rising Sun, Minister for Foreign Affairs of His Majesty the Emperor of Japan.

The Bearer.

No.

TRADUCTION.

Nous soussigné, prions les autorités compétentes de laisser passer librement la personne mentionée ci-dessus, allant à et de lui donner aide et protection en cas de besoin.

le jour du mois de la année de Meiji.

Ministre des Affaires Etrangères de Sa Majesté l'Empereur du Japon.

Le porteur.

No.

Überſetzung.

Der Unterzeichnete erſucht die betreffenden Behörden, die oben erwähnte Perſon, welche nach geht, frei und ungehindert reiſen, auch nöthigenfalls ihr Schutz und Beiſtand angedeihen zu laſſen.

den Meedji.

Miniſter des Auswärtigen Seiner Majeſtät des Kaiſers von Japan.

Der Inhaber:

Passport of Shōhichi Saka, 33-years-old, a commoner from Yokohama, with his third son Yositarō, 5-years-old, and his fourth son Eizō, 3-years-old. Dated 26 January 1885.

RECRUITMENT

Marquis Hirobumi Itō, Prime Minister of Japan in 1885.

Most of the early Japanese immigrants to Hawai'i came from southwestern Japan with the major contributing prefectures being Hiroshima, Yamaguchi, Kumamoto, Fukuoka, and, after 1900, Okinawa. By 1924, when Congress sealed off the United States and its territories from the Japanese, there were just over a quarter of a million *issei* and their children in America, with approximately one-half of them living in Hawai'i.

Conventional wisdom tells us that the emigrants came because of poverty in their villages and the hope of improving their lives, perhaps by saving money and returning to Japan to purchase land for their families. Although a relationship between economic distress and emigration must surely exist in the case of the Japanese, direct correlations are extremely difficult to establish.

Japan of the 1870s and 1880s was a new nation in extraordinary flux. The Meiji oligarchy had to provide compensation to an entire class of *samurai* in exchange for taking over its exclusive rights to political military power. In the countryside, villages felt the effects of massive inflation and, after 1881, a deliberate deflation that caused rice prices to fall nearly 50 percent in 3 years. When R. W. Irwin began recruiting sugar plantation laborers in 1884, there was unemployment, bankruptcy, rioting, political upheaval, and a prolonged depression that seemed to have no end in sight.

Irwin became the essential figure in the era of government-contract labor (*kanyaku imin jidai*) from 1885 to 1894. His efforts led to enormous personal profit and the emigration of nearly thirty thousand Japanese to Hawai'i. After lengthy and difficult negotiations with both the Japanese and Hawaiian governments, Irwin returned to Japan in September 1884 with a contract proposal, a credit line of $40,000, and a list of employers seeking laborers and servants. The Japanese approved the arrangement with the understanding that it was not an official act between two governments, but rather a voluntary agreement between the emigrants and Irwin, acting as a representative of the Hawaiian government. This permitted the Meiji officials to pursue their own foreign policy, aimed at achieving equality with the Western powers.

In October 1884, Irwin wrote to the Governor of Tokyo, outlining the specific steps for emigrants to follow, from application to approval. Then, in December 1884, the Japanese Foreign Ministry distributed its "Information Regarding Emigration" throughout the country, which explained details of the contract, application procedures, and conditions in Hawai'i. It explained that the people were "sincere and gentle by nature." Moreover, it

Robert Walker Irwin (1844–1925), Yokohama, 1884 (Shinichi Suzuki, photographer; courtesy of Hawaii State Archives).

Born in Pennsylvania, Irwin was a descendant of Benjamin Franklin. He was stationed in Yokohama as an agent of the Pacific Mail Co. in 1866, and later was involved with other business firms including Mitsui Bussan of Japan, established in 1876. In 1867 he was appointed as Vice-Consul of Hawaiʻi, in 1881 as Consul General, Minister Plenipotentiary, in 1882 as agent for Japan of the Bureau of Immigration during Kapena's visit, and as Minister Resident and Special Agent of the Bureau of Immigration for the Hawaiian government in 1884. He played a major role in negotiations between the Japanese and Hawaiian governments, as well as in the recruitment and transportation of the government contract laborers from Japan to Hawaiʻi.

noted that the school system was "excellent," and that polished rice would be provided at less than 5 cents per pound, comparable to prices in Japan. Other terms of the contract included: free passage to Hawaiʻi; lodgings and food provided while in quarantine waiting to be sent to a plantation; employment as an agricultural laborer for 3 years; wages at $9 per month ($6 for wives), with $6 per month food allowance ($4 for wives and $1 for each child, up to two children), and firewood, lodging, and medical care provided; the working month to be 26 days of 12 hours in the mill or 10 hours in the field; 25 percent of wages to be deducted for savings in a specified bank in Hawaiʻi and deposited through the Japanese Consul. The savings, with earned interest, were intended to secure return passage, which was the responsibility of the immigrants.

Irwin had anticipated 600 in this initial recruitment, but more than 28,000 Japanese applied. Nearly half of the 944 selected for the first boatload were from Yamaguchi, the home prefecture of the Foreign Minister, Count Kaoru Inouye, who was well aware of its severe economic problems and pressures. Nevertheless, the decisions to emigrate were intensely individual ones and involved considerations such as love of adventure, avoidance of the new military conscription, personal or domestic dissatisfaction, and even — rather than simply "making it" — the dream of making money to invest in order to "strike it rich."

During the initial period (1885–1894), some 29,000 Japanese arrived in Honolulu in twenty-six boatloads. These *kanyaku imin* were immigrants who were recruited and sent under direct government auspices. The Meiji government was interested in emigration as a "safety valve" to reduce tensions in the countryside, but it also sought the foreign capital sent home by overseas workers and the knowledge of modern agricultural techniques with which the emigrants would presumably return. Both governments had reason to look favorably on the recruitment of Japanese for contract labor and, like Irwin, individuals stood to profit from the traffic. There were, therefore, overwhelming incentives to reach an agreement in spite of the numerous conflicts that ensued between the first Japanese arrivals and sugar plantation management.

The Convention of 1886, signed on 28 January in Tokyo, added clarification and some protection for the immigrants and was made retroactive to include the earlier arrivals. Negotiations that led to the Convention began when Katsunosuke Inouye, son of Foreign Minister Kaoru Inouye, was sent to Hawaiʻi as a Special Commissioner in June 1885 to look into allegations of mistreatment of laborers — especially the case of five men who had died on a plantation in Pāʻia, Maui, probably as a result of abuse and sickness. The Convention established Yokohama and Honolulu as the sole ports of debarkation and entry, with the Kanagawa *kenrei* or governor to act on behalf of the Japanese government, and Irwin to act as Special Agent of the Hawaii Bureau of Immigration. All immigrants were to be under contract subject to approval of the Kanagawa *kenrei*. Free steerage passage was assured. Further, the Hawaiian government was to employ a "sufficient number" of inspectors, interpreters, and Japanese doctors for the laborers. While not formally part of the Convention, both parties agreed that adequate hospitals and burial grounds would be provided and that 30 percent of immigrants would be women. The Convention also guaranteed a number of immigrant rights in the Kingdom of Hawaii, including the rights of suffrage and naturalization. Only a year after the Convention was signed, these rights were unilaterally abrogated in the Bayonet Constitution of 1887, when King Kalākaua was forced to give up much of his authority to the foreign planters.

In September 1887, the Convention was revised to allow planters to recover their costs of transporting laborers by requiring male immigrants to pay $75.00 ($3.00 per month) over 2 years to the Hawaiian government. Later immigrants were required to bear a smaller share of the total cost, although they also received lower wages (pay with food allowance dropped from $15.00 in 1887 to $12.50 in December 1891) and were forced to suffer more deductions to cover the cost of the inspectors, interpreters, and doctors.

Villagers were recruited through formal government announcements, word of mouth, newspaper accounts, and, after 1900, a number of influential "guidebooks" to Hawai'i. Interested individuals applied through local offices and obtained exit permits from prefectural governments. After receiving passports from the Foreign Ministry, they travelled at their own expense to Yokohama, where individual contracts were signed between emigrants and a representative of the Hawaiian government. After the rigorous medical inspection and the boat trip of 10 to 14 days, the Japanese were subject to another medical examination in Hawai'i, were quarantined, and then were required to sign contracts with individual plantations through the Hawaiian government's Bureau of Immigration.

Within a year after the first boatload had arrived, prospective emigrants were being more selectively screened. The Kuka village office in Oshima district in Yamaguchi prefecture, for example, began to recruit "pure" farmers, to narrow the search to those between the ages of 25 and 30 rather than the more generous 20 to 40, to discourage those men who tried to take children without their wives, and to prohibit men who were supposed to serve in the military during the contract period. In 1894, the process was turned over to private emigration companies, which flourished until 1905.

Before 1886, private companies had been processing emigrants leaving for the United States mainland and the Pacific islands, but the Convention made the Japanese government directly responsible for the movement to Hawai'i. A combination of pressure from private companies and the burden of the administrative work persuaded the Meiji government to turn the operation over to the entrepreneurs. In the course of just over a decade, these companies arranged for the emigration of about ninety thousand Japanese to Hawai'i. Business was so profitable that Jōji Nakayama, the corrupt head of the Hawai'i immigration bureau's Japanese section, resigned his $6,000 per year post to return to Japan and enter the private field in 1895. Nakayama failed in his bid to exploit this market, but by 1898, five major emigration companies had a monopoly on all Japanese leaving for Hawai'i. These companies enjoyed huge profits from various fees charged to the emigrants, including service charges, interest on funds advanced as "show money" (Hawaiian laws required immigrants to have $50 cash on hand to "show"), life insurance fees, and fixed deposits for return passage in the branch of the Keihin Bank that they had established in Honolulu. Further, for each emigrant, they collected commissions from fees charged for passage on steamships, from railroad companies for travel in Japan, from inns where emigrants stayed while awaiting passage, from doctors who administered examinations, and, finally, from plantations to whom they supplied the laborers.

Some of the founders of these emigration companies included politicians who became leaders of the Seiyukai political party in Japan, and it is assumed that some of the profits found their way into the party itself. The extent of ruthless exploitation was widely known

Detail of the mount for Irwin's photograph.

23

Robert W. Irwin and his wife Iki, Japan, 11 February 1889 (courtesy of Hawaii State Archives).

The 17-year-old Iki, an adopted daughter of the Takechi family, accompanied her husband when he resigned from the Pacific Mail Co. and moved to Nagasaki to work for another company in 1869. The Japanese government did not legalize marriage between a foreigner and a Japanese woman until 1873, and the Irwins' marriage was officially registered in 1882.

and condemned. The Keihin Bank routinely profited by refusing to release funds owed to the immigrants or by delaying their release, even in emergencies. In one celebrated case, the friends of an *issei* who had died tried unsuccessfully to secure funds to use for funeral expenses. They finally succeeded by carrying his corpse into the bank and confronting the officials.

The Japanese language newspapers led the fight to end the corruption by organizing a Reform Association on 7 May 1905. The Association organized a mass protest meeting which agreed to send detailed exposés to major newspapers in Tokyo. Further, the Japanese government was petitioned to investigate the companies and the bank. Finally, in August 1905, the Keihin Bank was ordered by the Foreign Office to cease its unfair practices and the emigration companies went out of business. The final phase of immigration, until total exclusion of the Japanese in 1924, was conducted without the involvement of any private companies.

CONVENTION OF 1886

Whereas, a large number of the subjects of His Majesty the Emperor of Japan, have emigrated to the Hawaiian Islands, and whereas, it is not unlikely that others of His Imperial Majesty's subjects may desire to take advantage of the system of free and voluntary emigration which has been established and which it is intended by this Convention to confirm; and whereas, it is equally the desire of His Majesty the King of the Hawaiian Islands and His Majesty the Emperor of Japan, to afford to emigrants the most ample and effectual protection compatible with the Constitution and Laws of Hawaii; His Majesty the King of the Hawaiian Islands and His Majesty the Emperor of Japan being resolved to treat upon these important subjects, have for that purpose appointed their respective Plenipotentiaries to negotiate and conclude an Emigration Convention, that is to say:

His Majesty the King of the Hawaiian Islands, Robert Walker Irwin, Knight Commander of the Royal Order of Kalakaua, His Majesty's Chargé d' Affaires and Consul General at Tokio and His Majesty the Emperor of Japan, Count Inouye Kaoru, Jusammi, His Imperial Majesty's Minister of State for Foreign Affairs, First Class of the Order of the Rising Sun etc. etc. who, after a reciprocal communication of their respective full powers, found in good and due form, have agreed upon and concluded the following Articles:

Article I

It is mutually agreed between the Contracting Parties, that the several stipulations contained in this Convention, shall, so far as the same are applicable, embrace as well the subjects of His Majesty the Emperor of Japan who have already emigrated to the Hawaiian Islands, as those who may hereafter emigrate thither.

Article II

The Government of His Majesty the Emperor of Japan agree that in pursuance of the provisions of this Convention, and so long as the same remains in force, Japanese subjects may freely emigrate to the Hawaiian Islands. But nothing herein contained shall be held to deprive His Imperial Japanese Majesty's government of the right in individual cases, to prohibit such emigration, or at their pleasure generally to limit, suspend, or prohibit such emigration, if in their judgement the exigencies of the State or the welfare of Japanese subjects, justifies such action. It is, however, understood, that this right shall not be arbitrarily exercised, neither shall it be enforced against intending emigrants, in respect of whom the Japanese Government shall have given the permission provided for in Article III hereof.

Article III

All emigration under this Convention, shall be carried on between the Ports of Yokohama and Honolulu. The Kenrei of Kanagawa, shall in all matters connected therewith, represent and act on behalf of the Japanese Government. His Hawaiian Majesty's Government engage to appoint a Special Agent of the Hawaiian Board of Immigration to reside at Yokohama. The appointment of such Agent shall be subject to the approval of the Japanese Government.

It shall be the duty of the said Agent to correspond and consult with the said Kenrei upon all matters connected with the subject of Japanese emigration to Hawaii, and he shall moreover, be charged with the duty of making all necessary arrangements with reference to the embarkation and transportation of intending emigrants. Whenever emigrants are desired, the said Agent shall give the said Kenrei at least one month's previous notice, setting forth the number and class of persons desired, to which notice the said Kenrei shall without unnecessary delay reply giving the determination of His Imperial Majesty's Government in that behalf. In default of such notice or in default of a favorable reply thereto from the said Kenrei, the concluding paragraph of the last preceding Article hereof, shall not apply.

Article IV

All emigration under this Convention, shall be by contract. The contracts shall be for periods not exceeding three years and shall be in accordance with a form to be approved by both Governments. The contracts shall be concluded at Yokohama by and between the Special Agent of the Hawaiian Board of Immigration in the name and on behalf of the Hawaiian Government, and the intending emigrants, and shall be approved by the Kenrei of Kanagawa. During the continuance of any such contracts, the Hawaiian Government shall assume all the responsibility of employer towards the emigrants and shall consequently be responsible for the due and faithful performance of all the conditions of such contracts. And at the same time the said Government of Hawaii guarantees to each and every Japanese emigrant the full and perfect protection of the Law of the Kingdom, and will endeavor at all times and under all circumstances to promote the welfare and comfort of such emigrants.

Article V

His Hawaiian Majesty's Government agrees, moreover, to furnish all emigrants under this Convention, free steerage passage including proper food from Yokohama to Honolulu in first class passenger Steamers. The Steamers selected for the purpose of transporting such emigrants shall be approved by the Kenrei of Kanagawa.

Article VI

In order to ensure the proper fulfillment of the terms of the Contracts entered into between the Board of Immigration of the Hawaiian Kingdom and any Japanese emigrants, and to afford full protection to such emigrants in the enjoyment of their rights under the

Original brocade envelope of the 1886 Convention.

Found among King Kalākaua's personal possessions, the envelope was kept by Mrs. J. Frank Woods, who was related to the King's family through her former husband, Prince Jonah Kūhiō Kalaniana'ole.

The Convention of 1886 (courtesy of Hawaii State Archives).

The Japanese government saw the need to determine immigrants' rights and warrants at a government level, to counteract existing problems and as a basis for preventing future problems.

Laws of the Hawaiian Kingdom, His Hawaiian Majesty's Government will provide and employ, during the continuance of any of the contracts aforesaid, a sufficient number of Inspectors and Interpreters who shall be able to speak and interpret the Japanese and English languages, and the services of such Interpreters shall at all times be rendered without charge to such emigrants, in the Courts of the Hawaiian Kingdom, in any suits arising out of or concerning any such Contracts, in which such emigrants may be plaintiffs, defendants, complainants or accused.

Article VII

The Government of His Hawaiian Majesty will, during the continuance of any of the Contracts provided for by this Convention, employ a sufficient number of Japanese physicians, to attend the emigrants, and will give to the said physicians the status of Government physicians, and will station them in such localities as may from time to time appear to be desirable in order to afford the emigrants all necessary medical aid.

Article VIII

His Hawaiian Majesty's Government further agree that the Diplomatic and Consular Agents of Japan in Hawaii, shall at all times have free and unrestricted access to all Japanese emigrants; they shall be afforded every facility to satisfy themselves that the Contracts are being fulfilled in good faith and they shall also have the right, in case of violation thereof, to ask and obtain the protection of the laws and the local authorities of Hawaii.

Article IX

The well being, happiness and prosperity of Japanese subjects emigrating to Hawaii, being equally objects of solicitude to both the Contracting Parties, His Imperial Majesty's Government consent that his Hawaiian Majesty's Government shall have the right to send back to Japan all evil-disposed, vicious or vagrant Japanese subjects in Hawaii, who may create trouble or disturbance or encourage dissipation of any kind among the emigrants or who may become a charge upon the State.

Article X

The present Convention shall be ratified and the ratification shall be exchanged at Honolulu as soon as possible.

Article XI

The present Convention shall take effect immediately upon the exchange of the ratifications thereof, and shall remain in force for the period of five years and thereafter until six months previous notice shall have been given by one of the Contracting Parties to the other of its intention to abrogate it.

In testimony whereof the respective Plenipotentiaries have signed the present Convention in the English language, and have hereunto affixed their seals.

Done at the City of Tokio, this twenty-eighth day of the first month of the Nineteenth year of Meiji, corresponding to the twenty-eighth day of January in the Eighteen hundred and eighty-sixth year of the Christian Era.

(Signed) Inouye Kaoru (L.S.)
(Signed) R. W. Irwin (L.S.)

Japanese Consulate, Nuʻuanu Avenue, Honolulu, 1887.

The consulate opened in Honolulu in 1884, and this building was acquired by the first Consul General, Tarō Andō, in 1886. He and Mrs. Andō are shown here on the porch. Andō arrived on the third ship, *City of Peking*, on 14 February 1886, and delivered the Convention to be signed in Hawaiʻi.

Political cartoon of the 1887 Revolution.

The Bayonet Constitution, which Kalakaua was forced to sign under pressure from White businessmen in Hawaiʻi in 1887, denied the suffrage rights that the 1886 Convention had guaranteed to Japanese.

Message of the governor of Hiroshima to the departing immigrants, Hiroshima, 1885.

As you set sail for work in Hawaii, we hope each and every one of you will be diligent in observing the following admonitions. When you arrive in that country you are to observe all of its rules, preserve your health, and be single-minded in your work. You must be particularly careful of your conduct so that your country is never dishonored. Further, regard thrift above all and save your money. These you will do so that you may, on the day of your return to Japan, proceed to your villages garbed in silks and honor.

25 May 1885
Hiroshima Kenrei, Sadaaki Senda

Colonel Curtis P. I'aukea, 1887.

I'aukea was sent to Japan in May 1884 to serve in the same capacity and with the same mission as Mr. Kapena. I'aukea's instructions were given to him by the Foreign Office:

You are aware how persistently the Japanese government has maintained that it is impossible for them "to enter upon the subject of the proposed convention until after the revision of the existing treaties with Western powers had been concluded" ... You have therefore to present the matter to His Excellency the Minister under a new phase. (Board of Immigration 1886:224).

John M. Kapena, Honolulu, ca. 1880 (J. J. Williams, photographer).

Appointed as Envoy Extraordinary and Minister Plenipotentiary to Japan in 1882 for immigration negotiations, John Kapena had the following orders issued to him by the Minister of Foreign Affairs for Hawai'i, Walter Murray Gibson.

You will point out, Mr. Minister, to Japanese officials the excellent character acquired by the Japanese race in this kingdom, and, at the same time, mention the kind and friendly regard entertained among His Majesty's subjects, foreign as well as native, towards a race which will blend and assimilate with the Hawaiian people. (Report of the President, Board of Immigration, 1886:223)

Mr. Kapena, while at Tokio, had several interviews with the Japanese Minsiter of Foreign Affairs Inouye ... but, for the time, nothing more was done, as it was found necessary to postpone any further negotiations, on account of the existence of certain stipulations in treaties then in force between Japan and other Powers, which would have conferred upon the latter countries the same privileges as might be granted to Hawaii (Board of Immigration 1886:224).

The newspaper advertisement (right column, vertical Japanese text):

公許 アメリカ行募集

さるべく候

（注意）小生は合衆國布哇縣政府の公許を得て
募集するものなれば御安心の上御申込みな

四國屋事
漢城旅館

市哇ホノル、府 郵函九五〇

募集人 芳我日下
舗主事

弗さへ御持参相成らば乗船できるよう御取
計ひ申すべく候につき至急御申込被下度候

の内貳拾参弗は御立替へ申候間 金拾五

に行く人には御便利を計りて切符代参拾八弗
定期の初航海などこの濵船にて米國シヤトル

右オリムピア號はゼームスグレフィス會社が

船賃の現金は拾五弗

濵船はオリムピア號
、出發は貳月貳十七日

ホノルルの

Newspaper advertisement recruiting workers for Seattle
(*Yamato Shimbun*, Honolulu, 10 February 1906).

Freed from labor contracts, people could choose their place of
employment. As a result, many people moved to the United
States mainland in search of better paying jobs. Professional
recruiters actively lured laborers in Hawai'i to move to
greener pastures. Between 1901 and 1907, more than fifty
thousand people moved to San Francisco and Seattle from
Honolulu.

RECRUITING LABORERS FOR AMERICA
(authorized by Territory of Hawaii)

Steamship *Olympia*.
Departing Honolulu on 27 February 1906

The steamship Olympia of the James Griffiths Co. will be sailing to Seattle on its inaugural voyage. Since only $15 will be
required in cash, there will be a balance of $23 towards the
total fare of $38. Please respond immediately.

Recruiter/Manager: Kusaka Haga
Shikokuya aka Kanjo Ryokan
P.O. Box 950 Honolulu

The Morioka Shōkai, Honolulu, 1899 (courtesy of Yoshitami
Tasaka).

Five major private immigration companies took over the process of emigration of Japanese to Hawai'i in 1894. From left,
Yōkichi Tasaka, Iga Mōri, Miss Lindy, Makoto Morioka, Saburō Adachi, Hamon Mizuno.

Raising of American flag, Wailuku, Maui, at annexation ceremony in 1898.

Annexation of Hawai'i by the United States in July 1898 resulted in the legal prohibition of contract labor through the
Organic Act.

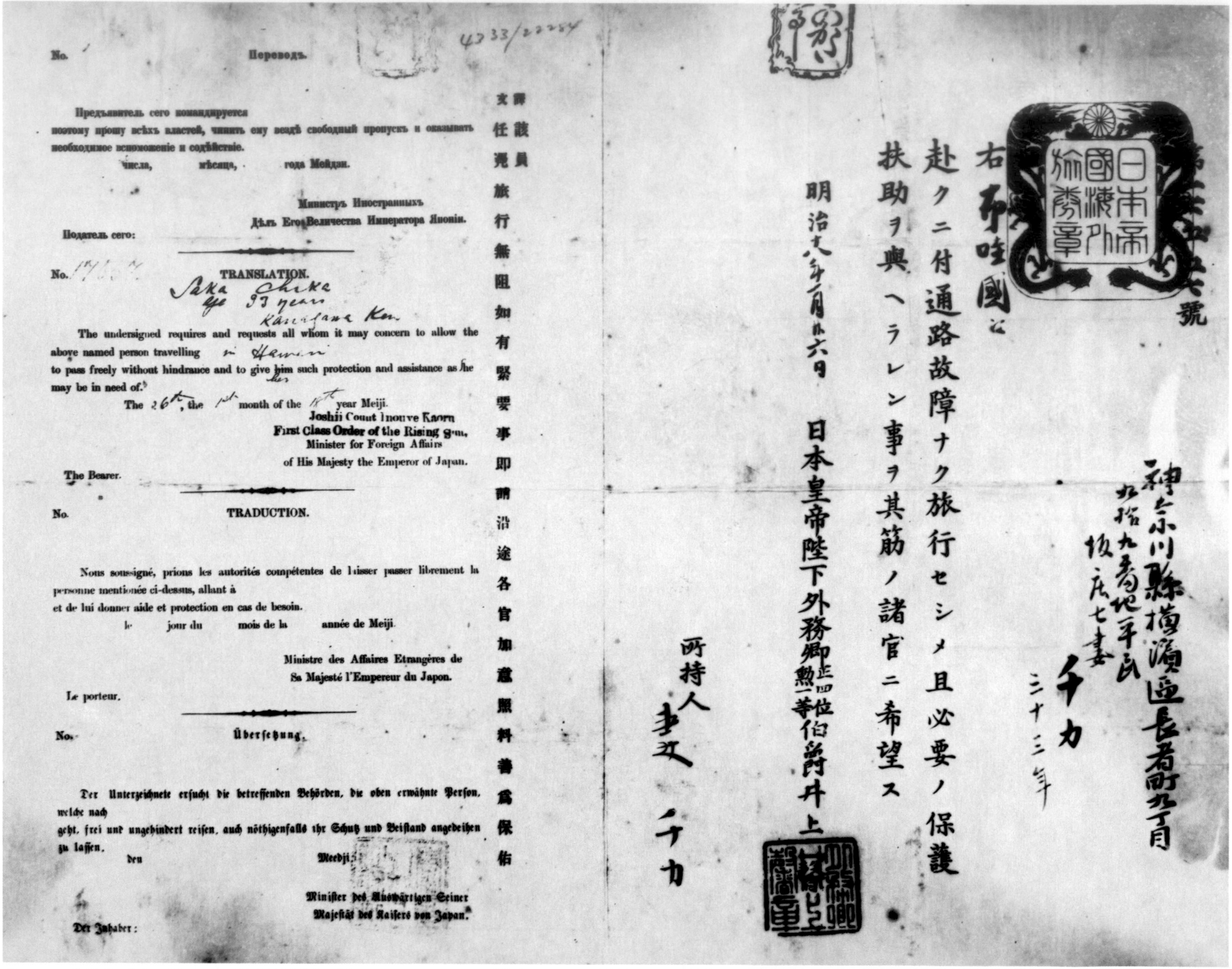

No. Перевод.

Предъявитель сего командируется
поэтому прошу всѣхъ властей, чинить ему вездѣ свободный пропускъ и оказывать
необходимое вспоможеніе и содѣйствіе.

числа, мѣсяца, года Мейдзи.

Министръ Иностранныхъ
Дѣлъ Его Величества Императора Японіи.

Податель сего:

No. 181757

TRANSLATION.

Saka Chika
age 33 years
Kanagawa Ken

The undersigned requires and requests all whom it may concern to allow the
above named person travelling in Hawaii
to pass freely without hindrance and to give him such protection and assistance as she
may be in need of.

The 26th, the 1st month of the 18th year Meiji.

Joshii Count Inouye Kaoru
First Class Order of the Rising Sun,
Minister for Foreign Affairs
of His Majesty the Emperor of Japan.

The Bearer.

No.   TRADUCTION.

Nous soussigné, prions les autorités compétentes de laisser passer librement la
personne mentionnée ci-dessus, allant à
et de lui donner aide et protection en cas de besoin.

le   jour du   mois de la   année de Meiji.

Ministre des Affaires Etrangères de
Sa Majesté l'Empereur du Japon.

Le porteur.

No.   Übersetzung.

Der Unterzeichnete ersucht die betreffenden Behörden, die oben erwähnte Person,
welche nach
geht, frei und ungehindert reisen, auch nöthigenfalls ihr Schutz und Beistand angedeihen
zu lassen.   den

Meedji

Minister des Auswärtigen Seiner
Majestät des Kaisers von Japan.

Der Inhaber:

Passport of Chika Saka, 33-years-old, Shōhichi's wife, a commoner from Yokohama. Dated 26 January 1885.

This Memorandum of Agreement, between the Hawaiian Government, represented by R. W. Irwin Special Commissioner and Special Agent of the Bureau of Immigration, and _Saka Shohichi_ voluntary passenger per Steamship _City of Tokio_ from Yokohama to Honolulu Witnesseth:

1st. The Hawaiian Government agrees to furnish steerage passage from Yokohama to Honolulu, free of expense to _S. Saka_ and _Chika_ his wife, and to his two children said _Chika Saka Shohichi_ and his family having expressed a desire to go to Honolulu as voluntary passengers. This free passage includes ordinary food on the voyage.

2nd. On arrival at Honolulu the Hawaiian Government agrees to obtain employment for the said _S. Saka_ as an agricultural laborer for 3 years and also similar employment for _Chika_ his wife if desired. Until such employment has been obtained, the Hawaiian Government will give the said _S. Saka_ his wife and two children aforesaid lodging commodious enough to secure health and a reasonable degree of comfort and an allowance of six Dollars per month to the said _S. Saka_ and four Dollars per month to the said _Chika_ his wife and one Dollar per month for food to each of his said children.

The Hawaiian Government will furnish to the said _S. Saka_ and his family as aforesaid cleaned rice at a price not to exceed five cents per pound, and fuel for cooking free of expense.

3rd. The Hawaiian Government guarantees to the said _S. Saka_ wages at the rate of nine Dollars per month, and to the said _Chika_ his wife, at the rate of six Dollars per month, payable in Hawaiian or United States Gold or Silver coin, with allowance for food and lodging as in Art 2. But the said _S. Saka_ must furnish blankets and bed clothing for himself and his family.

4th. The Hawaiian Government agrees to furnish the said _S. Saka_ and his family good medical attendance and medicines free of cost to him.

5th. The Hawaiian Government guarantees that twenty six days of ten (10) hours each in the field or twelve hours each in the sugar house, shall, within the meaning of this agreement constitute one month's service as an agricultural laborer. The hours of service shall be counted from the regularly established moment for departure to work in the field or in the sugar house and shall include the time occupied in going to and from work.

6th. The said _S. Saka_ and his family shall be exempted from all and every kind of personal tax for 3 years from the date of arrival at Honolulu.

7th. Twenty five per cent of the sum received by the said _S. Saka_ and _Chika_ his wife as wages shall be handed over to the Japanese Consul at Honolulu who will duly receipt therefor and deposit the same in the name of the said _Saka_ in the Hawaiian Government Postal Savings Bank, to be kept on interest at the rate of 5o/o per annum, and not to be withdrawn, except the Japanese Consul recognizes the absolute necessity of such withdrawal and signifies his approval in writing of the application of the said _Saka_ therefor.

Signed and sealed in triplicate at Yokohama this _26_ day of _January_ 1885. One copy to be retained by each of the parties hereto, and one to be left in the custody of the Kanagawa Ken Rei.

His Hawaiian Majesty's Special Commissioner and
Special Agent of the Bureau of Immigration

I hereby certify that the above Agreement
has been signed and sealed by both parties
in my presence.

KANAGAWA KEN REI.   Voluntary Passenger

Labor contract of Shōhichi and Chika Saka, signed between R. W. Irwin, His Hawaiian Majesty's Special Agent and Special Commissioner of the Bureau of Immigration, and Shōhichi Saka, with certification by the governor of Kanagawa Prefectural Government. Dated 26 January 1885.

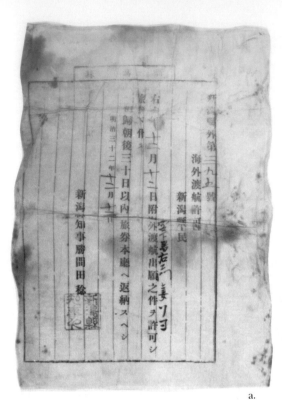

32

a.

b.

c.

INSPECTION CARD. No. 175

(IMMIGRANTS AND STEERAGE PASSENGERS)

Ship "LADY JOICEY" Dec., 28., 1899.
Left Yokohama

Name of Immigrant Riyo Miyashata

Last Residence Niigata Ken

INSPECTED AND PASSED AT YOKOHAMA.	PASSED AT QUARANTINE HONOLULU.	PASSED BY IMMIG. BUREAU. HONOLULU.

VACCINATED.

DEC 11 1899

SANITARY HAWAII

此札ヲ所持スル人ハ布哇國ニ於テ檢
疫所ニ止留ル、事ヲ免ガル、故ニ失
ワザル樣ニ注意スベシ

Keep this card to avoid detention
at Quarantine at Honolulu.

A set of documents for emigration, 1899: (a) exit permit for
Soyo Miyashita, Niigata; (b) passport for Soyo Miyashita; (c)
vaccination certificate for Soyo Miyashita; (d) labor contract
of Haruemon and Soyo Miyashita with Makoto Morioka, a
private immigration company; (e) labor contract of Mr. and
Mrs. Miyashita with Olaa Sugar Co., 1900.

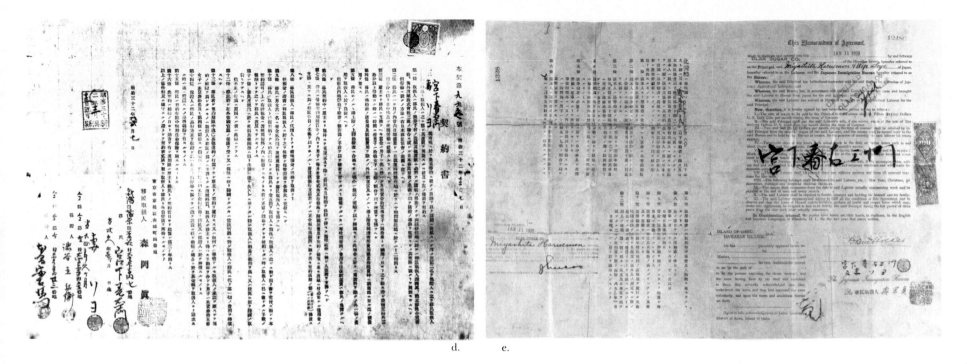

d.   e.

33

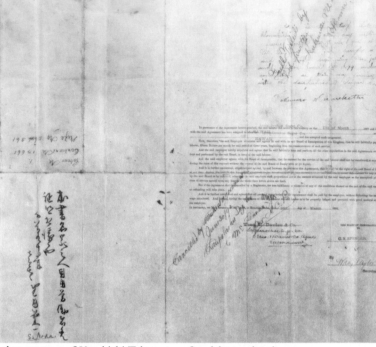

Labor contract of Umekichi Takemoto, a free laborer, dated 1891; terminated by mutual agreement with Laupahoehoe Plantation, then recontracted with Kukaiau.

Passport and certificate of free labor issued to Shigeichi Katahara, 1897.

Notice of health examination requirements for emigrants issued by the Shimane prefectural government.

General information for departing emigrants issued by the Shimane prefectural government.

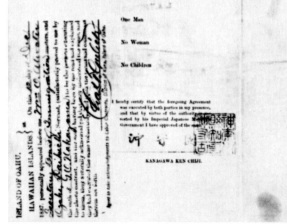

Labor contract between Daikichi Ozaki and the Reciprocity Sugar Co., Hāna, Maui, dated 1887.

Whereas a certain Agreement was entered into, at Yokohama, Japan, on the............................November 1887, between ROBERT W. IRWIN, His Hawaiian Majesty's Minister Resident and Special Agent of the Hawaiian Bureau of Immigration, and.., in which it was agreed, among other things, that the Hawaiian Government would obtain for the said............................, employment in Hawaii as an agricultural laborer upon the terms and conditions in said Agreement contained, And whereas, the said............................, did arrive in this Kingdom on the................1887.

Now therefore these presents, witnesseth, that in pursuance of said agreement the Hawaiian Government has assigned the said.. as anagricultural laborer to............................, in the Island of............................ and that the said............................ has consented to, and accepted such assignment.

Signed and sealed at Honolulu, the............................A. D. 1887.

THE BUREAU OF IMMIGRATION.

BY

L. A. THURSTON,
PRESIDENT.

In pursuance of the Agreement hereto attached, the said _Ozaki Daikichi_........did arrive in this country on the _11 Dec._ 1887, and in accordance with the said Agreement has been assigned to labor for _Reciprocity Sug. Co. as a laborer._ at _Hana, Maui_............................and has accepted such assignment.

Now, therefore, the said _Reciprocity Sug. Co._ stipulates and agrees to and with the said Board of Immigration of this Kingdom, that he will faithfully pay to the said............................Dollars per month for said period of three years, beginning from the commencement of such service.

And the said employer hereby stipulates and agrees that he will faithfully keep and perform all the other stipulations in the said Agreements set forth, to be kept and performed by the said Board, in favor of the said laborer.

And the said employer agrees with the Board of Immigration, that the contract for the service of the said laborer shall not be transferred to any third party during the term of this contract without the consent of the said Board of Immigration or its Agent.

And it is further understood, stipulated and agreed, by and between the parties to this Agreement, that it shall be the right of the said Board of Immigration, at any time, during the time in this Agreement stipulated, for its duration, upon the representation of the said laborer, to cancel this contract for any cause deemed by the said Board to be sufficient, refunding the said employer such proportional sum of the amount advanced by the said employer as the unexpired portion of the time of service agreed upon may bear to the whole time herein above set forth.

But if the Agreement shall be cancelled by a Magistrate, for non-fulfillment or violation of any of the conditions thereof on the part of the said employer, then no refunding will take place.

And it is further understood and agreed that all personal taxes levied by the Government shall be paid by the employer, without deducting the same from the wages stipulated. And further, during the continuance of this Agreement the said laborer is to be properly lodged and provided with good medical attendance by the employer.

In testimony, we have hereunto set our hands, at Honolulu, Oahu, this _12_ day of _Dec._ 1887.

THE BOARD OF IMMIGRATION.

BY

L. A. THURSTON,
PRESIDENT.

By _Wm. O. Atwater_
Secty

移住民事務局長

一千八百八十七年十一月　日本横濱

一　拂ヲ布哇國駐剳公使兼移住民事務局特
　派委員ロベルト、ダブリュー、アルウヰン民ト
　布哇政府ハ　　　　ノ間ニ眼結ヶタル約定書中
二　雇傭セシム可キ　　　ノ約欸ヲ　農夫トシテ
一　千八百八十七年　月　日當國ニ到

　若シレニヨリ赤哇政府ハ右約定ニ陸セシ令玆
二　遣粉スル事ニ其ヶ又　　　島
二　返粉ノ義ヲ承諾シ　　　右
一　拾ヶ記名調印ス　　　農夫トシテ

西暦一千八百八十七年　月　日『　ノヘ』府

Japanese immigrants on the bridge to Quarantine Island, Honolulu, 1893 (courtesy of Hawaii State Archives).

The immigrants had to walk down the "China Bridge" to enter the Immigration Station on the sandy island a mile offshore in Honolulu Harbor. The immigrants were kept in the station, surrounded by a fence, from 1 to 2 weeks to meet the quarantine requirement of 18 days following departure from Japan. When the epidemic of bubonic plague struck Honolulu, the confinement period was extended.

ARRIVAL

The *City of Tokio* arrived in Honolulu at 9 o'clock in the morning on 8 February 1885, under the command of Captain Jeff Maury. After nearly 2 weeks of uneventful sailing across the Pacific from Yokohama, all aboard were thankful for their safe arrival and the enthusiastic welcome they received. Among the passengers were the 944 government contract laborers eagerly awaited by the Hawai'i sugar planters, as well as the man who had arranged their recruitment, Robert W. Irwin, and his wife and daughter. Accompanying this *ikkaisen*, or "first boat" of Japanese immigrants, was the first Japanese Consul, Jirō Nakamura, with his wife, and Viscount Tadafumi Torii who was assigned to the consulate. Another passenger—who was to become more important to the *issei* immigrants than the official Japanese government representative — was Jōji Nakayama, the future inspector-in-chief of the Japanese section of the Hawaiian government's Bureau of Immigration.

The first newspaper account of the Japanese arrival noted that observers at the dock were "struck with their robust, healthy appearances. They all wore a cheerful, contented look, . . . and soon settled down into their shore quarters and made themselves at home."

Consul Nakamura immediately drafted a report, dated 8 February 1885, to the Japanese government. He was pleased, he said, that the 944 laborers had all arrived without incident and that there had been nothing worse than a few instances of seasickness during the entire voyage. He was grateful that Irwin had made provision for familiar Japanese foodstuffs and for occasional snacks of milk, bread, and Japanese crackers. There had been a miscarriage by one of the two pregnant women on board, but she had been well treated by the doctor. There was one puzzling case, the Consul went on, involving an infant who had evidently been abandoned and who was discovered only after the ship had left port. All in all, however, Nakamura had the highest praise for the consideration shown the Japanese and especially for Irwin's kindness and attention to detail.

The Japanese were taken to the quarantine station at the Immigration Depot where they were required, once again, to sign their labor contracts with the sugar plantations through the Hawaii Bureau of Immigration. They remained in quarantine for several days, undergoing health examinations. On 10 February the *Daily Pacific Commercial Advertiser* took time to reflect on the significance of the Japanese:

> The arrival of the first installment of the Japanese immigrants is the most important event that has happened in Hawaii for many years. . . . Next to the ratification of

S.S. *City of Tokio*. Photo of original painting (courtesy of Peabody Museum, Salem, Massachusetts).

S.S. *City of Tokio* (1874–1885) was owned by Pacific Mail Steamship Co. and built by Roach and Son of Chester, Pennsylvania, in 1874. She weighed 5,079.62 tons and was 408 by 47 feet with a single screw, a top speed of 15 knots, compound engines, four masts, and two funnels. Under Captain Jeff Maury, she arrived in Honolulu on 8 February 1885 with the first government contract laborers. The ship was wrecked on 24 June 1885 in Tokyo Bay.

Table 3a
THE FIRST BOAT ARRIVALS
HOME PREFECTURE AND SEX

HOME PREFECTURE	ADULTS MALE	FEMALE	CHILDREN MALE	FEMALE	TOTAL
Yamaguchi	311	67	25	17	420
Hiroshima	140	43	23	16	222
Kanagawa	83	37	18	6	144
Okayama	37				37
Wakayama	19	1	1	1	22
Tokyo Group	86	10	2	1	99
TOTAL	676	158	69	41	944

SOURCE: Compiled by K. Sinoto from Japanese Consulate records.

Table 3b
AGE AND SEX STATISTICS FOR THE FIRST GROUP OF JAPANESE IMMIGRANTS TO HAWAI'I

AGE (YEARS)	MALES	FEMALES	TOTAL
0–4	35	28	63
5–9	22	7	29
10–14	8	2	10
15–19	7	9	16
20–24	131	39	170
25–29	162	52	214
30–34	176	39	215
35–39	151	19	170
40–44	38	3	41
45–49	10		10
50–	2		2
Unknown	3	1	4
TOTAL	745	199	944

SOURCE: Compiled by Kazuyoshi Nakayama for HIHPC from Japanese Consulate records.

Table 3c
FAMILY STATISTICS FOR THE FIRST GROUP OF JAPANESE IMMIGRANTS TO HAWAI'I

STATUS	NO. OF UNITS	NO. OF INDIVIDUALS
Couples only	76	152
Nuclear families	74	251
Nuclear families with a spouse's sibling	2	7
Singles		534
TOTAL		944

NOTE: Within this group there were 22 marriages, 10 divorces, and 67 births between 1885 and 1906.
SOURCE: Compiled by Kazuyoshi Nakayama for HIHPC from Japanese Consulate records.

the Reciprocity Treaty it must be acknowledged by all parties to be the chief event of the reign of Kalakaua . . . it is to the King himself that we owe this successful ending to a long diplomatic endeavor.

The writer was quick to credit Irwin for his efforts in Japan leading to the successful negotiations:

> Those who have had the opportunity of observing his work among the newly arrived immigrants, his energy, his tact and best of all his success among them, cannot but sing his praises as "the right man in the right place." In his hands we feel sure that the future of Japanese immigration is absolutely safe.

In the same issue, another article, "A Bit of Japan," focused on life in the Immigration Depot for the *ikkaisen* or "first boat" immigrants:

> The first thing that attracts the attention of the visitor to the depot is the fairness of the skins of the immigrants. . . . Many of them, the women especially, are actually white, and they are all very clean.

Their clothing, which varied considerably, was described, and special attention was directed to the *geta* or wooden clogs "the Japs. mount themselves on pieces of wood cut rudely into the semblance of a shoe sole."

The new arrivals cooked their own food, and numerous fires could be seen burning in small holes dug in the sands of the immigration compound. The *Advertiser* writer observed that the 108 children were "happy, contented looking like little old men and women. They are to be seen playing at keeping house, making gardens, finding the sands of Hawaii as well adapted to their purpose as those in Japan." Finally, the article concluded on an optimistic note: "They bathe, dress, and sleep in quiet, and everything seems to show that they will rapidly become domesticated here."

On 11 February, 3 days after their arrival, the Japanese hosted King Kalākaua and a group of his officials as well as the U.S. Minister and his wife. Irwin had organized an exhibition of *kendō* (Japanese fencing), acrobatic feats on an upright ladder, various musical performances and, most impressive to the guests, *sumō* wrestling matches replete with officials, a proper ring with sand, and "East" and "West" teams of twenty brawny men each. Tubs of *sake* were piled high for participants and guests alike, along with some boxes of "Japanese snap biscuits" (probably *senbei*). The wrestlers concluded the mini tournament with a:

> sort of dance of triumph by the leading ones in the East (the winners). Fastening around their waists red, yellow, and blue blankets (in imitation of the gorgeous silk wrappings which Consul Irwin informs us the professionals wear on such occasions), they commenced a slow, stately ring dance. [The "gorgeous silk wrappings" are the *keshō mawashi* traditionally worn by professional *sumō* wrestlers.]

The Japanese appear to have been enthusiastic and hopeful, although there must have been some concern over the large, crude, barrackslike building in which they were housed.

The *issei* called it the *senningoya* (literally, "hut for 1,000 people") but could not have known that some of the plantations would provide similar quarters for their work force and pack several hundred men, women, and children into a single building.

In general, however, there was a very positive atmosphere surrounding the initial arrival of the Japanese in February 1885. After all, as one reporter overheard an observer at the *sumō* exhibition say, "such people on a plantation would help make things lively, and there certainly was a fine display of muscle, pluck and good nature."

After being released from the Immigration Depot, the immigrant laborers were sent to their designated work sites. Most were shipped to sugar plantations — sixteen on Hawai'i, six each on Maui and Kaua'i, and one each on O'ahu and Lāna'i. Ten individuals were employed by private families as cooks and servants, and two went to work as servants in the royal household.

The Honolulu Immigration Station (colored postcard), 1890s.

Honolulu in 1884, as seen by the immigrants when their ship approached its destination (courtesy of United Japanese Society of Hawaii).

Baggage inspection at Immigration Office, ca. 1910–1915.

Interpreter Tomizō Katsunuma, at right, was a licensed veterinarian, trained on the United States mainland. He came to Hawai'i in 1898.

Japanese immigrants at Quarantine Island, ca. 1895 (J.J. Williams, photographer; courtesy of Hawaii State Archives).

Toyokichi Nakamura, right foreground, was a *gannenmono* who served as an interpreter.

Table 3d
Movement of Individuals From the First Group of Japanese Immigrants to Hawai'i

YEAR	RETURNED HOME	MOVED TO MAINLAND	DIED	TOTAL
1885	1		18	19
1886	26		21	47
1887	39	15	7	61
1888	290	34	6	330
1889	80	24	4	108
1890	21	1	4	26
1891	24		2	26
1892	22	11		33
1893	22	6		28
1894	12		2	14
1895	13		2	15
1896	9			9
1897	11		1	12
1898	3			3
1899	1			1
1900				
1901	3			3
1902	2		1	3
1903	1			1
1904	2			2
1905	2		1	3
1906	1			1
Unknown	10		6	16
TOTAL	595	91	75	761

Source: Compiled by Kazuyoshi Nakayama for HIHPC from Japanese Consulate records.

Table 4
Statistics for the Second Boat Arrivals on the Yamashiro Maru, 1885

HOME PREFECTURE	ADULTS		CHILDREN		TOTAL
	MALE	FEMALE	MALE	FEMALE	
Hiroshima	377	8	1	4	390
Kumamoto	275	1			276
Fukuoka	133	13	3		149
Kanagawa	6	2	2	2	12
Niigata	30	7			37
Chiba	6	1	1		8
Shiga	72	2			74
Gunma	10				10
Wakayama	31	1		1	33
TOTAL	940	35	7	7	989*

*Appears as 988 in accompanying Table 5.
Source: Compiled in 1983 by K. Sinoto from Japanese Consulate records.

Table 5
Japanese Immigration to Hawai'i Under Government Contract, 1885–1894

ARRIVAL DATE	NO. OF IMMIGRANTS	VESSEL
Feb. 8, 1885	944	*City of Tokio*
June 17	988	*Yamashiro Maru*
Feb. 14, 1886	927	*City of Peking*
Dec. 11, 1887	1,447	*Wakanoura Maru*
June 1, 1888	1,063	
Nov. 14	1,081	*Takasago Maru*
Dec. 26	1,143	
Mar. 2, 1889	957	*Omi Maru*
Oct. 1	997	
Nov. 21	1,050	
Jan. 9, 1890	1,064	*Yamashiro Maru*
Apr. 2	1,071	
May 22	1,068	
June 17	596	*Sagami Maru*
Mar. 11, 1891	1,093	*Yamashiro Maru*
Mar. 30	1,081	*Omi Maru*
Apr. 28	1,091	
May 29	1,488	*Yamashiro Maru*
June 18	1,101	*Miike Maru*
Jan. 9, 1892	1,098	
June 25	1,124	*Yamashiro Maru*
Nov. 28	989	
Mar. 6, 1893	729	
June 6	1,757	
Oct. 9	1,631	*Miike Maru*
June 15, 1894	1,491	
TOTAL	29,069	

SOURCE: Japanese Consulate records.

Japanese laborers at Immigration Depot, 1890s (Gilman Collection).

The laborers were identified by contract numbers; a husband and wife were assigned the same number.

43

Shingen-bukuro, drawstring cloth bag for travelling, ca. 1913.

Woman's luggage made of bamboo and rattan, widely used for travelling, ca. 1910.

Yanagi-gōri, suitcase made of willow (*Salix koriyanagi*) branches, consisting of two parts, a "box" and a lid, making it expandable.

Yanagi-gōri was usually tied with rope to secure the cover. The owner's name, home address, and the destination — Honolulu — are written on the cover.

Table 6
MAJOR JAPANESE IMMIGRATION COMPANIES AND THEIR OPERATIONS 1894–1908

COMPANY NAME	HOME OFFICE LOCATION	YEAR ESTABLISHED	NO. OF GROUPS PROCESSED	NO. OF PEOPLE PROCESSED
Yuki Ogura	Osaka	1894	3	2,500
Kobe Toko Goshi Gaisha	Kobe	1894	11	909
Kaigai Toko Goshi Gaisha	Hiroshima	1896	61	10,731
Makoto Morioka	Tokyo	1896	51	8,148
Kumamoto Imin Goshi Gaisha	Kumamoto	1896	46	7,738
Nippon Imin Goshi Gaisha	Kobe	1896	21	5,800
Tokyo Imin Goshi Gaisha	Yokohama	1897	14	3,382
TOTAL				39,208

NOTE: These seven companies were officially permitted to operate by the Japanese government. However, the annexation of Hawai'i to the United States in 1900 prohibited contract labor, and later, in 1905, the Reform Association, organized among Japanese in Hawai'i, protested the companies' exploitation of their countrymen. Subsequently, operations of the companies diminished until they were all closed by 1908.

SOURCE: Compiled by K. Sinoto from *Hawaiian-Japanese Annual* for 1906.

View of Honolulu Harbor from Punchbowl showing the Immigration Station on Quarantine Island off Honolulu Harbor, ca. 1890s.

44

Japanese immigrants in quarantine, February 1885.

Cooking was going on, the food being in vessels of quaint and pretty shape and design placed over fire kindled in holes dug in the soft sand. These people eat no meat, their diet consisting almost entirely of fish, with which they are abundantly supplied. Rice is with them an important article of food and they like all kinds of vegetables. They cook in messes, and there is the usual amount of bustle about the numerous fires, that is inseparable from the preparing of food the world over. (*Daily Pacific Commercial Advertiser*, 10 February 1885).

Map 1

QUARANTINE ISLAND, 1901
(M. D. Monsarrat, Surveyor)

Map showing the location of Quarantine Island from a 1901 map of Honolulu, M. D. Monsarrat, surveyor.

Queue of men in *kimono* at Immigration Depot, 1890s (Gilman Collection).

Japanese immigrants in Immigration Depot, ca. 1899 (F. Davey, photographer).

Map 2

Downtown Honolulu in 1894
(Drawn by Rev. Takie Okumura)

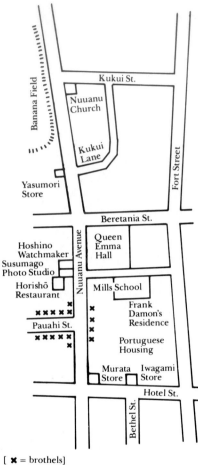

[✖ = brothels]
Downtown Honolulu, 1894
by Rev. Takie Okumura

Map drawn by Rev. Takie Okumura in 1894, from his book *Rakuen Ochiba.*

Caucasians lived on the east side of Nuʻuanu Avenue and Chinese and Japanese resided on the west side. The center of the Japanese establishment was between Nuʻuanu and River streets. The "red light" district is marked with Xs.

Table 7

Important Events in Hawaiʻi 1778–1924

750 ca.-1250 ca.	Polynesians settle in the Hawaiian Islands: introduction of food and medicinal plants including sugarcane and domesticated dogs, chickens, and pigs.
1778	Capt. James Cook discovers Hawaiʻi on his third expedition.
1786	First English traders stop in Hawaiʻi on their way to China.
1791	Don Francisco de Marin introduces vegetables and fruits.
1795	Kamehameha I unites the islands, except Kauaʻi and Niʻihau.
1802	Chinese on Lānaʻi produce sugar with stone crushers.
1819	Death of Kamehameha I; American whaling ships begin to stop in Hawaiʻi; Abolition of worship of religious idols and *kapu* system.
1820	First company of American missionaries arrives.
1824	Death of Kamehameha II and Queen Kamāmalu in London during their official visit.
1825	Wilkinson (English) starts cultivating coffee and sugarcane.
1827	First Catholic missionaries arrive; First printed laws are released.
1832	First general census is taken by American missionaries.
1835	First successful sugar plantation begins at Kōloa, Kauaʻi.
1839	Declaration of Rights; Seven Japanese from the shipwrecked *Chojamaru* are brought to Hawaiʻi. They work on sugar plantations on Mauʻi while in Hawaiʻi. Recollections of one of them, Jirokichi, are recorded in "Bantan" ("Bandan") after their return to Japan in 1843.
1840	First constitution is proclaimed.
1842	United States recognizes independence of Hawaiʻi. Captain Paulet seizes Hawaiʻi for Britain.
1843	Britain's Admiral Thomas restores sovereignty to Kamehameha III.
1848	The Great Mahele — Division of Land.
1850	Foreigners can own land; Royal Hawaiian Agricultural Society is formed; Master and Servants Act in effect.
1852	First 152 Chinese contract laborers arrive.
1853	First interisland steamer, S.S. *Akamai,* starts service.
1854	Death of Kamehameha III.
1860	First Japanese Envoy to United States on *Powhatan* makes emergency stop at Honolulu. Kamehameha IV proposes Japanese immigration to Hawaiʻi.
1863	Death of Kamehameha IV.
1864	Bureau of Immigration is created by the Hawaiian government; New constitution declared by Kamehameha V.
1866	Van Reed (American businessman in Japan) is appointed as consul general of Hawaiʻi to Japan; Robert W. Irwin becomes an agent for Pacific Mail Co. in Yokohama, Japan.
1867	U.S. Minister R. B. Van Valkenburgh, representing Hawaiʻi, signs the temporary Japan-Hawaii Friendship agreement; Van Reed starts recruiting Japanese contract laborers for sugar plantations in Hawaiʻi.
1868	First 148 Japanese contract laborers *(Gannenmono)* arrive in Hawaiʻi.
1870	Forty Japanese laborers return home at Japanese government's expense after a labor dispute on the plantation.
1871	Japan-Hawaii Friendship and Commerce treaty is signed.
1872	Death of Kamehameha V.
1873	William Lunalilo succeeds to the throne.
1874	Death of King Lunalilo; David Kalākaua is elected king.
1876	Reciprocity Treaty with U.S. in effect, lifting the tariff on Hawaiian sugar to U.S; Japanese Warship *Tsukuba* visits; Kalākaua asks Capt. Ito to convey the interest of Hawaiʻi in having Japanese immigrants come to work on the sugar plantations.
1878	First Portuguese immigrants arrive.
1879	Construction of ʻIolani Palace begins.
1881	King Kalākaua embarks upon a world tour accompanied by W. C. H. Judd and W. N. Armstrong; He visits Japan and meets Emperor Meiji with proposals of Japanese immigration to Hawaiʻi, marriage of a Japanese prince and a Hawaiian princess, and his idea of a Polynesian Federation; German immigrants arrive to work on sugar plantations.
1882	John M. Kapena is sent to Japan to extend an official invitation to Kalākaua's forthcoming coronation; R. W. Irwin is appointed Hawaiʻi's agent of the Bureau of Immigration in Japan; ʻIolani Palace is completed.
1883	King Kalākaua's coronation: Japanese delegates, Magohichiro Sugi, Masakata Ishibashi, Shogo Nagasaki, attend.
1884	Curtis Iʻaukea stops in Japan on the way back from attending Russia's Alexander III's coronation; Iʻaukea and Irwin return to Hawaiʻi to prepare the draft of an agreement for Japanese immigration.
1885	First installment of 944 government contract Japanese immigrants arrive on the *City of Tokio* on 8 February; Second installment of 989 arrives on *Yamashiromaru* on 17 June; Japanese section is created under Bureau of Immigration, Hawaiian government.
1886	Convention of Japanese Immigration is signed.
1887	Mass meeting of Honolulu citizens requesting dismissal of Gibson Ministry; Bayonet Constitution is proclaimed by the Reform government; Suffrage right of Japanese people is denied; Rev. Miyama (Methodist) starts the first Christian Mission for Japanese in Honolulu.

1889	Robert Wilcox attempts to overthrow the Reform government.
1891	Death of King Kalākaua; Queen Lili'uokalani succeeds to the throne.
1892	Senator O. W. Smith of Hawai'i speaks against increased Japanese population in Hawai'i.
1893	Queen Lili'uokalani is deposed by Provisional government; Warship *Naniwa* arrives to protect Japanese in Hawai'i, where Japanese league is organized to retrieve suffrage right.
1894	Private immigration companies take over recruitment of Japanese laborers; Constitution of Republic of Hawaii in effect.
1894	Sino-Japanese war.
1895	Sino-Japanese war ends; Robert Wilcox's attempt to restore the Queen's power; Abdication of Queen Lili'uokalani.
1896	Japanese Immigration Bureau closes.
1897	Landing refused to approximately 1,000 Japanese immigrants arriving on three boats; Reading test (in Japanese) is imposed upon Japanese immigrants.
1898	Spanish-American War, troops are sent to Philippines; Annexation of Hawai'i to U.S. is approved by President McKinley.
1899	First Spanish immigrants arrive; Death of Princess Ka'iulani; Epidemic of bubonic plague in Honolulu.
1900	The Great Chinatown Fire destroys downtown Honolulu; Territory of Hawai'i is established; Contract labor is prohibited due to application of United States laws to Hawai'i; First Okinawan immigrants arrive on S.S. *China*.
1903	First Korean immigrants arrive.
1904	Mass weddings (wharf marriages) become mandatory; Russo-Japanese war.
1905	Russo-Japanese war ends; Reform association is organized among Japanese in Hawai'i protesting the exploitation by Immigration Co. and Keihin Bank.
1906	First Filipino immigrants arrive.
1907	Moving of Japanese from Hawai'i to United States mainland is prohibited by Presidential order.
1908	Root-Takahira Gentlemen's Agreement restricted Japanese immigration to United States; Japanese government restricts emigration of their people; Nine Japanese leper patients sent home on the *Kasado Maru*.
1909	First major strike by Japanese laborers.
1912	Wharf marriages are criticized.
1913	Anti-Japanese land acts in effect in California.
1917	United States participates in World War I, Japanese enlist in United States Army. Five Japanese teachers are refused entry into Hawai'i.
1918	World War I ends; "Patriotic Movement" in United States; Prohibition law is imposed; Wharf marriages cease.
1919	Japanese Language School regulatory Act is submitted to the local government; Labor union organizes among Japanese sugar workers.
1920	Second major labor strike on O'ahu involving Japanese and Filipino laborers; Suffrage is given women by the nineteenth amendment to the United States Constitution.
1921	Japanese Language School act is imposed; Hawaii Sugar Planters' Association reduces wages for sugar plantation laborers; Japanese language schools file suit against foreign language school restrictions on the basis of unconstitutionality (in 1927, they win their case in the U.S. Supreme Court); Pan-Pacific Newspaper Conference discussion between anti-Japanese forces from the West Coast and local supporters of the Japanese about possible assimilation of Japanese in America.
1923	United States government sends labor committee to observe Hawaiian situation.
1924	Albert Johnson's Japanese Exclusion Act passes Congress; Period of restricted immigration of Japanese to United States, including Hawai'i, ceases.

SOURCE: Compiled by K. Sinoto

Family with shamisen at the Immigration Depot, 8 February 1885 (Dr. E. Arning, photographer).

47

48

Dock scene with Japanese contract laborers waiting for the steamer in Honolulu, ca. 1899.

"These people are on their way to the island of Hawaii where an extensive new sugar plantation was recently opened. They are brought to the Islands under contract to work for a certain period of years." (Bryan 1899:443).

Table 8
JAPANESE IMMIGRATION TO HAWAI'I, 1868–1924

EARLIEST IMMIGRANTS 元　年　者 One Shipload of 148 サイオト号で来布の148名	GOVERNMENT CONTRACT PERIOD 官 約 移 民 時 代 Approximately 29,000 Arrivals 約29,000名が来布	PRIVATE CONTRACT PERIOD 私 約 移 民 時 代 Approximately 57,000 Arrivals 約57,000名が来布
1868 **1885**	**1894**	**1900**
The first group of Japanese workers arrived in Hawaii in 1868. Their contracts were for three years, at four dollars per month. Because of their complaints about the unexpectedly harsh conditions of plantation life, the Japanese government would not agree to the resumption of immigration until 1885.	Immigrants were contracted to the Hawaiian government's Board of Immigration through its agent in Japan. Upon arrival in Hawaii their contracts were reassigned by the Board to various plantations. The average wage was $15.00 per month for men.	In April 1894 the Japanese government turned over immigration to government-licensed private companies. These immigration companies all too frequently exploited their fellow countrymen through intricate financial arrangements which resulted in an immigrant's initial contract period being spent in paying off "debts" to the company. The average wage was $12.50 per month for men.
最初の日本人移民がハワイに到着したのは1868年である。1ヵ月4ドルの報酬で3年間の労働契約であったが予想以上にきびしい耕地の労働条件に対して不満がとなえられたため日本政府は1885年に至るまで移民の再開に同意しなかった。	移民は日本駐在の代理人を通してハワイ政府の移住民局との間に契約を結びハワイ到着後更めて移住民局によってそれぞれの耕地との契約が交付された。当時男子1ヵ月の報酬は15ドルであった。	1894年日本政府は移民の取扱いを政府承認の会社に任せた。これらの移民会社は往々にして渡航費用に関する複雑な手続きを通じて同胞から搾取し移民は契約期間を会社への返済のために働きつづけるという結果をまねいた程である。この当時男子の報酬は1ヵ月12.5ドルであった。

FREE IMMIGRATION PERIOD 自 由 渡 航 時 代 Approximately 71,000 Arrivals 約71,000名が来布	RESTRICTED IMMIGRATION PERIOD 呼 び 寄 せ 移 民 時 代 Approximately 61,000 Arrivals 約61,000名が来布	BAN ON ASIAN IMMIGRATION 移 民 禁 止 時 代
1900 **1908**	**1924**	
In 1900 Hawaii came under U.S. laws which prohibited contract labor importation. While there was a great influx of Japanese immigrants during this period, there was an almost equally great outflow drawn by higher wages on the U. S. mainland. Average wages went from $15.00 to $18.50 per month for men.	Resentment of "cheap labor" on the west coast led to the "Gentlemen's Agreement" of 1907-08 under which Japan "voluntarily" placed severe restrictions on emigration. Only immediate relatives of immigrants and returning former immigrants were permitted entry. Over 20,000 "picture brides," whom Japanese men in Hawaii had married in absentia, arrived during this period. At the time of the Great Plantation Strike of 1920 the basic wage for common laborers was $20.00 per month.	The Immigration Law of 1924 excluded all Asians from U. S. immigration quotas. Japanese were not included in the quotas until after World War II.
1900年にハワイは米国属領となり米国の法律の適用により契約労働者の導入は禁じられた。この時代を通じて多数の日本人移民がハワイに来たが一方多くの人々が米本土の高賃金にひかれ移住していった。当時の男子1ヵ月の報酬は15ドルから18.5ドルであった。	米国北西岸にあふれた低賃金労働者の群に対する反感は1907年から1908年にかけて日米間の紳士協定により日本政府に自発的にきびしい移民制限を行わせた。このためハワイにすでに住んでいる移民の家族或は以前にハワイに住んでいたことのあるものだけが入国を許された。この時代に20,000人以上の写真結婚による花嫁達がハワイに来た。1920年における耕地の大ストライキ当時一般労働者の報酬は1ヵ月20ドルであった。	1924年の移民法によりすべての東洋人移民が禁止された。その結果第二次大戦後に至るまで日本人移民は移民割当のわくからはずされていた。

SOURCE: Compiled by HIHPC.

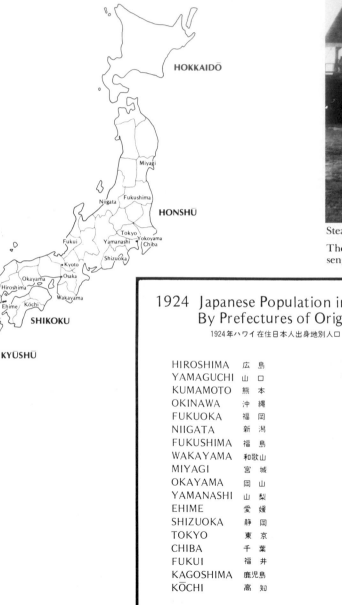

50

Steamer *Kinau* at Hilo Bay, pre-1900.

The interisland steamer anchored out in the bay and the passengers came ashore in landing boats.

1924 Japanese Population in Hawaii By Prefectures of Origin 1924年ハワイ在住日本人出身地別人口		
HIROSHIMA	広 島	30,534
YAMAGUCHI	山 口	25,878
KUMAMOTO	熊 本	19,551
OKINAWA	沖 縄	16,536
FUKUOKA	福 岡	7,563
NIIGATA	新 潟	5,036
FUKUSHIMA	福 島	4,936
WAKAYAMA	和歌山	1,124
MIYAGI	宮 城	1,088
OKAYAMA	岡 山	727
YAMANASHI	山 梨	581
EHIME	愛 媛	538
SHIZUOKA	静 岡	487
TOKYO	東 京	461
CHIBA	千 葉	434
FUKUI	福 井	396
KAGOSHIMA	鹿児島	381
KŌCHI	高 知	364

SOURCE: Compiled by HIHPC.

Jōji Nakayama, head of Customs House in Yokohama in 1872, appointed Consul General of Japan in Rome, Italy, in the same year, member of the Imperial Household Staff in 1876.

Nakayama came to Hawai'i in 1885 on the first boat; he was appointed head of the Japanese section of the Hawaiian government's Bureau of Immigration.

Kōloa Landing, Kaua‘i, ca. 1910.

52

Laborers and steam plow, pre-1900.

In the 1880s the steam plow replaced plows drawn by horses or oxen. The plows worked in pairs, with one on each side of a field and usually more than a thousand feet apart. One engine pulled a gang plow across the field, and the other drew it back. After the land was plowed and harrowed, with all the weeds turned under, the double mould-board plows were used to make the furrows for planting seed cane.

PLANTATION WORK

The plantation economy dominated Hawai'i for the period roughly spanning the mid-nineteenth to the mid-twentieth centuries. A small group of businessmen, predominantly American, established tight control over sugar production and marketing through a set of interlocking directorates among the major businesses. These corporations or "factors" eventually became known as the Big Five: American Factors (earlier, H. Hackfeld & Co.), C. Brewer, Theo. H. Davies, Castle & Cooke, and Alexander and Baldwin. They prospered as agents for plantations by handling the shipping and sales of sugar, purchasing equipment and materials, financing expansion, and insuring the operations. In time, they purchased nearly all of the sugar plantations and diversified into transportation, utilities, insurance, banking, and retailing. This control over the economy permitted the *haole* (White) owners and managers extraordinary power in every other sphere of human activity in Hawai'i, from wages and living conditions to eventual annexation of the islands to the United States in 1898.

By 1890, there were seventy-two plantations in Hawai'i producing 259,789,462 pounds of raw sugar for transport to refineries on the West Coast. The Hawaiian Islands, however, were not particularly suited to sugar cultivation. Places like the American South, the Caribbean, and other islands in the Pacific enjoyed more sunshine, larger reserves of native labor, better terrain, and more abundant rainfall. The entrepreneurs who invested in sugar were, therefore, subject to difficult conditions in trying to produce profits as well as sugar.

Sugarcane cultivation was extremely labor intensive. The industry was constantly on the search for technology that would reduce its reliance on masses of cheap labor, but these developments took time. When the Japanese arrived in the mid-1880s, plantations were beginning to use railroads more widely to transport laborers to the fields and cane to the mills. The stationary steam plows were a major advance in the arduous task of preparing land for planting, but cutting the seed cane, planting, irrigating, fertilizing, weeding, cutting, and loading the harvested cane into wagons, railroad cars, or flumes all remained backbreaking labor. The mills required a wide range of skills: attending to machines used in washing and crushing the stalks to extract the juice; boiling and clarifying the juice; condensing and crystallizing the sugar; and, finally, bagging and transporting the product for shipment to refineries in California. Support services involving carpenters, electricians, ironworkers, mechanics, and other skilled workers were required, and the Japanese soon began entering positions in all of these areas.

Bangō, the Japanese word for number, was the term used to describe a laborer's plantation identification tag. Ethnic background was indicated by both *bangō* shape and number.

Clearing a hillside in ʻŌlaʻa, island of Hawaiʻi (courtesy of United Japanese Society of Hawaii).

Plowing, Lihue Plantation, Kauaʻi, ca. 1890 (T. P. Severin, photographer).

Since so many of the costs of producing sugar were fixed or beyond their control, planters devoted considerable attention to the amount of labor needed, strategies to minimize labor costs, and appropriate means of hiring and controlling the workers. For Hawaiʻi, where the native population was declining rapidly, the use of contract or indentured labor was clearly advantageous. Planters had nearly as much control over such laborers as did slaveowners—without the cost of sustaining old, sick, or unproductive slaves. Nor did planters have to face the political and social criticism associated with the system of slavery. Contracts held workers to the plantations for a fixed number of years (eventually set at 3) with criminal penalties for runaways, including fines and imprisonment, and in the early years, additional periods of servitude.

The large number of individual plantations and the wide range of geographic and climatic conditions, as well as variation in management philosophy and style, meant that wide differences in treatment of workers would inevitably emerge. The treatment of contract laborers in Hawaiʻi was relatively humane when compared with conditions in places like Peru, Cuba, or other islands in the Pacific. Still, laborers were rarely seen as human beings, and it was the responsibility of the managers and the *luna* (field overseers) to extract the utmost work at the least cost. The *luna* was assigned to groups of laborers and was responsible for recording the time worked, supervising the day's tasks, and controlling the work force.

Conforming to the strict discipline of this industrial agriculture was physically, culturally, and socially devastating to the Japanese workers. Their lives had been full of backbreaking struggle, assuredly, but in Japan they had some periodic relief, if only because of the seasonal nature of agriculture there. In Hawaiʻi, the Japanese found that doctors employed by the plantations held the power to determine whether they were too ill to work. There was an endlessly predictable schedule: 6 days per week; 10 hours in the field or 12 hours in the mill. Whistles, bells, and sirens determined waking and resting; *luna* with whips dictated the pace of work. A typical day would find male workers rising at 4:30 A.M. to dress and have breakfast, with women getting up even earlier to prepare breakfast and the lunches to be taken to work. Work started at 6 A.M. and ended at 4:30 P.M. with half-an-hour for lunch.

Hawaii koku de wa yo	In this country, Hawaiʻi
Jikan ga tayori	Our lives are counted out by the clock.
Uchi e kaereba	But when I come home
Omae ga tayori.	It's you alone I can count on.

Such songs, called *holehole bushi*, were composed by Japanese immigrant workers to express their most deeply felt emotions regarding work and life in Hawaiʻi. *Bushi* is the Japanese term for song or melody, and *holehole* is Hawaiian for dried sugarcane leaves and, by extension, the work of stripping them from the stalks to facilitate harvesting the cane. *Holehole* work was considered less physically demanding than other field work and was routinely assigned to women, who were probably the spontaneous composers of most of these early songs.

Plantation work was performed by successive waves of immigrant labor from many different countries after the 1850s, when it became evident that native Hawaiian labor would not be sufficient to support the growing production. Recruiting many different immigrant groups to work on the plantations was a strategy employed to prevent any single group from dominating the labor force. This policy of divide and rule was encouraged as a means of preventing "any concerted action in case of strikes, for there are few, if any, cases of Japs, Chinese, and Portuguese entering into a strike as a unit." While the abundant supply of Japanese labor was a blessing, their increasing numbers in the plantation work force encouraged planters to go to other sources in Puerto Rico, Korea, and the Philippines. Of 39,587 sugar workers in 1901, there were 27,531 Japanese, or about 70 percent of the total.

The planters controlled the work force through a combination of strategies, including a judicious mixture of brute force — in the form of *luna* and policemen — and paternalistic efforts to keep the workers satisfied. In 1905, for example, Kahuku Plantation established a day-nursery for Japanese children and infants, to release mothers to work in the fields. Ewa followed suit with a free kindergarten at about the same time. This policy became especially noteworthy after the major strikes of 1909 and 1920; in addition, more movies were shown and youth organizations and activities were subsidized. In 1922, a popular almanac observed, "the Boy and Girl Scout movement for the benefit of the children has been undertaken and its extension is recommended as the best medium to promote Americanism, and teach loyalty to our country *and the plantation*" (emphasis added).

For the plantation workers the question of wages was almost always uppermost. The first male contract laborers in 1885 received $9 per month and the equivalent of $6 in food (women received $6 in wages and $4 for food) for a total of $15. This amount fluctuated between $12 and $15 in the period 1894–1899. There were major distinctions in pay scales according to sex, nationality, and status (whether contract or free labor). In 1899, the year before all contract laborers were released by the Organic Act, there were 5,471 free Japanese workers and 17,547 under contract. The vast majority of these laborers had arrived in the 1898–1899 biennium, when nearly thirty thousand Japanese came to Hawai'i.

Most of the Japanese in sugar plantation work were assigned tasks of the meanest kind and the most meager wages, but there were also those who earned considerably more than their fellow immigrants. At one extreme was the chief inspector of the Japanese section of the Hawaii Bureau of Immigration, who, although not a plantation worker himself, depended wholly on contract labor for his position. Jōji Nakayama was officially paid $250 per month, but he enriched himself through a variety of schemes in which he profited from the Japanese immigrants. For some time, until forced to desist by the Hawaiian government, Nakayama required men to pay him for permitting their wives to join them in Hawai'i. As one of the *holehole bushi* noted:

Dekasegi wa kurukuru	The workers keep on coming
Hawaii wa tsumaru	Overflowing these Islands.
Ai no Nakayama	But it's only middleman Nakayama
Kane ga furu.	Who rakes in the money.

Even among the laborers in the fields and mills, there were distinctions that emerged very quickly. On some plantations, younger and stronger workers were paid slightly more (usually 10 cents per day) to set faster paces for their fellow workers. These "*hippari* men"

Planting seed cane (*pulapula*).

Irrigation on a sugar plantation (*hanawai*), ca. 1899 (Bryan 1899:484).

The worker is Chinese.

Flume of sugar plantation near Onomea Bay, island of Hawai'i, ca. 1899 (Bryan 1899:517).

This flume, used for carrying water and sugarcane to the mills, is supported by a 200-foot-high trestle.

(from the Japanese *hipparu*, "to pull along") inspired considerable hatred for collaborating with the plantation management. In an unusual "dialogue" of *holehole bushi*, the *hippari* man is made to sing:

Tsuite kinasare	Keep up with me
Monku wa yamete	And stop your grumbling
Kuchi de horehore	You can't do *holehole*
Suru jya nashi.	With your mouth.

In retort, the others would sing:

Tsuite ikaryo ka	Why should I keep up
Omae no ato e	With the likes of you?
Ore nya mashinkin	You get the extra cash
Aru jya nashi.	Not me.

In the fields, angry workers threw sticks and stones at *hippari* men, forcing them to slow down. In one incident, in December 1893, four Japanese bound and beat one *hippari* man who had broken his promise not to set a fast pace on Ewa Plantation.

The planters found the wage system unsatisfactory since "it does not stimulate the ambition of the laborer, and, indeed, tends to reduce the amount of labor furnished by each laborer to the product of the least efficient and most thriftless." One of the most promising innovations was the development of the *ukepau* and *ukekibi* systems to encourage worker responsibility and incentive. The former (*uke*, Japanese for contract; *pau*, Hawaiian for completed) provided for agreed upon work quotas for the day. Workers could return to their camps before the end of the 10-hour day, as long as assigned tasks were completed. By the 1890s, this system had evolved into one in which laborers were paid on a piecework basis; those who cut and loaded cane were paid according to weight, and those who did planting or weeding were paid according to the amount of seed cane planted or number of rows weeded.

The system was further refined by 1895. In *ukekibi* (*kibi*, Japanese for sugarcane) a group of laborers contracted to cultivate a section of planted cane, often 50 to 100 acres, until harvest. Plantations provided the land and machinery for heavy work, such as plowing the field and transporting the cane to the mill, as well as fertilizer and water. Housing, medical care, and fuel for cooking were also provided, and a base allowance of perhaps $10 per month was advanced for living expenses. In return, the group organized itself without the feared and hated *luna*, and managed the whole process of work at its own pace. Occasionally, especially ambitious families would tend small *ukekibi* fields in addition to working for wages. The plantation harvested the cane from 18 months to 2 years after planting. The cane was weighed as it left the field or at the mill, and the workers were paid the market price, less the amount advanced. *Ukekibi* contracts at various times and places could vary widely in scale and coverage. Although there were charges that plantations cheated them, the *ukekibi* workers' earnings were usually higher than those of wage-laborers.

Eventually, especially after the 1909 strike, the planters placed more emphasis on a bonus system which was calculated on the basis of the price of sugar and became publicized as a type of profit-sharing plan. Like the *ukepau* and *ukekibi* systems before it, the bonus system was designed to keep workers from leaving sugar work and to encourage them to become a more dependable source of labor. To accomplish this end, bonuses were paid to those who completed a minimum of 20 workdays per month and to those who remained on the plantation until certain times, particularly until after the harvest.

Plantation work was hard and sometimes brutal. It was always tedious and monotonous. And, as will be seen, Japanese workers resorted to various means to make the conditions more bearable and the compensation more just and equitable. At the same time, they and their families concentrated on making the best of life in the plantation camps by moving on to better jobs and by creating or recreating social and cultural practices that would improve the quality of their lives.

Group of laborers on the Lihue Plantation, Kaua'i, ca. 1899.

"Those in front are Germans and Portuguese, next to them are the Japanese while the Chinese bring up the rear. Race prejudices are so bitter, especially between the Japanese and the Chinese, that they have to be kept separate in their work and habitations as far as possible." (Bryan, 1899:503).

Japanese woman irrigator, Pu'unēnē, Maui, ca. 1912 (R.J. Baker, photographer).

Women frequently used hoes to tend irrigation ditches and to control the flow of water.

Plantation field workers, Puʻunēnē, Maui, ca. 1912 (R. J. Baker, photographer).

SKETCH SHOWING LOCATION of New "KAULA" CAMP

Map 3
KAʻULA CAMP, HĀMĀKUA, ISLAND OF HAWAIʻI, 1909
(Theo H. Davies Collection, Bishop Museum Business Archives).

Table 10
CHANGES IN LABOR CONTRACT CONDITIONS THROUGHOUT THE GOVERNMENT CONTRACT PERIOD, 1885–1894

DATE	NO. OF ARTICLES RE: CONDITIONS	III WAGES		VII DEPOSITORY OF MONEY DEDUCTED FROM WAGES	XI AMOUNT DEDUCTED FROM WAGES			AUTHORIZED BY
		MALE	FEMALE		RATE OF DEDUCTION	ANNUALLY	MONTHLY UP TO...	
Jan. 1885	7	$9.00 + 6.00 food allowance	$6.00 + 4.00 food	Japanese Consulate in Honolulu, bank under Hawaiian government	25%	—	—	R. W. Irwin, Hawaiian Minister Resident, and Special Agent of the Bureau of Immigration
Nov. 1887	12	$15.00	$10.00	Japanese Consulate, Ministry of Finance, Japanese Government	25%	$75.00	$3.00	
May 1888	12	$15.00	$10.00		15%	$55.00	$2.20	
Oct. 1888	12	$15.00	$10.00		15%	$65.00	$2.60	
May 1890	12	$15.00	$10.00	Japanese Consulate in Honolulu	15%	¥15.50	¥ .50	
June 1892	12	$12.50	$10.00		15%	¥15.50	¥ .50	
Nov. 1892	12	$12.50	$10.00	Yokohama Shōkin Ginkō (Specie Bank), Honolulu Branch	15%	¥15.50	¥ .50	
Oct. 1893	11	$12.50	$10.00		15%	Article XI was eliminated		Naozō Ōnaka acting for R. W. Irwin
June 1894	11	$12.50	$10.00		15%			

SOURCE: Compiled by K. Sinoto in 1984 from Labor Contracts.

Olokele irrigation ditch, Kaua'i, ca. 1900–1910 (A. Gartley, photographer).

Japanese women workers (*hō hana*) during government contract period (courtesy of United Japanese Society of Hawaii).

Japanese women weeding (*kālai*) in Honomū, island of Hawai'i (courtesy of United Japanese Society of Hawaii).

Cutting cane (*kachiken*) (R. J. Baker, photographer).

Fluming sugarcane, island of Hawai'i, ca. 1920 (R. J. Baker, photographer).

A portable wooden flume was set up in the field to transport cut cane. Flume-making was one of the major responsibilities of the plantation carpenters, and the skill of the Japanese in this task was highly regarded.

Group scene at Ewa Plantation, O'ahu, ca. 1920.

Laborers of various ethnic groups pose for a photograph with their luna, at the far left.

Field worker collecting cut cane (*liliko hāpai*), Pu'unēnē, Maui, ca. 1912 (R. J. Baker, photographer).

Laborers wore protective clothing in the fields to shield themselves from the sun, rain, wind, heat, and dust and, most of all, from abrasions caused by the sharp edges of the cane leaves.

Plantation workers, probably on their lunch break, Puʻunēnē, Maui, ca. 1912 (R. J. Baker, photographer).

The man at left is holding a cane knife.

Cane field workers, Puʻunēnē, Maui, 1912 (R. J. Baker, photographer).

The couple found a place to have their lunch on a plantation railroad car that transported cut cane to the mill.

Cane knife, ca. 1913.

The hook was used to pick up cane stalks from the ground.

Enamelled two-tiered lunchpail with lid, in denim carrying bag, ca. 1903.

Commonly used to carry lunch to work; the bottom container was for rice; the top was for other foods, such as cooked vegetables, *tōfu*, and dried fish.

Hauling cane (*hāpai kō*), Ewa Plantation, Oʻahu, ca. 1896.
Cane stalks were hauled by workers in the early years.

Harvesting cane, Ewa Plantation, Oʻahu, ca. 1897.
The introduction of machinery for harvesting and hauling cane eased the tedious, backbreaking aspects of hand labor.

Japanese water carriers, ca. 1899 (Bryan 1899:466).
Every plantation employed men to carry drinking water to the laborers in the fields.

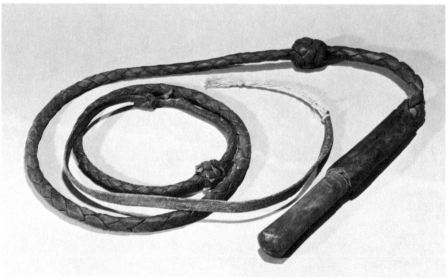

Leather whip, similar to the ones used by luna (overseers) to drive laborers.

Hauling cane at Lihue Plantation, Kaua'i, ca. 1890.

Overseers on horseback supervised laborers at work. Whips, such as the one held by the man in the center, were often used to drive human beings as well as oxen.

Group of plantation overseers or luna, Makaweli, Kaua'i, ca.
1912.

Railroad track repair gang, Wailuku, Maui, 1912 (R.J. Baker, photographer).

Spreckels Sugar Mill, Spreckelsville, Maui, ca. 1890

The Spreckels Sugar Co. was known for fair treatment and better working conditions. People wanted to work there when their contracts with other plantations were fulfilled.

Holehole bushi song:

Jōyaku kiretara yō
Kinau ni notte
Yukoka Maui no Spreckels e

When my contract expires,
I wish I could go to Spreckels
aboard the ship *Kinau*

Ookala Plantation, island of Hawai'i, ca. 1880s (J.J. Williams, photographer).

Extensive railroad systems were instrumental in transporting cut cane to the mills.

Boiler room under construction at Makee Mill, Keālia, Kaua'i, ca. 1900.

Steam was produced in the boiler room to generate power to run the mill. Horizontal return tubular boilers (HRT) which sit atop the fire boxes are missing; only the ash pits and fire boxes with fuel entrances are shown here.

66

Workers stationed beside sugar centrifugals, Kahuku Mill, O'ahu, ca. 1913.

Sugar centrifugals separated massecuite (cane juice with a 90 percent sugar content) into raw sugar and molasses.

Steam engines, Kahuku Mill, O'ahu, ca. 1913.

Steam engines turned the rollers of the sugar mill which ground the cane, separating the fiber (bagasse) from the juices. Bagasse was used as fuel to stoke the boiler room.

Blacksmith shop, Hana Plantation, Maui, 1904 (H. C. Ovenden, photographer).

Foundry workers, Waialua, Oʻahu, ca. 1910.

Foundry work was important in supporting the plantation's
capacity to construct and repair essential machinery and tools.
Second from left, Kumagorō Onomura and his son; second
from right, Tsurumatsu Onomura.

Jirō Iwasaki, ʻŌlaʻa, island of Hawaiʻi.

Jirō Iwasaki was born in Fukui Prefecture in 1867. He came to Hawaiʻi in 1893 to export Hawaiian sugar to a Yokohama sugar wholesaler for whom he had worked. Soon after arriving, he contracted to clear land for Olaa Sugar Plantation and later to grow seed cane and to harvest cane under contract.

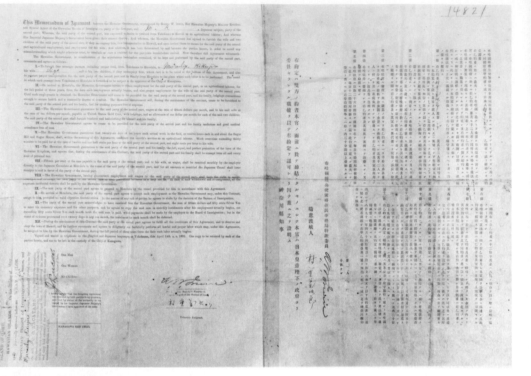

Labor contract of Kikujirō Murashige with Koloa Sugar Co., 1891, with completion certified in 1894.

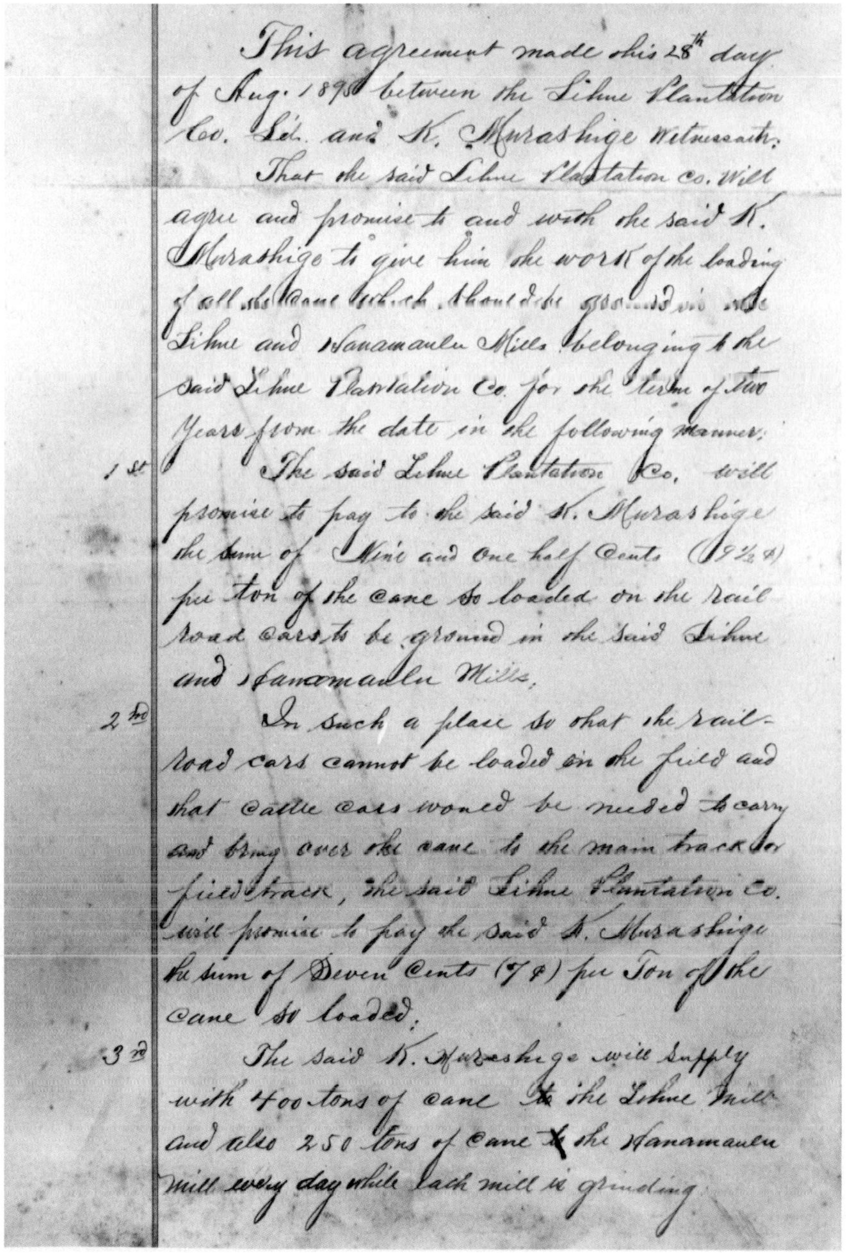

This agreement made this 28th day of Aug. 1895 between the Lihue Plantation Co. Ltd. and K. Murashige Witnesseth.

That the said Lihue Plantation Co. will agree and promise to and with the said K. Murashige to give him the work of the loading of all the Cane which should be ground in the Lihue and Hanamaulu Mills belonging to the said Lihue Plantation Co. for the term of two Years from the date in the following manner.

1st   The said Lihue Plantation Co. will promise to pay to the said K. Murashige the sum of Nine and One half Cents (9½¢) per ton of the cane so loaded on the rail road cars to be ground in the said Lihue and Hanamaulu Mills.

2nd   In such a place so that the railroad cars cannot be loaded in the field and that Cattle cars would be needed to carry and bring over the cane to the main track or field track, the said Lihue Plantation Co. will promise to pay the said K. Murashige the sum of Seven Cents (7¢) per Ton of the Cane so loaded.

3rd   The said K. Murashige will Supply with 400 tons of Cane to the Lihue Mill and also 250 tons of Cane to the Hanamaulu mill every day while each mill is grinding.

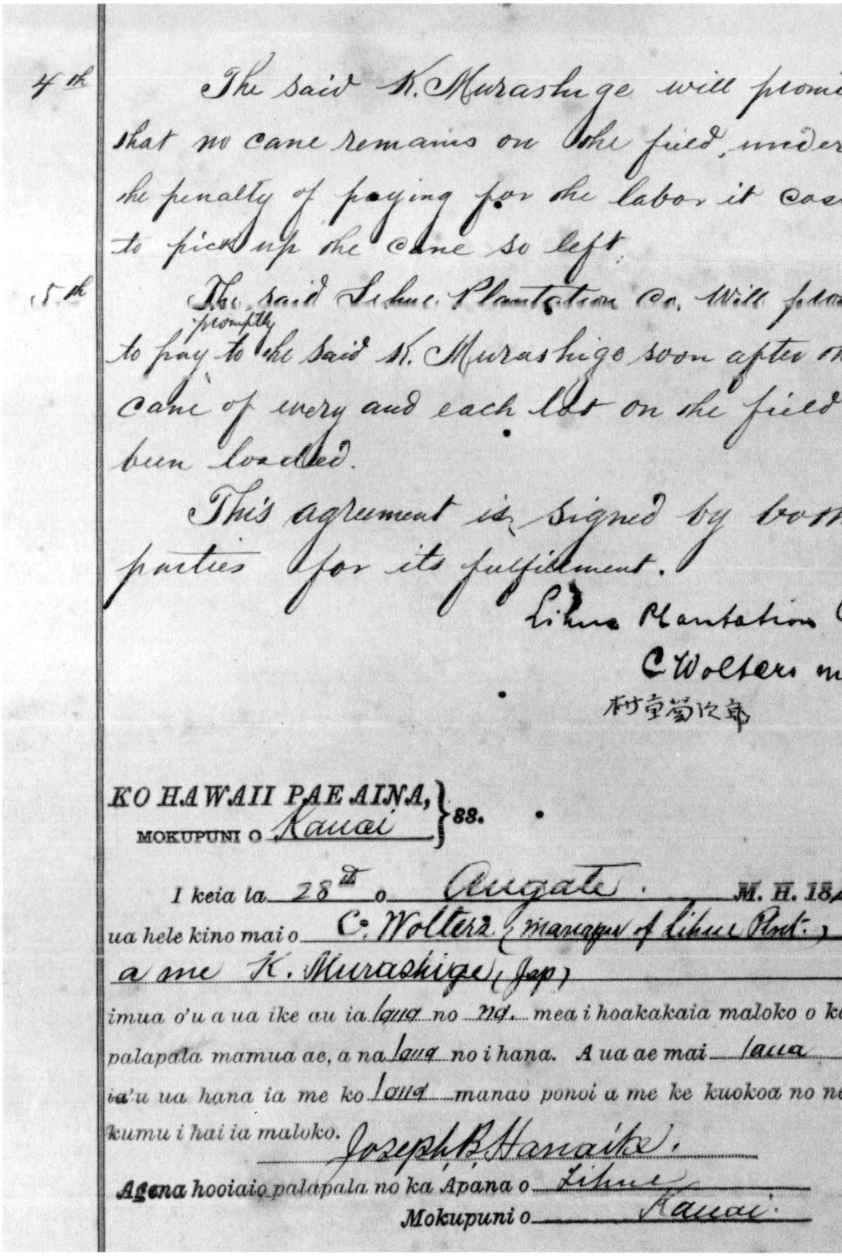

4th   The said K. Murashige will promise that no cane remains on the field, under the penalty of paying for the labor it costs to pick up the Cane so left.

5th   The said Lihue Plantation Co. will promise to pay promptly to the said K. Murashige soon after the cane of every and each lot on the field has been loaded.

This agreement is signed by both parties for its fulfillment.

Lihue Plantation Co.
C. Wolters manager

村室当次郎

KO HAWAII PAE AINA, } ss.
MOKUPUNI O Kauai

I keia la 28th o Augate M. H. 1895
ua hele kino mai o C. Wolters (manager of Lihue Plant.)
a me K. Murashige (Jap.)
imua o'u a ua ike au ia laua no na mea i hoakakaia maloko o ka palapala mamua ae, a na laua no i hana. A ua ae mai laua ia'u ua hana ia me ko laua manao ponoi a me ke kuokoa no na kumu i hai ia maloko. Joseph B. Hanaike.
Agena hooiaio palapala no ka Apana o Lihue
Mokupuni o Kauai.

Cane loading contract of Kikujirō Murashige with Lihue Plantation, in English and Hawaiian, 1895.

69

Advertisement for laborers by Kikujirō Murashige in *Yamato*,
13 November 1895.

A few ambitious people became entrepreneurs themselves
when their plantation contracts expired.

Recruiting advertisement for Kahuku Sugar Plantation,
Yamato, 20 June 1896.

Early entrepreneurs, ʻŌlaʻa, island of Hawaiʻi, ca. 1890s (courtesy of Y. Baron Goto).

Center, Juzō Sakamaki; second from right, Jirō Iwasaki.

約條番號 モ六三九

岸川象藏殿

横濱正金銀行

明治廿六年一月四日

行記帳高二有之候也
年十二月三十一日ニ於ル當銀
月迄御預入高元利金ニシテ同
右ハ貴殿ニ於テ明治廿五年十
一金　拾九圓六拾ノ錢九厘

預金額通知書

〔本書ハ賣買抵當又ハ融通ノ
これはうりかいひきあてまたはゆづうのとおりぬりものがい
用ニハ賣買抵當又ハ融通ノ
効ナキモノゝ事〕

Receipt for savings issued to Kikuzō Kishikawa by the Yokohama Shōkin Bank, Honolulu, 1893.

71

No. 11101   Honolulu, Dec. 31st 1888

小方松二

Received of Mr. Templeman

for your account the sum of $ 10.00

being 25 per cent. of your wages for till Oct / 88

which is deposited to your credit at 5 per cent. interest.

TARO ANDO.

$11.20   H. I. J. M.'s Diplomatic Agent and Consul General.

CONSULATE GENERAL OF JAPAN

Japanese Consulate General's receipt to Matsuji Ogata for 25 percent of his wages withheld as savings, 31 December 1888.

C. Brewer's Honolulu plantation mill (1898–1946) located at ʻAiea, Oʻahu, ca. 1902.

Workers' cottages and a long house surround a Japanese temple in the foreground, with the mill and cane fields in the background. This area has also been referred to as Aiea or Halawa Plantation.

PLANTATION LIFE

Not long after the *City of Tokio* docked in Honolulu with the first boatload of Japanese contract workers, the man who had arranged their arrival drafted a "circular" directed to all plantations. The Japanese, Robert W. Irwin insisted, were not laborers but small farmers whose farms were being "held in trust by relations, and should they like Hawaii and find themselves well treated, their intention [was] to remain here with their families." Irwin further suggested that the Japanese could be led by the "silken thread of kindness," and that they should not be driven by overseers, but supervised by their own leaders. He said they would repay such consideration with uncompensated work in emergencies, with a willingness to repair their own homes, and "a great many things that were not required by their contracts." Unfortunately, the Japanese, like other immigrants before and after them, were thrust into a plantation society that made it impossible for their lives to proceed as smoothly as Irwin envisioned.

At the very top were a few privileged *haole* owners and managers. In between the owners and the masses of laborers was a group of predominantly *haole*, Portuguese, and Hawaiian overseers (*luna*). Next came an ethnically mixed group of skilled workers such as carpenters, mechanics, and locomotive engineers. Finally, there were the field and mill workers, who, for the three decades between 1890 and 1920, were primarily Japanese. The plantation structure, in this broad view, had a castelike quality that encouraged the perpetuation of an image of the Japanese as a completely downtrodden group. The view looks significantly different, however, when examined from the standpoint of the Japanese as a complex, evolving ethnic community.

Laborers received, as part of their contracts, free housing, medical care, and cooking fuel from the plantations. The quality of housing varied enormously, from the sprawling estates of the managers to comfortable bungalows for *luna*, down to quarters that ranged from bad to intolerable for early contract laborers, depending on conditions at different plantations. At its worst, plantation housing was miserable. The more fortunate workers were given materials and time off from work to construct huts for themselves along traditional Japanese lines, thatched with sugarcane leaves. Others were horrified to find barrackslike buildings in which men, women, and children were indiscriminately thrown together in groups sometimes exceeding one hundred. In some of these areas cooking was done outside over wood fires set in dirt. By the turn of the century, many plantations built

Map 4

AIEA SUGAR PLANTATION, 1914
(courtesy of Tsuneichi Yamamoto)

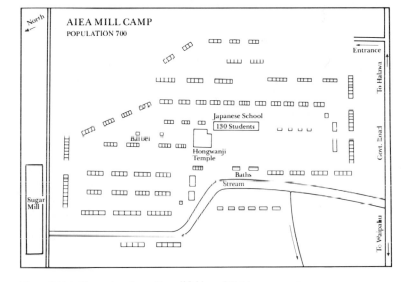

Map of Aiea Plantation from *Hawaii Ichiran*, 1914 (courtesy of Tsuneichi Yamamoto).

Hawaii Ichiran (A Glance at Hawaii), by Atsuchi "Nekketsu" Takei, contains information about plantation camps in Hawai'i.

Japanese plantation barber, ca. 1898 (F. Davey, photographer).

Barbering was one of the earlier professions started within the plantation community, and the trade was eventually dominated by the Japanese, even in the cities.

clusters of dwellings called camps, with perhaps five or six "longhouses," approximately 18 by 30 feet and divided into a dozen rooms. In one popular configuration, four of the rooms went to couples, while the other eight were assigned to single men. The couples lived in quarters measuring 6 by 6 feet, and the single men occupied rooms half as wide, with barely enough space in which to sleep. The quality of housing improved dramatically after the 1909 and 1920 strikes, and kerosene replaced wood as cooking fuel, making life somewhat more bearable in the twentieth century.

Medical care was extremely uneven, varying with individual managers' human qualities, as well as with distance from adequate hospitals and clinics. There were many complaints by the Japanese that *haole* doctors forced them to work in spite of illness and that the language barrier resulted in problems of diagnosis and treatment. In response to Japanese concerns, the Meiji government sent Katsunosuke Inouye as a special commissioner to investigate and negotiate solutions. Inouye was given the authority to withhold the 989 Japanese, if satisfactory arrangements were not forthcoming. He urged that Japanese doctors be retained, and this was agreed to by the Hawaiian government. In 1886, therefore, Jōji Nakayama was able to note the successful recruitment of eight Japanese doctors and ten interpreters to work under the Bureau of Immigration, and to be assigned to different plantations to treat the workers. Later, travelling peddlers carried traditional Japanese medicines, and Japanese workers shared folk treatments with Hawaiian natives and immigrants from other countries.

Japanese women prepared all meals for their families and, in some cases, also cooked for a few bachelors to earn additional income. For most of the single men, however, there was a system in which the plantation arranged with individuals among contract laborers, usually a couple, to cook for large groups of men. Such cooks, called *ōgokku*, received wages as regular laborers, a facility, and the fuel needed for preparing meals for perhaps twenty to thirty men. Each man paid about $4 or $5 per month for breakfast, *bentō* lunches to be taken to work, and dinners. In some camps, the cooks bought the food for the month and prorated the cost for the men at the end of the month.

The variety of ingredients was extremely limited and the Japanese immigrants generally faced a simple and repetitive diet. Protein was relatively expensive and rarely eaten. Some chicken and eggs were consumed and there was occasional beef or pork as well as fresh fish, but most of the protein was provided by soybeans and canned sardines or salmon. Homemade *tōfu* (soybean curd), *aburage* (fried *tōfu*), and small dried fish called *iriko* were major sources of protein for the laborers, and these items found their way into many of the meals.

The lack of fresh vegetables familiar to the Japanese diet convinced the first contract workers to urge subsequent immigrants to bring a variety of seeds. By 1900, one published source listed a variety of vegetables being grown by the Japanese in Hawai'i such as lettuce, green onions, turnips, string beans, eggplant, pumpkin, *daikon* (Japanese radish), *gobō* (burdock), and *shiso* (beefsteak plant). Early photos of Japanese camps near Hilo indicate that the Japanese were growing pumpkins, whose vines were allowed to climb and spread over their thatched huts. Indeed, the Japanese term for pumpkin, *bobura* (Kumamoto dialect), became a permanent part of the language in Hawai'i. It was used, at first, to denote all the Japanese, and later, those Japanese who were considered "country bumpkins."

Rice, of course, was the staple starch, and such an important part of the diet that its price was set at 5 cents per pound in the earliest contracts. Unfortunately, the polished variety preferred by the Japanese lacked the essential vitamin B1, which was not supplied by the rest of the diet, with the result that beriberi became a real problem.

On a typical day, the contract laborer faced a menu that did not change much from the one before or the one to follow. Breakfast consisted of rice, pickled vegetables (*tsukemono*), *miso* soup made with soybean paste and noodles, and tea. Lunch included rice and tea with *okazu* (entrees) such as *gobō* or cabbage cooked with *aburage; gobō* or cabbage cooked with dried fish or shrimp, dried codfish, or salted salmon. For their main meal, dinner, the *issei* could look forward to rice and tea with *tsukemono* and some dish prepared with a bit of dried fish or canned fish with fresh vegetables. Pork, beef, or chicken sometimes enriched their dinner on weekends or special occasions.

An 1889 inventory, compiled in the course of settling the affairs of a storeowner in Hono-ka‘a, Hawai‘i, indicates something of the Japanese diet and the cost to the laborers, who were paid between $12 and $15 per month:

canned salmon	1 dozen	$2.00
canned sardines	1 dozen	1.50
dried shrimp	1 lb.	.25
dried mushrooms	1 lb.	.38
dried seaweed (*nori*)	1 lb.	.06
soy sauce	1 barrel	3.25
mochi flour	1 lb.	.06
polished rice	1 lb.	.05

Most of the laborers from Japan had brought a single wicker basket (*yanagigōri*) which contained all their worldly goods, including clothes for rest and work. They wore traditional *kimono* in their quarters and around the plantation camps, but work clothes had to protect field laborers against the sun and rain, the sharp leaves of the sugarcane, and stinging insects such as the centipedes, scorpions, and yellow jackets that made their homes in the fields. For the men, *ahina* (denim) was prized for its durability and was used to make shirts and trousers, while straw hats and raincoats were regular parts of the outfit. The women often wore blouses made of Japanese cotton *ikat*, which was widely used in their home prefectures. Skirts were made of woven striped cotton, which was also imported, and there was usually an apron made of *ahina* for additional protection. Men and women wore *tekko* to cover their hands, *tabi* for their feet, and *kyahan* to wrap around their legs. A minor industry revolved around women who designed, sewed, repaired, and laundered these clothes.

The contract labor period, extending from 1885 to 1900, was noted for the degree of social disorganization characteristic of frontier areas. The overwhelming numbers of single males in their twenties and thirties added to the problem. Since there was a nearly constant ratio in this period of four males to each female, there were just enough women for men to fight over and persuade or coerce into the lucrative business of prostitution. By 1910, after the arrival of many "picture brides," the ratio had been improved to three to one and, by 1920, to three males for every two females. *Sake, onna, bakuchi* — liquor, women, and gambling — were virtual trademarks of the early period. Tarō Andō, Japanese Consul General from 1886 to 1888, noted in a report to Tokyo:

Outdoor kitchen of a Wainaku Japanese house, island of Hawai‘i, ca. 1890 (C. Furneaux, photographer).

Japanese houses with pumpkin vines growing over the roofs, Wainaku, island of Hawai‘i, ca. 1890 (C. Furneaux, photographer).

Seeds of some familiar vegetables were probably brought by the immigrants who arrived on the third boat in February 1886.

Early plantation bath, ca. 1890s (W. T. Brigham Collection).

Women washing clothes, early 1900s.

The undersigned went on a field trip to the plantations as soon as reaching Hawaii. The reputation of the Japanese is not too good. . . . The majority of them have no families to return to after a day's hard work and out of sheer loneliness seek solace in gambling, drinking and the companionship of women with questionable morals. Gambling in some plantations has reached a point where all night sessions are common.

Some of the most revealing commentaries survive in the *holehole bushi*. One such verse described Consul General Andō, who claimed to be interested in reforming the Japanese community. He was a heavy drinker who later converted to Christianity and led the temperance movement. Andō's personal commitment and good intentions did little, however, to improve the situation.

Hizamoto ni bakuchi	Gambling right under your nose
Mameya wa sakan nari	Whorehouses all over
Ome ni mienu ka	Can't see anything, Andō
Kuraki Andō.	Staying in the dark?

Other *holehole* rationalized the prostitute's life:

Sanjūgosen no	Why settle for 35 cents
Hore hore shiyō yori	Doing *holehole* work all day
Pake san to moi moi surya	When I can make a dollar
Akahi kala.	Sleeping with the Chinaman?

It was often said that the plantation managers arranged to have groups of prostitutes brought in regularly, especially on payday. Nor was illicit sex limited to organized prostitution. Cases of women being "stolen" from their husbands were reported, and there were some who simply ran away from unhappy marriages.

Asu wa Sande jya yo	Tomorrow is Sunday
Asobi ni oide	Come over and visit
Kane wa hanawai	My husband will be out watering the field
Washa uchi ni.	And I'll be home alone.

Beginning in 1888, *sake* was imported, and the Japanese made a great deal of liquor at home, ranging from beer and wine to hard whiskey such as *'ōkolehao*, made from roots of the ti plant. Gambling was conducted informally on all plantations but quickly became a function of tightly organized gangs. By the 1890s, some of the gangs that controlled both gambling and prostitution had moved their bases of operation to Honolulu, where the *Pacific Commercial Advertiser* and other English language newspapers were highly critical:

Since the advent of the Japanese to this country there has been growing under the very noses of the good people of this city an evil. . . . We refer to the large increase of the Japanese prostitutes in the city. . . . What becomes of the Japanese who leave the plantations and do not return to Japan? Fully one thousand of these men can be accounted for as idlers who are living on the earnings of Japanese women.

By the turn of the century, some plantation managers were brazen enough to threaten law enforcement agencies who might attempt to arrest gamblers.

The moral and social disorganization among the Japanese persuaded both the Japanese and *haole* leaders that organized religion had, a useful role to play in Hawai'i. The Japanese immigrants were overwhelmingly Buddhist, but the first churches to be established for them were Christian. Dr. C. M. Hyde of the Hawaiian Mission Board introduced Bible classes and English language lessons to help spread Christianity among the *issei*, with little success. Some progress in converting the Japanese was made when Rev. Kanichi Miyama arrived from the San Francisco Methodist Church Conference in 1887. Miyama appealed to the workers' sense of individual and national pride to turn them away from gambling and drinking. In 1888, Rev. Taizō Shimizu also arrived from San Francisco to provide assistance to Dr. Hyde. In the same year, Rev. Jirō Okabe was transferred to Hilo, where he remained until 1892, when he moved to Honolulu. Rev. Takie Okumura came to Hawai'i from Japan in 1894, a few years after graduating from Dōshisha University in Kyoto.

Okumura quickly became the most important Christian leader in the Japanese community and extended his influence well beyond the boundaries of the religious world. He began his work in Hawai'i by assuming leadership of the Japanese Christian Church in Nu'uanu until 1904, when he created a separate mission in Honolulu's Makiki area. He also established one of the earliest Japanese language schools in Hawai'i in 1896. Okumura was a courageous and articulate leader whose outspoken views on several major issues involving the process of "Americanization" of the Japanese made him perhaps the most controversial figure in the history of the Japanese in Hawai'i.

The Buddhists were somewhat slower to organize in Hawai'i, although a Jodo-Shinshu priest, Sōryū Kagai, arrived in 1889 on an informal visit to review the situation. Kagai reported to his Hongwanji superiors in Kyoto that the Japanese in the islands needed a mission, but that such a branch should extend some recognition to the Christian God in a way that would not conflict with Shintō or Buddhism. Kagai felt this approach was necessary because Christians had made an earlier entry into the Japanese immigrant community and to prevent possible criticism of Buddhism as an alien religion. Hongwanji leaders refused to accept this view, however, and it was not until 1894 that the first Buddhist temple was established by Gakuo Okabe of the Jodoshu. Okabe's temple was built in the plantation town of Hāmākua on the island of Hawai'i

Since most of the immigrants had come from the southwestern prefectures where Jodo-Shinshu adherents were predominant, it was inevitable that this denomination would become important. In 1897, Keijun Miyamoto arrived to conduct another survey in response to appeals from the immigrants. Miyamoto found that "unofficial" priests had been performing religious functions and that unscrupulous individuals had been busy defrauding Japanese by soliciting donations for nonexistent causes. Hongwanji headquarters immediately designated Hawai'i a mission site and Hōni Satomi was sent as the first official priest. In 1899 Yemyō Imamura arrived to assist Satomi. Imamura took over leadership in 1900 to begin a long and distinguished career in Hawai'i. Other Buddhist sects followed, with Ni-

Opening day of Olaa Temperance Society at Iwasaki Camp, island of Hawai'i, 1911 (Iwasaki Collection).

The Olaa Temperance Society was organized by Jirō Iwasaki in 1911.

Jōdō Mission under construction in Wailuku, Maui, 1913.

Kohala Church, island of Hawai'i, ca. 1899 (Okumura Collection).

Rev. Shigefusa Kanda, a native of Hokkaido and a graduate from Dōshisha University, Kyoto, who came to Hawai'i in 1893, was minister and founder of the church.

chiren in 1900, Soto in 1903, and Shingon in 1914, but Jodo-Shinshu was to remain the center of Buddhist activity in Hawai'i.

Plantation managers were quick to see the benefits of organized religion and, although they preferred Christianity, were generous in donating land for churches and temples as well as financial support. Religion helped stabilize the work force and sometimes succeeded in persuading laborers that their rewards should be expected in the next life rather than in the next pay period. By 1901, Buddhist temples in Waipahu and Kahuku were receiving donations from planters. This practice was widespread until the massive 1920 strike, when the Buddhist leadership actively supported the Japanese workers.

The first Shintō shrine, the Yamato Jinja, was built in 'Ōla'a on the island of Hawai'i in 1898. Shintō remained closer to its religious and ideological roots, perhaps because it was being so systematically turned into an ideology of ultranationalism by political leaders in Meiji Japan.

Although it was difficult to recreate the whole range of cultural events in Hawai'i, the Japanese managed to celebrate some of the most important occasions and perpetuate the most important traditions. In the early years, however, all Japanese men and women were in their twenties through forties, and all the children were very young; there were no grandparents to remind everyone of the days gone by and there were no graveyards of ancestors, or cultural monuments, to provide a sense of stability. Still, musical instruments like the *shamisen* and *shakuhachi* were brought out for performances, and dances were rehearsed and enjoyed. Boys' Day and Girls' Day were eagerly celebrated, and the New Year celebration was the occasion for much drinking and socializing.

The most important cultural event was also the most controversial. Each year the entire Japanese community rallied to celebrate the birthday of the Emperor Meiji on 3 November, which was newly designated as a national holiday by the Meiji government. On this *tenchōsetsu*, all work would stop, even though the plantations did not, at first, recognize it as a holiday. In 1891, for example, Wray Taylor, secretary to the Hawaiian Board of Immigration, complained to the Japanese consul general that "much trouble has been caused, and expense incurred in several plantations, on November 3, the anniversary of the birth of the Emperor of Japan, by the laborers refusing to work." By the mid-1890s, however, the plantations were forced to concede the right of Japanese laborers to celebrate *tenchōsetsu* and official contracts acknowledged the change.

The *ikkaisen* (first boat) immigrants included Japanese who knew *sumō* and *kendō* well enough to perform for King Kalākaua and his officials when they visited the immigration compound on 11 February 1885. Both of these vigorous traditions were carried on by the Japanese in plantation camps. One master swordsman from Miyagi, Hanemon Furuyama, was specifically sent by his prefectural government to train sugar workers in *kendō* in order to develop discipline and moral character. In 1896, only a decade after their arrival, the Japanese organized the first all-Hawai'i *sumō* tournament, indicating that the sport was flourishing throughout the islands. Indeed, it was noted that many non-Japanese enjoyed the matches and that young men of other nationalities were participating in the training and competition. *Judo* became popular in the early 1900s and was eventually adopted as a school activity by many Japanese youths.

Of the Western sports, baseball became the favored activity after 1901, when Rev. Okumura organized the first Japanese team from students at his boarding school. Within a few years there were leagues organized to accommodate Japanese teams challenging similar teams from other plantations or made up of players from other ethnic groups. The plantations encouraged such activity, although active support became more noticeable in the 1920s when it became necessary to create better conditions that might persuade the second-generation *nisei* to remain on the plantations.

Literary and dramatic expression remained unorganized until the late 1890s. As early as 1893, Yoshijirō Iwamoto from Yamaguchi performed *ukarebushi* (lengthy songs sung to musical accompaniment) at plantations for workers who were celebrating the completion of their contracts. Amateur drama groups began performing, accompanied by *jōruri* music, in the urban centers of Honolulu and Hilo before the turn of the century, and the community even built a Japanese theater in 1889 in Honolulu. In 1900, a local troupe was organized to perform *shimpa* (modern plays) for local audiences, and a steady stream of silent films from Japan began to make the rounds of various plantation towns. The silents created a need for skilled narrators, the *benshi*, who memorized the scripts and performed all the roles, sometimes to the accompaniment of a *shamisen* player. Local poets gained a measure of fame in the islands, especially after the newspapers began publishing their writings in the 1890s. The first full-scale history of the Japanese in Hawai'i, *Shin Hawaii* (New Hawaii), by Hidegorō Fujii, was published in 1900 and contained a section of poetry including classical Chinese verse, *haiku*, *waka*, traditional Japanese satirical *senryū*, and two *holehole bushi*. In this poetry, references to plantation work and life are readily detectable. Fujii included one poem by Sasakura Ushu, for example, which set a Hawaiian theme to the traditional pattern for *waka*:

> *Yū na yū na nakumushi no ne no yukashisa ni*
> *Kibi no hitomura karinokoshitsutsu.*

> Every evening, touched by the nostalgic sound of chirping insects,
> I left a stand of sugarcane for them while cutting the rest.

One of the noted poets of that early period was Rokumei Sanjin, whose witty *senryū* took the Japanese nationalism of the times into the Hawaiian cane fields.

> *Fukoku no kyōhei*   Sturdy soldiers of a wealthy nation,
> *Kata ni hō*   A hoe on the shoulder,
> *Koshi ni kennaifu.*   Cane knife at the belt.

For the women, there was little room for participation in recreation and cultural activities except for the small group of *issei* and *nisei geisha* who entertained at teahouse parties. The *holehole bushi* thus assume greater importance as the major surviving legacy of *issei* women's perspectives on plantation and immigrant life in Hawai'i.

By the turn of the century, the Japanese community had evolved into a complex society still largely based on the sugar plantations but with increasingly diverse occupations. There was every indication that the Japanese would remain as a permanent part of the Hawaiian

Plantation *sumō* match, ca. 1900.   79

Sumō was probably introduced to Hawai'i by the *gannenmono*. After the arrival of contract laborers, this traditional form of wrestling became a popular recreation among Japanese workers and was enjoyed by other people in the community.

The first Japanese baseball team, Honolulu, 1903 (Okumura Collection).

In 1901, the JBS team was organized by Rev. Takie Okumura from among boarding students at the Okumura Home. The team changed its name to Excelsior in 1904.

Mrs. Matsu Higa with children, Pāhoa, island of Hawai'i, 1916 (courtesy of Takenobu Higa).

Matsu came to Hawai'i in 1912. From left, daughter Hatsu, sons Takeo and Takenobu.

80

scene. The tendency to stay and settle was much weaker in the first years, with about 75 percent of the contract laborers arriving in 1885–1890, finding their way back to Japan or moving to the United States mainland. The annexation of Hawai'i in 1898 indirectly pushed the Japanese into more permanent status. Aware that United States laws preventing contract labor would take effect with the implementation of the Organic Act in 1900, sugar planters rushed to import more Japanese workers. In 1898–1899 alone, approximately thirty thousand Japanese arrived in Hawai'i, doubling their total population in the islands. This influx created a critical mass of people whose collective needs and activities generated the momentum for establishment of educational, cultural, financial, and social institutions, which further reinforced the determination to make Hawai'i home.

Initially recruited as contract laborers before 1900, the first group of Okinawans to arrive in Hawai'i in 1900 soon became free laborers. By 1924, when the United States prohibited all further Japanese immigration to America, there were nearly twenty thousand Okinawans in Hawai'i. Okinawa had been an independent kingdom, heavily influenced by Chinese and Japanese cultures over many centuries, before being absorbed as a Japanese prefecture in 1879. Okinawans fought for political and economic equality, including the right to suffrage, with the Japanese who were in control. When economic conditions worsened, Kyūzō Tōyama, a leader of the People's Rights Movement, sought to convince the Japanese government to allow impoverished Okinawans the right to emigrate to Hawai'i.

In Hawai'i, Okinawan communities within the plantations assumed their own identities because of their unique language and cultural and historical traditions, and in response to prejudice from *naichi* (other Japanese). One result was the development of related but separate institutions, including social groups and churches.

Although the ratio of men to women was still far from balanced in 1900, more than 30 percent of the Japanese were married, a percentage that put them on a level with the Hawaiians and well above the comparable figures for *haole,* part-Hawaiians, and Chinese. The basic family units for the maintenance of a permanent settlement of Japanese in Hawai'i were set in place. The subsequent arrival of thousands of *shashin hanayome,* "picture brides," for the rest of the single men would add dramatically to the Japanese population and further increase the establishment of family and neighborhood services.

In 1908, the Japanese government issued roughly equal numbers of passports to men and women leaving for Hawai'i (1,706 to females and 1,915 to males). Between that year and 1924, 32,000 women and 27,738 men left Japan for Hawai'i, a total of 59,378 people. Of the 32,000 women who entered Hawai'i in that period, it is probably safe to assume that more than 20,000 arrived as "picture brides."

Arranged marriages were customary in Japan, as in most of the world, so the exchange of photographs to facilitate the negotiations taking place across the Pacific was not particularly remarkable. In some cases, the prospective bride and groom had known each other, and the decision to marry was not difficult. In most cases, the men in Hawai'i sent photos to their parents or relatives in Japan for help in finding a suitable wife. Go-betweens *(baishakunin* or *nakōdo,* and, in Hawai'i, the term *shimpai* came into general use from its meaning, "to worry or care about")* assumed responsibility for the arrangements, and the bride's name was entered into the groom's family register *(koseki tōhon)* to legalize the marriage. After waiting for 3 to 6 months, the brides proceeded to Hawai'i where from 1904 to 1912, they were forced to participate in mass weddings, performed at the wharf by Christian ministers, and sometimes involving the ludicrous spectacle of a sudden "marriage" between a father and the daughter he had come to meet. One newspaper editorial in the *Hawaii Shimpō* of 22 February 1907, protested:

> If the Japanese government reports that a woman is married to a man, although the ceremony was performed while he was living in the Hawaiian Islands and she in Japan, the immigration authorities have no right to insult the Japanese government's endorsement of that marriage.

Frederick Kinzaburō Makino, the founder of the *Hawaii Hōchi*, attacked this practice in the inaugural issue of his paper in 1912:

> The most important event in the life of a person is one of getting married. The freedom of choosing an appropriate religious service solemnizing the event should be allowed the individual if there is freedom of religion and if there is recognition of individual right.

Vigorous community protest finally convinced immigration authorities to end this practice in 1917.

The picture-bride practice was not without its problems. The system was occasionally manipulated to allow for importation of prostitutes into Hawai'i. There were numerous instances where the photos were seriously outdated or dramatically retouched. In some extreme instances, one or both parties became so disillusioned with the real person that arrangements were simply ignored at dockside, with women wanting to return to Japan or men and women simply walking away from one another. For thousands of women, however, this was the way to adventure, away from the confines of the village in Japan. Life on the plantations might not have been objectively described by the men luring brides to Hawai'i, but most *issei* women managed to adjust and raise their children in a new world.

Japanese laborer and his wife, ca. 1899 (Bryan 1899:474).

A letter from an immigrant's family in Japan announcing the departure of his wife for Hawai'i.

Japanese house in Wainaku, island of Hawai'i, ca. 1890 (C. Furneaux, photographer).

Wainaku village, island of Hawai'i, ca. 1890 (C. Furneaux, photographer).

Many early Japanese contract laborers lived here. These Japanese women are apparently being interviewed by a visiting Caucasian woman. A pile of firewood is seen on the left.

Kimono-clad immigrants at Wainaku, island of Hawai'i, ca. 1890 (C. Furneaux, photographer).

The Japanese immigrants quickly adopted Western-style clothing for work, but at home they relaxed in traditional *kimono*.

Wainaku plantation village, island of Hawaiʻi, 1890s (J. A. Gonsalves, photographer).

A wooden flume and pipes to bring water from the hill are shown. A small building with banners in the center appears to be a community bath.

84

Wainaku village, island of Hawai'i, ca. 1890 (C. Furneaux, photographer).

Early Japanese laborers sometimes built their own houses with old boards, sugarcane leaves, and bamboo provided by the plantations. It was not a particularly difficult task for them, as they had often helped each other in building such thatched houses in Japan, and the construction here shows a distinct Japanese influence.

Workers' housing at Iwasaki Camp, ʻŌlaʻa, island of Hawaiʻi, ca. 1915 (Iwasaki Collection).

Jirō Iwasaki took a contract to clear the land for the Olaa Sugar Plantation soon ofter his arrival in March 1893. As many as eight hundred Japanese laborers flocked to work for him. The well-known Iwasaki Camp was established during that time.

Tsutō Tanji, about 20-years-old, Pu'unēnĕ, Maui, ca. 1907
(T. T. Kobayashi, photographer).

The photo was sent to Japan to Kiyo's family for arranging
their marriage.

Miss Kiyo Sasaki, about 18-years-old, Fukushima, Japan, ca.
1913.

The photo was sent to Mr. Tanji on Maui for arranging their
marriage.

Japanese family near Honoka'a, island of Hawai'i, ca. 1899. (Bryan 1899:526).

Some women are wearing Western-style clothing made of Japanese *ikat* material.

Mr. and Mrs. Tanji, Pu'unēnē, Maui, November 1914 (T. T. Kobayashi, photographer).

A "picture bride," photographed in Yamaguchi, Japan, ca. 1912.

Graph 1a

LENGTH OF STAY IN HAWAI'I BY HUSBAND BEFORE MARRIAGE

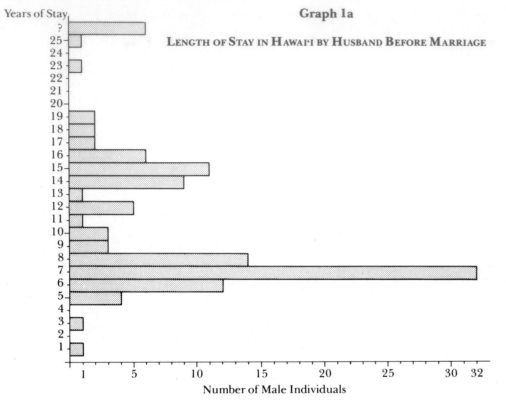

Years of Stay

Number of Male Individuals

Graph 1b

AGE DISTRIBUTION OF HUSBAND AND WIFE

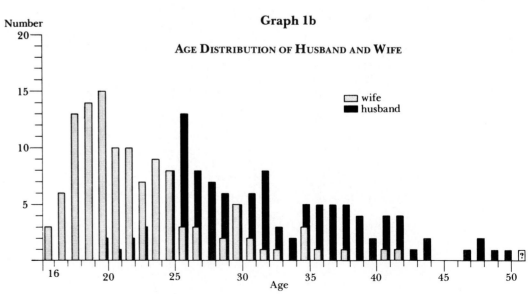

wife
husband

Number

Age

Graph 1c

AGE GAP BETWEEN HUSBAND AND WIFE

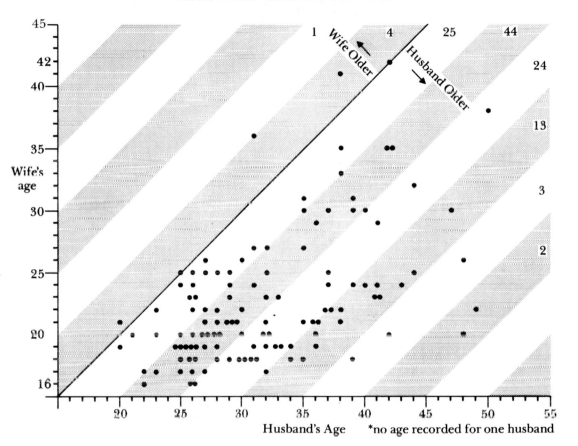

Graphs 1a–1c

STATISTICS ON 117 COUPLES MARRIED BETWEEN 4 NOVEMBER 1913 AND FEBRUARY 1914

SOURCE: Compiled by K. Sinoto, 1983, from marriage license records, Hawaii State Archives.

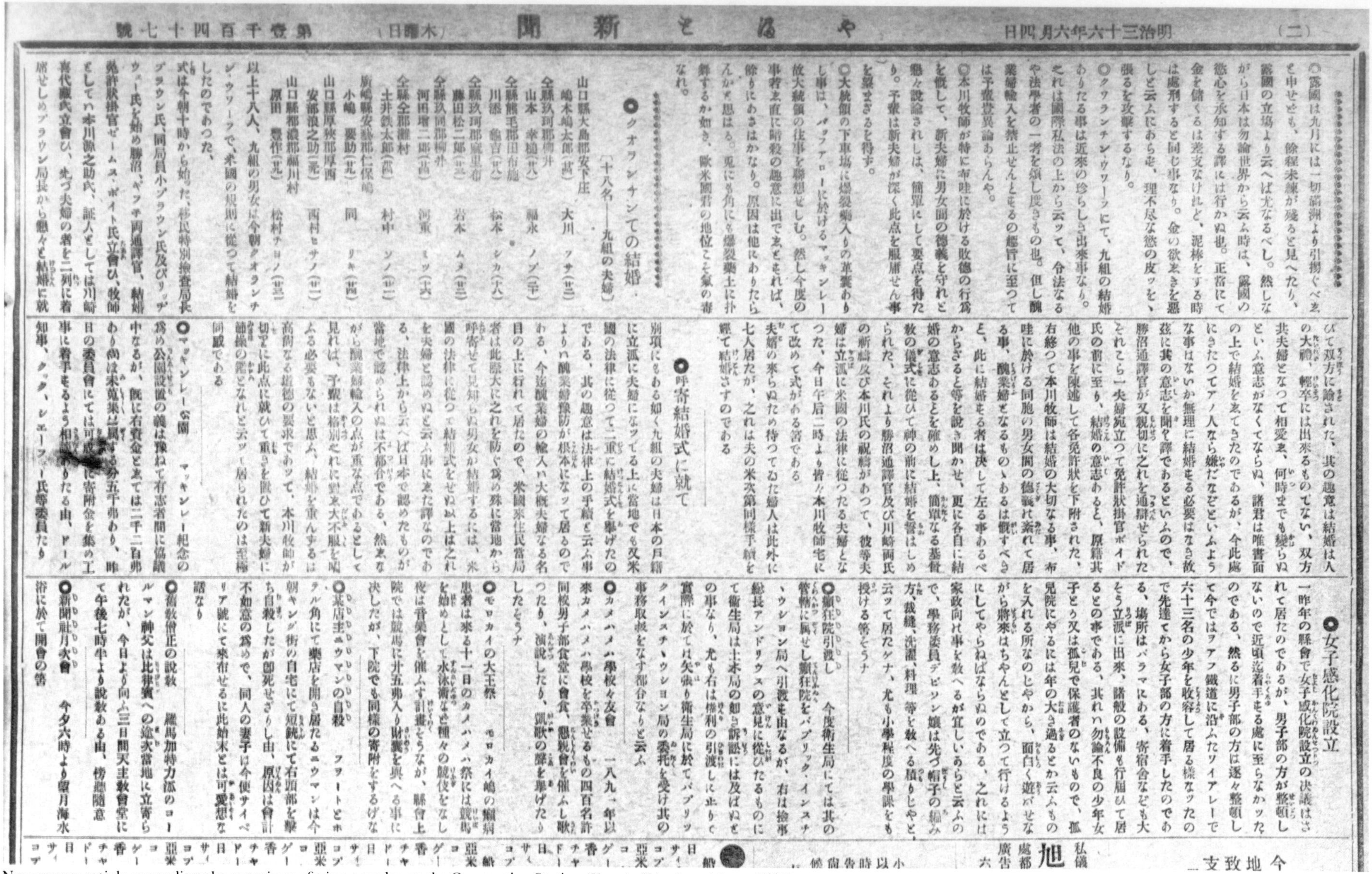

90

○クオランチンでの結婚

○呼寄結婚式に就て

○女子感化院設立

Newspaper article regarding the marriage of nine couples at the Quarantine Station (*Yamato Shim-bun*, 4 June 1903).

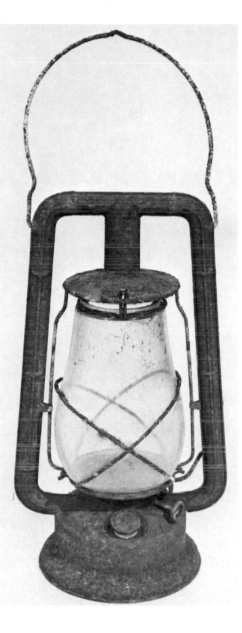

Hanging lamp.

Small lamp made from an ink bottle.

Small lamp.

Iron, heated with charcoal.

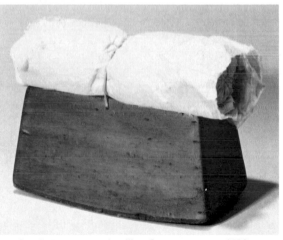

Handmade Japanese-style pillow for a woman, ca. 1892.

This type of pillow was designed for women who wore Japanese-style hairdos. The pillow was placed under the neck instead of the head.

Plantation camp, early 1900s (courtesy of United Japanese Society of Hawaii).

Newly married plantation couple, 'Ōla'a, island of Hawai'i, ca. 1910–1920 (M. Koga, photographer).

Although the groom wore a Western suit, the bride dressed traditionally in a Japanese wedding *kimono*.

McGerrow Camp Nursery, Pu'unēnē, Maui, ca. 1920 (courtesy of Alexander and Baldwin Sugar Museum).

Portrait of a Japanese family in Western dress, ca. 1890
(W. E. H. Deverill, photographer).

A Japanese girl with homemade doll (A. Gartley, photographer).

"As I have earned $62.50 during the period from 25 February to 30 June, I purchased a pocket watch for $7.00...." — excerpt from a letter sent home by a Japanese immigrant, July 1886 (Doi 1980:108).

Pocket watches were status symbols among plantation laborers.

Japanese family in front of their house (M. Koga, photographer).

Plan of plantation house for Japanese laborers, ca.1909 (Theo H. Davies Collection, Bishop Museum Business Archives).

10 FEET

24 FEET

12 X 12 FEET   12 X 12 FEET

18 FEET

VERANDAH
6 X 24 FEET

Japanese

Sewing box made of koa wood, for a bride, ca. 1912.

Handmade *tabako-bon*, tobacco smoking tray, pre-1912.

Lidded rice cooking pot atop stove made from a 5-gallon tin can.

Early immigrants were advised to bring basic utensils such as rice cooking pots, tea kettles, and basins. The manner in which Japanese immigrants prepared their own food in the quarantine station was described in an article in the *Daily Pacific Commercial Advertiser*, 10 February 1885.

Handmade *geta* (clogs), ca. 1907, utilizing locally available wood, leather, and nails.

96

Iron cooking pot for rice *(kama)* with wooden lid, American-made aluminum saucepan, and spoon.

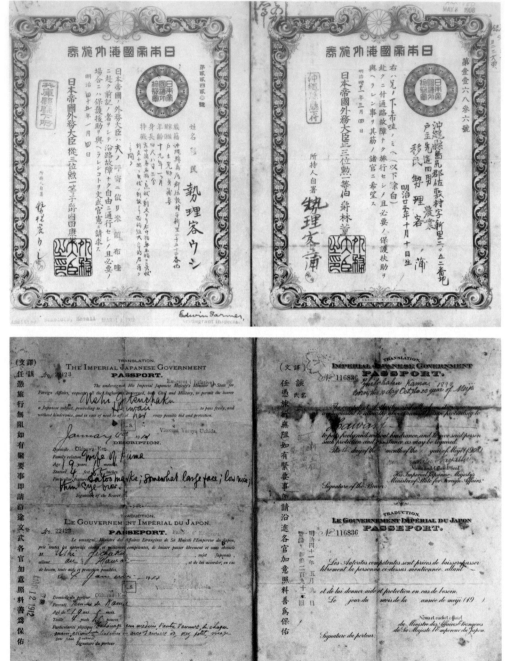

Passports of Kama Serikaku, 1907, and Ushi Serikaku, 1912 (courtesy of Michael Serikaku).

Boys' Day celebration, probably 'Ola'a, island of Hawai'i, ca. 1924.

From left: Wakamatsu Odani, Seimatsu Odani, Toshio Umetsu, Shigeo Umetsu. The *nobori* (banner) was painted by Tsuruji Umetsu.

Friends gathered for farewell to Mr. Arakawa (center) who made enough money by his taxi business to return to Okinawa, ca. late 1920 (courtesy of United Okinawan Society).

Table 11
AMOUNT OF MONEY SENT HOME BY JAPANESE IMMIGRANTS IN HAWAI'I 1892–1907

YEAR	AMOUNT (U.S.$)
1892	125,628.98
1893	434,927.87
1894	532,162.79
1895	484,618.61
1896	660,949.56
1897	776,527.23
1898	841,637.42
1899	1,380,704.61
1900	1,846,042.25
1901	2,462,932.62
1902	2,582,727.96
1903	3,011,009.04
1904	2,906,037.97
1905	3,644,085.00
1906	3,460,072.44
1907	3,688,588.60
TOTAL	28,839,264.86

SOURCE: Report of Consul General Saitō (Doi 1980; 173).

A receipt for money sent to Japan by Matsuji Ogata and signed by Jōji Nakayama, 4 February 1889.

Money sent by immigrants to their families in Japan was handled by the Japanese section of the Bureau of Immigration prior to the opening of the Yokohama Shōkin Bank in Honolulu.

MARRIAGE CERTIFICATE.

THIS IS TO CERTIFY

That _Rinzuchi Mizunaka_ of _Olaa Hawaii_

and _Sayo Miyamoto_ of Immigration Station _Honolulu_

were by me joined together in

▲ HOLY ▲ MATRIMONY ▲

according to the usages of the _Japanese M. E._ Church

and the Laws of _Territory of Hawaii_ on the _17_ day of _July_

in the year of our Lord _Nineteen_ hundred _Nine_

_____ } Witnesses.   _R. G. Nakagawa_
_____   Minister of the Gospel.

New York: EATON & MAINS.   Cincinnati: JENNINGS & GRAHAM.

Marriage certificate issued at Immigration Station on 17 July 1909.

Although their marriage was arranged through correspondence and was acknowledged in Japan by registering the name of the bride into her husband's family record, U.S. government required an official ceremony at the Immigration Station upon bride's arrival.

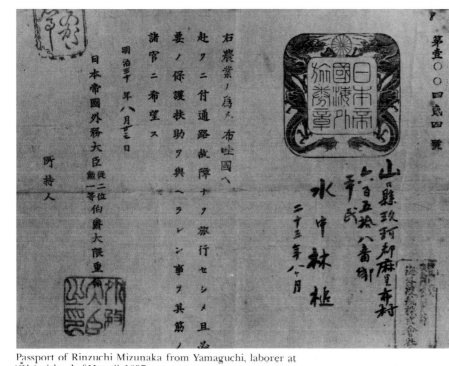

Passport of Rinzuchi Mizunaka from Yamaguchi, laborer at 'Ōla'a, island of Hawaii, 1897.

Dispensary, 1915 (Edgeworth Collection).

Dr. Shin Yamamoto.

Born in Nagasaki, Japan, he came to Hawai'i in 1890 employed by the Bureau of Immigration to care for Japanese plantation laborers. He later became the chief doctor of the Hilo Japanese Hospital which was established in 1889.

Passport of Sayo Mizunaka from Yamaguchi, 1909.

MEDICINE/MEDICAL CARE

The Japanese Hospital in Liliha on the third anniversary celebration of its founding and the completion of a new building, Honolulu, 3 November 1899 (Okumura Collection).

Dr. Sanzaburō Kobayashi, who was licensed in both Japan and the United States, came to Hawai'i in 1893 after practicing in San Francisco. He opened his own hospital with twelve rooms on Beretania Street in 1896. When the number of his patients grew to more than four hundred a year, Dr. Kobayashi built a new three-story building with twenty-five rooms and modern facilities at a cost of $7,000 on Liliha Street. It was completed on 3 November 1899 and was called the Japanese Hospital (*Nihonjin Byoin*).

Dr. Kobayashi's Japanese Hospital was purchased in August 1901 by the Immigration companies and donated to the Japanese Benevolent Society which merged it with their own hospital (built in Kapālama in 1900), and the name, Japanese Hospital, was retained. In 1918 the society built new facilities on Kuakini Street. In 1942, the name was changed to Kuakini Hospital which has continued to expand at the same location to serve the entire community.

大河原三郎君
小島春庇君
三田村敏竹君

小林亥三郎君
毛利伊勢君
小川運伯君

Dr. T. Mitamura Dr. S. Kojima Dr. M. Ogawara
Dr. U. Ogawa Dr. Iga Mori Dr. S. Kobayashi
Taken on Nov. 3rd. 18

Japanese doctors, Honolulu, 1899 (Okumura Collection).

Many doctors initially came to Hawai'i under the jurisdiction
of the Bureau of Immigration to administer to Japanese laborers on the plantations. Some stayed on and established private practices; from left: front, Drs. Unpaku Ogawa, Iga
Mōri, Sanzaburō Kobayashi; back, Drs. Toshiyuki Mitamura,
Shunan Kojima, Sanshirō Ōgawara.

Japanese medicine.

Even though free medical treatment was offered by plantations under the labor contract, familiar medicines were imported as early as 1892 and distributed by agents who visited plantation communities, leaving assorted medicines in a paper bag with each family. The bag had an inventory list on the back so that the agent could check the items used, for payment and replacement.

Uesu Hospital in Hilo, island of Hawaiʻi, ca. 1915.

Christmas, Japanese Christian Church, 1898 (Okumura Collection).

Ewa Plantation Hospital, Oʻahu, 1928.

Japanese Christian Church on Kukui Street, on the Emperor's birthday, Honolulu, 3 November 1898 (Okumura Collection).

The church was dedicated on 6 June 1897, after the building and the land were purchased with $8,000 donated from people here and in Japan.

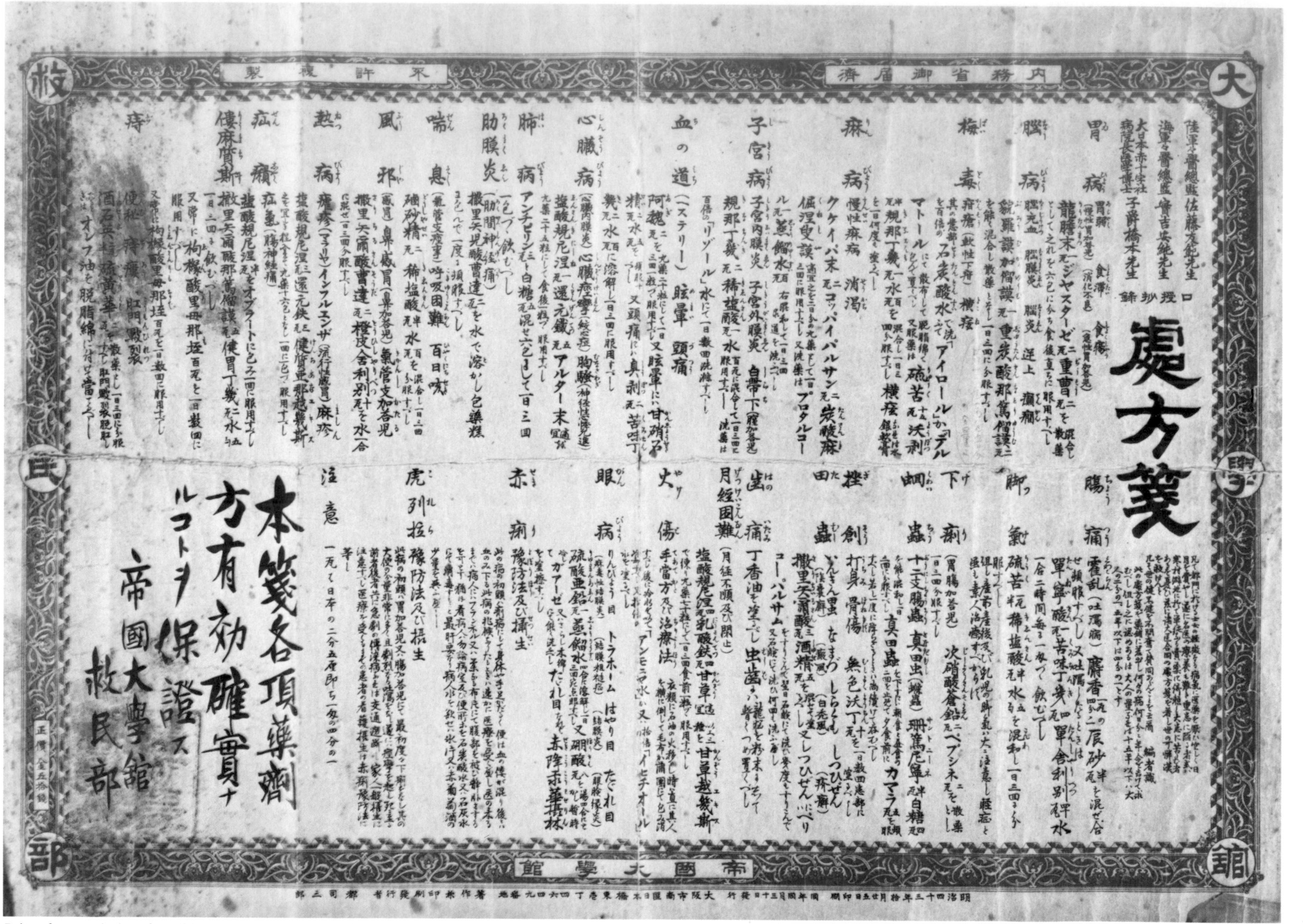

内務省御届済　眾許複製

陸軍々醫總監佐藤進先生
海軍々醫總監實吉安純先生
大日本赤十字社病院長醫學博士子爵橋本先生
口授　鈔錄

處方箋

胃病
腦病
梅毒
痳病
子宮病
血の道
心臓病
肺病
肋膜炎
喘息
風邪
熱病
疝癪
僂麻質斯
痔

腸痛
脚氣
下痢
蛔蟲
挫創
田蟲
歯痛
月經困難
火傷
眼病
赤痢
虎列拉
注意

本箋各項薬劑方有効確實ナルコトヲ保證ス
帝國大學館
救民部

帝國大學館

Printed prescription describing symptoms and medication, 1910.

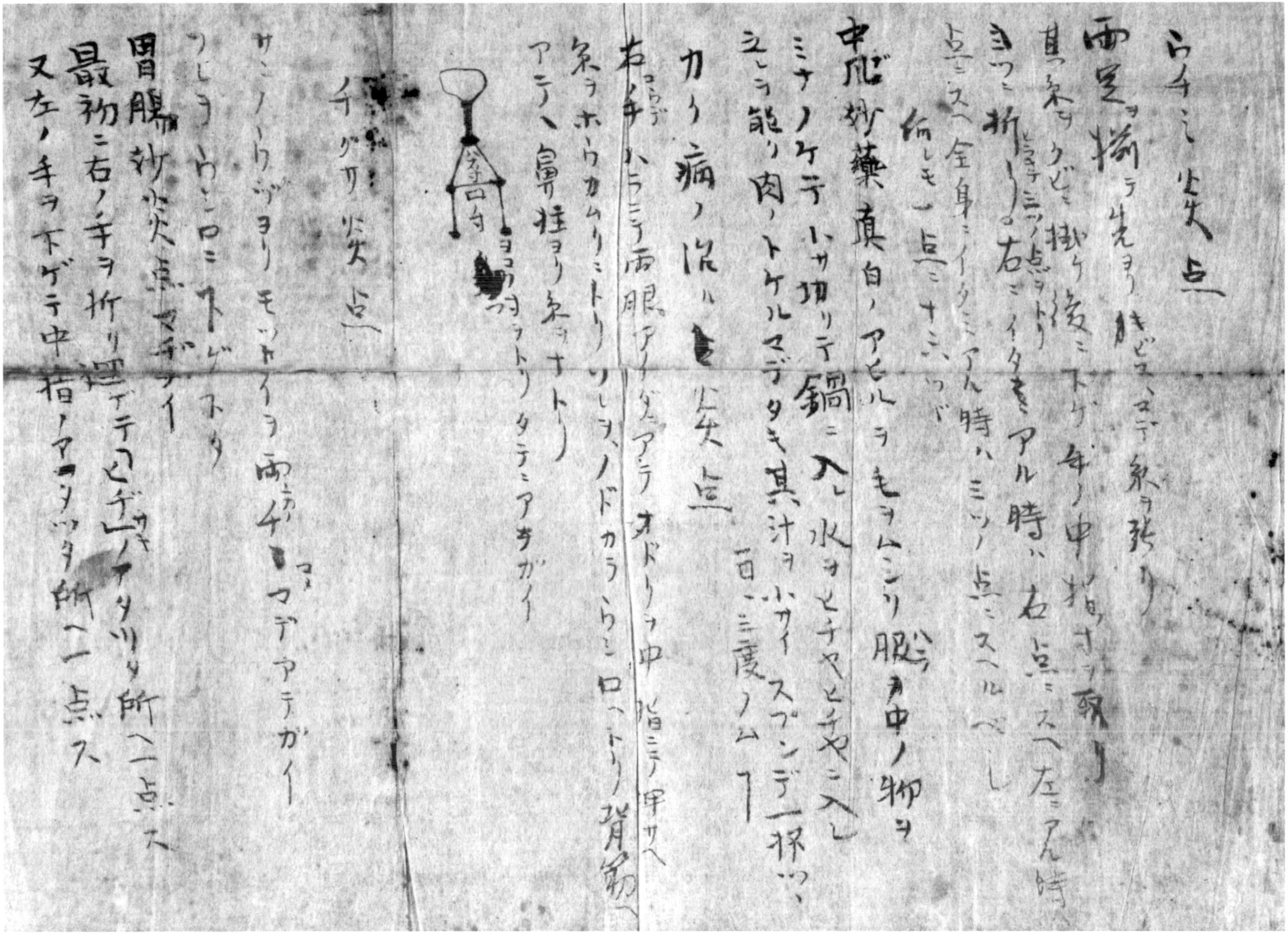

らうゑニ灸点

右足ヲ揃ヘ足ビューまデ象ヲ張リ
其ノ糸ヨリ心ニ掛ケ後ニトリ年ノ中指サヲ取リ
ヨツニ折リテ其ノ中ニ三ツ点ヲトリ
点ニス、全身ニイタミアル時ハ三ツ点ニスヘルベシ
点ニス右ニイタミヲアル時ハ右ニ点ニ左ニ左ニアル時ハ
何レモ一点ニスヘシ

中ニ妙藥眞白ノアヒルヲモツムシリ脇ノ中ノ物ヲ
ミナノケテ小サク切リテ鍋ニ入レ水ヲとッチャとチャと
之ヲ能ク肉ノトケルマデタキ其ノ汁ヲ小サイスプンデ一杯ニ
百ニ三度ノム

力ラ病ノ次ハ灸点
右手ハラニラ両眼アイダアラオドリヲ中指ニテ甲サヘ
気ヲホウカムリミトリシヲノドカラ口ニトリノ背動
アテハ鼻柱ヨリ気ニトリ
アニハ鼻柱ヨリ気ニトリタテミアサガイ

チグリ灸点

サニノウシヨリモツキラ両チーマデアテガイ
シヲワニロニトシデトリ

胃腸妙灸点サチヂイ
最初ニ右ノ手ヲ折リ廻デテヒヂニアタリタ所ヘ一点ス
又左ノ手ヲ下ゲテ中指ノマヽニアッタ所ヘ一点ス

Handwritten moxa instructions, used by a travelling candy
seller on Oʻahu, for giving moxa treatments to plantation
workers and their families, ca. 1900.

Moxa (a mugwort) is a burned herbal heat treatment applied
to the body's nerve centers.

New Year at the Japanese school that Rev. Okumura started in 1896, Honolulu, ca. 1899 (Okumura Collection).

Hana Sunday School with Mr. Nobuzō Imai, Maui, 1897.

Japanese evangelists, June 1898 (Okumura Collection).

Rev. Takie Okumura is standing on the left.

本派本願寺舊布哇別院

Honpa Hongwanji Mission, Fort Street, Honolulu.

The mission was started in 1898. The still existing Gandhara-style building was erected in 1918 by Rev. Yemyō Imamura, who succeeded Rev. Satomi in 1899 and dedicated his life to the mission. His efforts resulted in the establishment of missions in every town in Hawai'i. He also promoted Buddhism in English in order to reach out to the non-Japanese community.

Residence of Rev. Shigefusa Kanda, Kohala, island of Hawai'i, ca. 1899 (Okumura Collection).

Rev. and Mrs. Takie Okumura, Honolulu, ca. 1930s (Okumura Collection).

A native of Kochi and later a graduate of Dōshisha University, Rev. Takie Okumura arrived in Hawai'i in 1894. Married in 1886 to Katsu Ogawa, Rev. Okumura returned to Japan in 1896 to bring his wife and three children to Honolulu. Mrs. Okumura, mother of thirteen, assisted her husband in all his endeavors, particularly with the management of the Okumura Home.

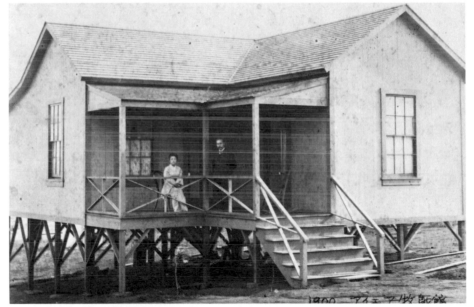

Minister's residence at Aiea Church, with Rev. and Mrs. Taihei Takahashi, 'Aiea, O'ahu, 1900.

Rev. Takahashi was a cousin of Rev. Miyama, who established the first Japanese Methodist church in 1887. Mrs. Takahashi taught at the Aiea and Ewa Japanese Schools.

Nichiren-shū mission, Ka'ū, island of Hawai'i, with Rev. and Mrs. Nunome on horseback, 1914.

The temple was dedicated in May, 1902.

Yamato Jinsha, a Shintō shrine, Hilo, island of Hawai'i, 1898.

Shrine builders were brought from Japan to participate in the construction of this shrine, completed on 3 November 1898 with $1,200 contributed by the community. These builders trained local Japanese carpenters in techniques and styles that were to influence future architecture in Hawai'i. This shrine was later renamed Hilo Daijingu.

Aiea Church Sunday School, 'Aiea, O'ahu, 1905.

Rev. Taihei Takahashi is at top right.

Olaa Hongwanji, established in 1902, island of Hawai'i, ca.
1915 (Iwasaki Collection).

109

Rev. Kanichi Miyama (1847–1936).

Rev. Miyama, a Methodist minister, came to Hawai'i from San Francisco in September 1887 to minister to Japanese immigrants. Many Japanese converted to Christianity under his strong influence, including the first Consul General of Japan in Honolulu, Tarō Andō. Rev. Miyama organized the Japanese Temperance Society in 1888.

Torii, gate of a Shintō shrine, Nāwiliwili Harbor, Kaua'i, post-1900.

This *torii* was constructed of wooden barrels, probably used as containers for imported *shōyu*, *miso*, or *sake*.

Traditional Japanese carpentry tools brought over from Japan and used locally by *issei* carpenters.

From upper left clockwise: *sumitsubo* (liner), *kebiki* (marking gauge), variety of *kanna* (planes), *nomi* (chisels), *yakigote* (branding iron), and *azebiki-noko* (fishtail saw).

Izumo Taisha, a Shintō shrine, Honolulu, 1906 (R. J. Baker, photographer).

Established in 1906 by Rev. Katsura Miyaō on Beretania Street, this shrine was later moved to its present location near Nuʻuanu Stream.

曾我部四郎

Rev. Shirō Sogabe.

Born in 1865 in Fukuoka, Japan, Sogabe graduated from Dōshisha University in Kyoto then came to Hawai'i in 1894 under the auspices of the Hawaiian Mission Board. Shortly after his arrival, he started his mission in Honomū. In 1897 he founded a boarding school, Honomu Gijuku, on the island of Hawai'i; this school educated many young men who became active in society.

今村惠猛

Rev. Yemyō Imamura (1867–1932) of Honpa Hongwanji Mission.

A Buddhist priest from Fukui, the Rev. Yemyō Imamura arrived in Hawai'i in 1899.

Handmade home Shintō shrine, ca. 1902.

Umetarō Ogata, a watchmaker who had a shop on River Street, Honolulu, made the shrine with tin from a 5-gallon can. The divine tablet is inside.

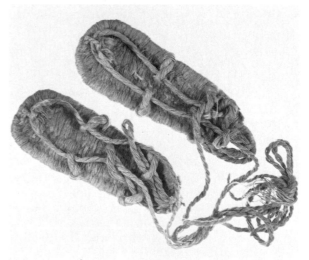

Slippers made of burlap fiber belonging to Rev. Shirō Sogabe of Honomū, ca. 1894.

One of seven pairs made for him; this is the only pair that was left when he returned from his mission to Kona.

天照皇大神

112

Funeral scene amidst cane fields, 1915 (Iwasaki Collection).

Kurtistown Jōdō Mission, island of Hawaiʻi, ca. 1905 (M. Koga, photographer).

Boys' Day celebration, Hāna, Maui, 1904 (H.C. Ovenden,
photographer).

116

Sumō participants, Hāna, Maui, 1904 (H.C. Ovenden, photographer).

Adult and children wrestlers posing for the photographer. According to an old folk belief, a baby boy attired in *sumō* garb and carried on the shoulder of a wrestler would be granted "strength" in life.

Edozakura, *sumō* instructor at Hawai'i Chūgakkō, Nu'uanu, O'ahu, ca. 1920 (courtesy of Yoshitami Tasaka).

Edozakura first visited Hawai'i in 1915 as a member of the second professional *sumō* group to perform in the islands. The following year, he was invited to return to teach *sumō*.

Homemade *sumō keshomawashi* (ceremonial apron) owned by wrestler Satsumanada.

Hanemon Furuyama, an official *kendō* instructor of Ryūkō-rhū (a school of *kendō*).

Furuyama was sent to Hawai'i by the Miyagi prefectural government to discipline Japanese immigrants through training in *kendō*. He opened his training center at Honomū soon after his arrival in Hawai'i in 1914 at the age of 57. He trained students at both Honomu-Gijuku and at Papaikou Japanese School.

Kōbukai *kendō* club members at Katō Jinsha Dōjō, Honolulu, 1915.

The club was founded in 1902 by Dr. Umekichi Asahina.

Archers, Honolulu, ca. 1910 (courtesy of Yoshiko Tsukiyama).

Dr. Umekichi Asahina, standing at left, arrived in 1885 and was the first Japanese dentist in Hawai'i. He participated in both archery and *kendō* activities.

Baseball at 'A'ala Park, Honolulu, 1908.

Excelsior baseball team, Honolulu, 1904 (Okumura Collection).

119

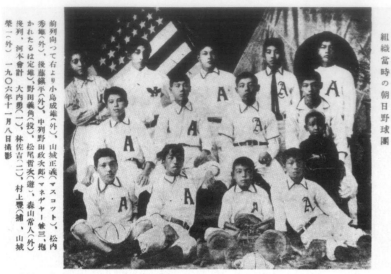

前列向つて右より小島成雄〈外〉、山城正義〈マスコット〉、松内秀繁〈外〉、後藤鎮平〈外〉　中列野田政次郎〈マネヤー兼三、抱かれたるは定雄〉、野田義角〈投〉、松尾哲夫〈遊〉、森山常人〈外〉後列、河本會計　大内勇〈一〉、林佐吉〈二〉　村上豊〈捕〉、山城榮一〈外〉　一九〇六年十一月八日撮影

組織當時の朝日野球團

Asahi baseball team, Honolulu, 1906.

The team was organized in 1905. From left: front, Chimpei Gotō, Hideo Matsuuchi, Masayoshi Yamashiro, Naruo Kojima; middle, Tsuneto Moriyama, Tetsuji Matsuo, Gikaku Noda, Masajirō Noda with Sadao; back, Eiichi Yamashiro, Yutaka Murakami, Sakichi Hayashi, Isamu Ōuchi, Mr. Kawamoto.

120

Group of people in a variety of sports attire, ca. 1900 (Okumura Collection).

Jōdoshu Temple Band, Pu'unēnē, Maui, ca. 1915 (courtesy of Alexander and Baldwin Sugar Museum).

Japanese play, Kekaha, Kauaʻi, 3 November 1908.

Japanese immigrants from Fukuoka prefecture performed
the play "Pistol Gōtō (Robber with Pistol), Sadakichi Shimizu."

Japanese musicians at Camp 5, Puʻunēnē, Maui, ca. 1908.

The group, named Komusō, travelled to various plantation camps.

Asahi Theater, Beretania Street, Honolulu, ca. 1915.

Opened in 1899 as the first Japanese theater ("Asahiza") in Honolulu, the theater was destroyed by the Chinatown fire in 1900 and rebuilt in 1908.

124

Rice Festival at Hāmākua Poko, Maui, 1907 (courtesy of Alexander and Baldwin Sugar Museum).

Children's *kabuki* theater group, Haʻikū, Maui.

Eirakuza Theater, Haleʻiwa, Oʻahu, 1912.

The theater was built in 1911 with modern facilities, including generated electricity and piped water. Tomitarō Aino from Yamaguchi prefecture was the owner.

A group of *onna-zumō* (women *sumō* wrestlers) from Japan who visited Hawai'i in 1911 (courtesy of Kiyoshi Okubo).

Banzai Club, Honolulu, ca. 1910 (Edgeworth Collection).

The sign in the center next to the picture of dice reads "Japanese Gambling Place."

Paauhau Japanese School, island of Hawai‘i, ca. 1907.

The children are dressed for a special occasion, with the boys in Western clothing and the girls in *kimono*.

JAPANESE SCHOOLS

The education of their children was an immediate problem for the *issei*. Those who intended to return to Japan wanted their children to be prepared for the adjustment as well as to be able to compete adequately within Japanese society. A whole range of basic information — as diverse as children's songs and myths, mathematics, Japanese history, Japanese language, and ethics — had to be transmitted if the children were not to lose touch with the complex culture of the homeland. Those parents who intended to remain in Hawai'i were concerned about the language gap, which threatened to widen as the years went by. The inability of the children to communicate in Japanese would mean that traditional family relationships could be maintained only at very crude levels, with discussions confined to simple sentences. The primary purposes of the early Japanese language schools, therefore, were to teach the children to learn their language, to know their heritage, and to "think and feel sympathy with their parents."

The Meiji leaders in Japan had been convinced early that formal education for the broader masses was an important part of building their "rich country and strong military." Their own search for knowledge had taken them to various countries and they had been particularly impressed with the educational systems of France and the United States. In 1890, the Meiji Emperor promulgated the Imperial Rescript on Education, which set the tone for generations of Japanese dedicated to the pursuit of formal schooling. The emphasis on compulsory mass education to produce a literate citizenry resulted in national policies requiring attendance. By 1872, Japanese children were required to complete four years of schooling. By 1885, the year when the first contract laborers came to Honolulu, 65.8 percent of males and 32.1 percent of females of school age were attending elementary school in Japan. In 1895, the figures had climbed to 76.7 and 43.9 percent and, in 1905, had reached an almost unbelievable 97.7 percent for males and 93.3 percent for females. It is not surprising, therefore, that so many of the *issei* would arrive in Hawai'i having received some basic formal education. An 1896 survey in Hawai'i determined that 69 percent of all immigrant males and 25 percent of females were literate in Japanese. Moreover, some 285 males and 28 females were able to read and write English, and 68 males and 6 females could read and write Hawaiian.

There were more than 100 children among the 944 Japanese aboard the *City of Tokio* in February 1885. In 1888, the first recorded attendance of Japanese in Hawai'i public schools included 54 of a total of 8,770 children of all nationalities. Within a decade, more than 260 Japanese children were enrolled in public schools, where lessons were conducted in English. By 1900, there were 1,500 Japanese in the school system, and more than 7,000 in 1910. By 1924, the 25,858 Japanese students constituted just over one-half of all students in Hawai'i. These numbers had a significant impact upon the public school system in Hawai'i,

A class of students at the Kula Japanese Language School, Maui, ca. 1899.

The school was founded by Seiji Fukuda (right) in May 1895. The teacher, Tamaki Gomi, is on the left. Next to him, in the middle row, is Raku Saka, a daughter of Mr. and Mrs. Shōhichi Saka, who arrived on the first boat. Her brother is second from the right in the back, and next to him is Yuki Fukuda, a daughter of the founder.

As seen here, children of other ethnic groups also attended the Japanese schools in areas where there were no public schools. Children dressed in either Western- or Hawaiian-style clothing, and some dresses appear to be made with Japanese *kasuri (ikat)* material.

The first Japanese Primary School on Oʻahu, with its founder, Rev. Takie Okumura, in *kimono*, 1896.

Rev. Okumura was inspired to establish the school by a little girl's comment. In response to his inquiry about her mother, the girl said in a mixture of English, Hawaiian, and Japanese, "Me mama hana hana yō konai." ("My mother is at work and is not able to come.") Hideo Kuwabara, in a dark suit, was the teacher.

Children exercising at Japanese Primary School, Honolulu, 3 November 1899 (Okumura Collection).

which had to accommodate these newcomers and, in the eyes of an anxious public, to compete for their attention and loyalty with the Japanese language schools.

Japanese language schools sprang up quickly in all communities where the Japanese populations had begun to increase. The first Japanese school was established on the island of Maui in 1895 by a merchant, Seiji Fukuda, who hired Tamaki Gomi as the instructor. Rev. Takie Okumura founded the second school, in Honolulu, in April 1896. With the help of a licensed teacher, Hideo Kuwabara, who was introduced by Rev. Shigefusa Kanda, Okumura provided instruction in Japanese for 1 hour each day after public school was over. When the initial enrollment of thirty increased, Okumura was able to solicit funds from the *haole* community to construct a larger facility in 1899.

Although attached to a Christian institution, the Okumura school was disassociated from its religious origins because of concern that the Buddhists would establish their own school, thus escalating Buddhist-Christian rivalry. Many of the earlier schools were started by Christians, but rumors that the Christian schools were openly attacking Buddhism convinced Bishop Yemyō Imamura that the Buddhists needed their own institutions. In 1902, the first Hongwanji school opened its doors on Fort Street in downtown Honolulu. By 1910, the Christian schools were greatly overshadowed by Buddhist and independent institutions.

The increase in numbers of Japanese language school students was steady and dramatic: in 1900, there were 1,552 children in 11 schools; in 1907, 4,966 students were attending 120 schools; by 1920, there were 17,541 youngsters studying Japanese in 143 schools; and the enrollment peaked in 1933 with 43,606 students in 190 Japanese language schools throughout the Territory.

Both Buddhist and Christian schools provided a basic curriculum including the language, history, folklore, culture, and ethics (*shūshin*) of Japan, but the Christian schools generally emphasized subjects more directly relevant to American life, including Christianity itself. The Buddhist schools tended to hold longer sessions — often 1½ hours in the morning and 2 hours in the afternoon — as well as summer programs that ran from 9:00 A.M. to 3:00 P.M., with a 2-week vacation. Some planters donated land for buildings and materials for construction as well as monthly subsidies, in order to maintain laborer morale and perhaps to facilitate the eventual return of the families to Japan. The schools became centers of activities for the Japanese community, including the celebration of Japanese holidays such as *tenchōsetsu*, classes and exhibitions in the martial arts, and lessons in music and dance.

Although there was some expression of opposition to the Japanese schools during the 1890s and later, the major confrontations began when it became clear that the second-generation *nisei* — American citizens by birth — were likely to remain on Hawaiian soil. In 1907 Christian clergymen, both American and Japanese, argued that the schools were a menace to the Americanization of the Territory, but attorneys who went through the textbooks with the help of a translator found nothing that fostered any anti-American spirit. Nonetheless, attacks against the Japanese schools intensified over the next two decades, until the United States Supreme Court intervened in 1927. Problems did not, however, originate only from the *haole* community.

The development of Japanese language schools in the first two decades of the twentieth century was marked by Christian-Buddhist competition within the *issei* community. Christian leaders advocated the merging of schools on the plantations to neutralize the Buddhist influence, but these overtures were rejected. At the same time, responding to accusations that their teachers promoted anti-American attitudes, Buddhist leaders publicly announced that their schools were dedicated to promoting good American citizenship among the growing numbers of *nisei*. Official pronouncements from Bishop Imamura's office as early as 1910 emphasized the Honpa Hongwanji's position of supporting Americanization.

The first Territorywide Japanese Educational Association was founded in February 1915 to unify the diverse language schools and to counter the attacks being mounted against Japanese language instruction. One of the Association's primary goals was the revision of textbooks to make them more consistent with the history, mores, and values of Hawai'i and America. Up to that time, textbooks had simply been imported from Japan. At the invitation of the Association, Professor Yaichi Haga of Tokyo Imperial University travelled to Honolulu in the summer of 1916. With the help of a scholarship (established when Prince Fushimi visited Hawai'i and donated $200 for education in 1907), he rewrote the textbooks to be more suitable for use in Hawai'i. Haga was assisted by Ryūsaku Tsunoda of the Hongwanji language school and Mitsuaki Kakei of Rev. Okumura's school. Nevertheless, his new edition pleased neither Americans—who noted that myths of Japan's divine origins remained—nor some Japanese, who were angered by removal of sections specifically praising Japan.

Ironically, the intensive efforts to convince the public that Buddhism and its Japanese language schools were perfectly compatible with American society convinced some that this was a deliberate attempt to mislead. Wallace R. Farrington, general manager of the *Star-Bulletin* (and later, Governor of the Territory), publicly congratulated the Hongwanji Mission at the dedication of its new building in 1918 for helping in the "natural assimilation of American ideals." Privately, however, he maintained that this was a new strategy to mislead Americans in order to strengthen Buddhism, which was "as definitely Japanese as the Evangelical or Catholic might be termed definitely American."

The first official attack on the language schools occurred in 1917, when immigration officials denied permission for five Japanese school teachers to disembark in Honolulu. These five were detained in the immigration compound as ineligible immigrants, although provisions in the law clearly allowed them to enter the country. Kinzaburō Makino of the *Hawaii Hōchi* retained attorney Joseph Lightfoot, who filed a petition for *habeas corpus* in the United States District Court. Although the five were freed, their case was defeated in the Territorial courts. The verdict was appealed to the Ninth Circuit Court of Appeals in San Francisco, where the decision was reversed. The United States Supreme Court upheld this decision, and the teachers were allowed to stay and work in Hawai'i. This setback did not deter opponents of the Japanese language schools, however, and the Territorial legislature became the arena for the battles to come.

World War I had produced a violent antiforeign prejudice in the United States, and the slogan "One Language Under One Flag" became the rallying cry against all foreign language schools, but especially against those in the German and Japanese communities. In 1918, twenty-one state legislatures introduced bills to control language schools. Public officials in Hawai'i launched the formal attack on the Japanese schools with proposals to place them under the direct supervision of the Territorial Department of Public Instruction.

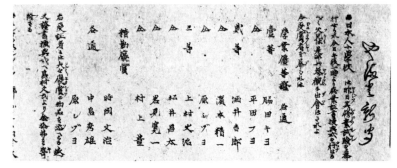

Advertisement for Japanese Primary School in *Yamato*, 5 May 1896.

Results of the term test, Japanese Primary School, reported in *Yamato Shimbun*, 3 October 1896.

Honpa Hongwanji Japanese Primary School, Honolulu, O'ahu, ca. 1912 (T. Shimizu, photographer).

Aiea Japanese Language School, O'ahu, 1897.

The teacher, Mrs. Takahashi, also taught at the Ewa Japanese School.

Then, in 1919, a Congressional committee of three members arrived to investigate the situation in response to a joint invitation extended by the Governor and the Superintendent of Public Instruction. The committee submitted a lengthy report, essentially recommending gradual abolition of the schools, and urging that they be controlled by the Department of Public Instruction and that teachers be required to pass standard English examinations. The first bill providing for such measures was introduced into the legislature in 1919; it failed to pass because of vigorous opposition from the Japanese community.

It was more, to be sure, than national antiforeignism that fed the animosity against Japanese schools. Both the schools and the Buddhist temples that sponsored so many of them had been strong supporters of the Japanese who struck the sugar plantations in 1920. Language school teachers were active in support work, which included raising funds for the strikers and their families, and school rooms were used for strike meetings. In less direct but equally important fashion, the schools were training grounds — so the English language papers such as the *Advertiser* claimed — for the next generation of Japanese to follow the lead of the Japanese language newspapers.

Between 1920 and 1923, the legislature and the Department of Public Instruction imposed increasingly severe controls on the language schools, requiring additional teacher qualifications, revisions of textbooks, discriminatory head taxes on students, and gradual elimination of classes for the lower elementary grades. In the face of the clear challenge to the very existence of the language schools, the Japanese were presented with two basic positions advocated by Kinzaburō Makino and his *Hawaii Hōchi* on one side, and by Yasutarō Sōga and his *Nippu Jiji* with Rev. Takie Okumura on the other.

In December 1922, Consul General Keichi Yamasaki summoned about forty leading citizens of the Japanese community to his offices to discuss the controversy and the appropriate response. The resolution adopted by this group, which included Sōga and Okumura, argued against any court challenges to the Territorial policies because "a legal contest . . . would work to the disadvantage of the Japanese schools and . . . would injure the feeling between Americans and Japanese in Hawaii." The Japanese government, as usual, was inclined to be cautious in these matters and counseled patience and accommodation. Interestingly, the planters were more likely to support the schools, fearing the loss of the bulk of their labor force if the schools were not available to the children of their Japanese workers. The planters, however, were accused of putting profits above loyalty to *haole* supremacy, and were not free to combat the antiforeign and anti-Japanese propaganda with any degree of comfort. In this atmosphere, the conservative approach — to avoid legal challenges — was understandable.

On the other hand, Makino was determined to test the constitutionality of these laws and consulted his old friend, attorney Joseph Lightfoot, about the possibility of success in the courts. Lightfoot and several other prominent *haole* attorneys represented the plaintiffs on 28 December 1922 when, led by the Palama Japanese Language School, 16 schools filed suit in the Territorial Circuit Court. The subsequent press war between the *Hawaii Hōchi* and the *Nippu Jiji* was vicious, and the issue divided the Japanese community as no other had before or since. In the Kaka'ako district, for example, the dispute created a serious rift that took decades to heal. Eventually, in spite of boycotts by *Hōchi* advertisers and pressure from many quarters, Makino and the test-case group were able to convince 88 of 146 schools to join the court challenge. In this, Bishop Imamura's decision to participate actively in the litigation proved to be important, partly because thousands of dollars were needed to support the effort through the appeals process.

Meanwhile, in 1923, the United States Supreme Court had ruled that Nebraska's attempts to abolish its German language schools were unconstitutional. This precedent was important in generating continued support for Japanese plaintiffs in Hawai'i. Finally, on 21 February 1927, the Supreme Court heard Lightfoot present the case for striking down the Territorial laws and policies, and agreed that they represented unconstitutional "parts of a deliberate plan to bring foreign language schools under a strict governmental control for which the record discloses no adequate reason."

The legal victory was savored by the Japanese community in a mass meeting in Honolulu. Some five thousand participants adopted a resolution emphasizing the willingness of the language schools to cooperate with the Department of Public Instruction on all matters. The group, meeting on 29 March 1927, went to great pains to affirm "our continued loyalty to America and our desire to rear our children as loyal, patriotic and useful citizens of the United States." At the podium, Makino addressed the crowd, reassuring them that

Americans feel it only proper that we took the action we did. . . . It behooves us, who live in this country, to understand the characteristics of the Americans. Individuals and organizations alike must never forget to stand up for their rights and freedom. . . . We ask that the Japanese schools cooperate with the Territorial government officials to strive to raise good American citizens capable of understanding both the English and Japanese languages.

Table 12

JAPANESE SCHOOL-AGE CHILDREN AND JAPANESE LANGUAGE SCHOOLS IN HAWAI'I, 1888–1940

YEAR	NO. OF CHILDREN	NO. OF SCHOOLS
1888	54	0
1900	1,552	11
1907	4,966	120
1915	13,553	135
1920	17,541	143
1933	43,606	190
1939	38,515	194
1940	40,000+	200

SOURCE: United Japanese Society of Hawaii 1971: 225.

Japanese children having lunch in school (courtesy of Hawaii State Archives).

Night school, where working Japanese studied the English language, 21 March 1902 (Okumura Collection).

軍艦千歳號

H. I. J. S. "Chitose" in Honolulu

132

千歳艦將校及日本人小學校生徒　明治三十二年四月三日

Officers of "Chitose" and Japanese School Children

Taken on Apr. 3rd 1899

Officers of the Japanese warship *Chitose* with Japanese Primary School children, 3 April 1899 (Okumura Collection).

1897
明治30年 エワ

布哇国エワ耕地
日本人
小學校生徒

Ewa Plantation Japanese School, Oʻahu, 1897.
Mrs. Taihei Takahashi, the wife of a Methodist minister, was the teacher.

Lihue Japanese School, Kaua'i, ca. 1905 (Okumura Collection).

Japanese language school in Honomū, island of Hawai'i, ca. 1910.

134

Table 13
JAPANESE SCHOOLS IN HAWAI'I: 1895–1932

YEAR FOUNDED	O'AHU	HAWAI'I	MAUI	KAUA'I	MOLOKA'I	LĀNA'I
1895			Kula			
1896	Honolulu Japanese School→Hawaii Chūō Gakuin					
1897	Aiea Ewa	Honomu Gijuku Kukuihaele				
1898		Kealakekua				
1899		Laupahoehoe		Lihue		
1900				Kealia Koolau		
1901	Kakaako Waipahu	Yashijima (Nā'ālehu)		Waimea		
1902	Fort Gakuen Moiliili Waialua	Honomakau (Jōdo shū) Pepeekeo	Hamakuapoko Wailuku Gakuen	Lawai Makaweli Koloa		
1903	Kahuku Puuloa Waimanalo	Kaumana Olaa		Hanalei Kilauea		
1904		Honaunau Honokaa Hakalau (Jōdo shū) Kukaiau Kukuihaele Ninole Pahoa Pauilo/ Hamakua Bansei Shōgakkō (Hilo) Mountain View	Kaanapali Puukolii Puunene	Hanapepe Heiwa Gakuen (Hongwanji, Līhu'e) Kekaha Wahiawa		
1905	Pearl City Waianae	Hawi Onomea Wainaku (Jōdo shū) Papala		Mana		
1906	Kawailoa	Chūō-kona (Kapulena)				
1907	Hawaii Chūgakkō Kalihi Kaaawa/ Kahana	Kohala Hongwanji Niulii Ookala Paauhau Papaikou	Kihei Paia			
1908	Hawaii Jōdo shū Heeia Wahiawa	Halawa Honomu	Keahua Spreckelsville Waihee Waikapu	Anahola Kapaa		

JAPANESE SCHOOLS IN HAWAI'I: 1895–1932

YEAR FOUNDED	O'AHU	HAWAI'I	MAUI	KAUA'I	MOLOKA'I	LĀNA'I
1909	Waikiki Laie	Hamakua Kaapahu Waiakea-uka	Haiku			
1910	Palama Gakuen		Hana Kahului Kaeliku	Pakala Wailua		
1911		Hookena Kamuela Papaaloa Wainaku	Keahua Kōran Jojuku (Wailuku)	Frear (Līhu'e)		
1912	Waipahu	Piihonua				
1913	Taishō Gakkō (Hale'iwa)	Hilo Jogakkō/ Chūgakkō Kapoho Napoopoo Papaaloa		Eleele		
1914	Kahaluu	Hilo Meisho- Chūgakkō Kapoho	Makawao Peahi (Ha'iku)	Kalaheo		
1915	Tōyō Gakuen	Hakalau Wailea	Pauwela			
1916	Kaimuki	Hilo Dokuritsu- Gakkō Kehena	Honolua		Molokai	
1917	Punaluu	Taishō (Keauho) Onomea	Honokowai Kaupakulua Wailuku (II)	Kukuiula		
1918	Palama					
1919	Kailua	Kohala				
1921	Ewa		Wahikuli			
1922	Luluku (Kāne'ohe)		Ulupalakua			
1923	Kakaako/ Alapai	Kealakekua		Kapaa		
1924	Aiea	Honomu				Lanai
1926	Waialae Halemano				Libby (Maunaloa)	
1927	Waiahole				Kualapuu Shōwa (Kauanakakai)	
1928	Kahala	Kazan (Volcano)			Kamalo	
1929	Manoa Heiwa Gakuen Kalihi-kai Shōwa (Wahiawa)	Waiakea Chūō (Hilo)	Shōwa (Jōdo shū, Lahaina)			
1930		Kaumana- Kyōwa (Hilo)				
1932	Kipapa Taihei ('Aiea)					

Public school in Hanalei, Kaua'i, with teachers Pringle and Wells, ca. 1890 (W. E. H. Deverill, photographer).

All school-aged children in Hawai'i were required to attend school. Classes were conducted in either English or Hawaiian until 1896.

135

SOURCES: Compiled by K. Sinoto in 1984 from Kihara 1935; Morita 1915; Watanabe 1935.

Japanese Kindergarten, Honolulu, ca. 1900 (Okumura Collection).

137

Children at Okumura boarding school, Honolulu, 1899 (Okumura Collection; R. Susumago, photographer).

By 1903, the boarding school accommodated 150 children between 6 and 12 years of age. Mr. Hideo Kuwabara, a licensed
teacher from Hiroshima, is at right. Rev. and Mrs. Takie Okumura are in front, center. The children's uniforms seem to be
modelled after the school uniforms of Japan.

138

A public school classroom in Waipahu, Oʻahu, ca. 1914.

Kukaiau School, island of Hawai'i, 1912.

The children are wearing black ribbons of mourning, following the death of the Emperor Meiji in 1912.

日本語讀本 卷六

Japanese-language textbook as revised by Dr. Haga.

Title page.

Table of contents.

日本語讀本 卷六附録

Title page of supplement.

Japanese school teachers, 1920 (J. M. Ōsumi, photographer).

This group of teachers had just passed the examinations required by the Territorial Legislature, which applied regulations and restrictions to the foreign language school.

140

		7.
接する	Sessuru	Being close to each other
包まれ	Tsutsumare	Being surrounded
如く	Gotoku	Like
賞して	Shōshite	Praising, admiring
		8.
亦	Mata	Also, too
咲ク	Saku	To bloom, to be in flower
		9.
從ふ	Shitagau	Follow
消長	Shōchō	Prosperity and decay
兩	Ryō	Both
壯な	Sakanna	Vigorous, high
耳目	Jimoku	Ear and eye
主要	Shuyō	Importance
如何に	Ikani	How much, how
難い	Gatai	Difficult
命令	Meirei	Order, command

		4.
貿易	Bōeki	Trade, commerce
困難	Konnan	Difficulty
地圖	Chizu	Map
前に	Sakini	Previously
引見して	Inkenshite	To summon, have an interview with
		5.
立志	Risshi	Fixing one's aim in life
適當	Tekitō	Proper, suitable
負ウテ	Oute	Carrying on the back
坂	Saka	A slope, an ascent, descent
		6.
競馬	Keiba	Horse-race
子供	Kodomo	Child, children
頭	Kashira	Leader, chief
傳はつて	Tsutawatte	Being spread

Example of supplement with English definitions.

大正十二年八月十八日印刷
大正十二年八月二十日發行
大正十三年九月一日訂正再版印刷
大正十三年九月三日訂正再版發行

版權所有

編纂兼發行者
　布哇　ホノルヽ教育會

校閲者
　芳賀矢一
　新保磐次
　山岸德平

納本者
　東京市神田區通神保町九番地
　合資會社　冨山房

社代表長者
　坂本嘉治馬

電話神田二一二四一・二一四二・二一四三番
振替貯金口座東京五〇一番

Publications information.

142

Members of the Hawaii Educational Board for Japanese language schools, O'ahu, 11 August 1916 (Okumura Collection; R. Yasui, photographer).

This photograph includes Dr. Yaichi Haga (left), a Tokyo University professor who was invited to Hawai'i to revise the Japanese school textbooks.

英語夜学校生徒岡部次郎君の渡米を送る　明治廿八年六月九日

Rev. J. Okabe & Scholars of Japanese Night School. Taken Jan. 9th 1895.

Night school students sending off Rev. Jirō Okabe, who was leaving for the mainland United States, 9 June 1895 (Okumura Collection).

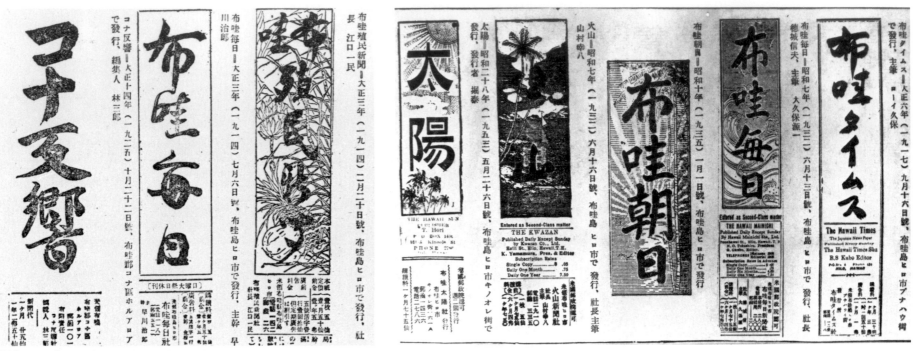

144

Title pages from various newspapers.

Kona Hankyō, Hawaii Mainichi, Hawaii Shokumin Shimbun, Kazan
Hawaii Asahi, and *Hawaii Times*.

JAPANESE LANGUAGE NEWSPAPERS

According to a popular Japanese saying, if there are as many as three Japanese living in the same place, a Japanese newspaper is published! Japanese in Hawai'i first published a newspaper in 1892, 7 years after their arrival, and many more followed, although only a handful endured. The surviving newspapers played various roles in the history of the Japanese in Hawai'i, and many of them were initiated as forums for the expression of ideas that would affect the masses.

Japanese newspapers served as the only major network through which the *issei* learned of important events in Hawai'i, reports of community affairs, and gossip about notable people within the Japanese community and outside it. The papers also related stories of the political changes sweeping their home country and the wars fought, although this news travelled by ship and was thus several weeks or more out-of-date. News from the United States mainland reached Hawai'i faster after the initiation of cable service in 1903 and the beginning of wireless communication in 1914. Thus, the papers—dozens of them over the years from 1892 on—fulfilled a wide variety of functions. They were educational in the broadest sense, providing instruction regarding life in a foreign land, as well as information about the wider world.

Newspapers helped direct the cultural growth of the community by publishing poetry and short stories written by the *issei* or by contemporaries in Japan. They reported on cultural events such as plays and exhibitions and provided calendars of upcoming events. Both Japanese and *haole* businesses supported the papers by purchasing advertisements.

For the immigrants who faced continual challenges to their struggle to improve their lives, the newspapers were critical sources of information. Every important political issue was treated in considerable detail, from voting rights and labor movements to the language school controversy of the 1920s. Japanese language papers could play these roles because the need for information and action was so great, and because there was a large pool of literate immigrants who could benefit from the publications. By the early twentieth century, when the members of the Japanese community constituted a complex society, their newspapers reflected the variety of regional and special interest groups in Hawai'i.

Nippon Shūhō was started in Honolulu by Bunichirō Onome—a former storeowner and coffee farmer—in 1892. A weekly mimeographed paper, it sold for 10 cents a single copy, and 35 cents for a monthly subscription. Onome started the paper to criticize the Bureau of Immigration for its arrogant officials and poor treatment of Japanese laborers. As one of six interpreters appointed by the Bureau of Immigration in 1886, he thus was familiar with the situation.

Hawaii Shimbun was published by Jūkichi Uchida, a Honolulu physician and the president of the Japanese League, which was organized in 1893 to regain the suffrage that had

Nippon Shūhō, 26 September 1892 (eighteenth issue).

This first Japanese-language newspaper was started on 3 June 1892 as a mimeographed weekly.

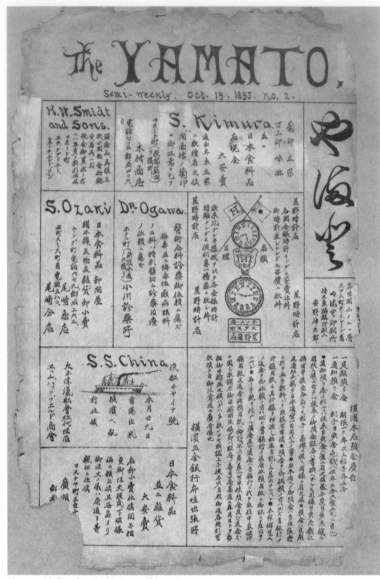

Yamato, 19 October 1895 (second issue).

Yamato, the antecedent of the *Hawaii Times*, started as a mimeographed semiweekly on 15 October 1895. It was published three times a week from July 1896, and daily from 2 May 1908.

been denied Japanese after passage of the Bayonnet Constitution. His newspaper actively supported the suffrage movement, albeit without success.

Hawaii Shimpō, the first typeset daily, was started in 1894 by Chūzaburō Shiozawa, who had been a storeowner in Wai'anae and Waipahu. Yasutarō Sōga, who later became the publisher of the *Nippu Jiji*, had worked for Shiozawa both in his store and on his newspaper staff. With the 1905 reform organization, *Hawaii Shimpō* led the way in criticizing the immigration companies for their exploitation in the recruitment of Japanese laborers. This joint effort resulted in the downfall of the immigration companies. Sometarō Shiba became Shiozawa's successor; he opposed the strike of Japanese laborers in 1909 and was slashed by a knife-wielding attacker. The paper was taken over by Tsuyoshi Hattori and Masao Segawa in 1916, continuing until the early 1920s as one of the leading newspapers. It changed to a weekly in 1926, and was discontinued shortly thereafter.

Yamato, a mimeographed semiweekly paper, was started by Shintarō Anno and Hamon Mizuno on 15 October 1895 as an organ of communication for the immigration company elite, with a few Japanese Meiji intellectuals on the staff. The title was changed to *Yamato-Shimbun* in 1896, and to *Nippu Jiji* in 1906, a year after it was taken over by Sōga, after the downfall of the immigration companies. During the 1909 labor strike on O'ahu, the *Nippu Jiji*, with a circulation of 1,000 became the major advocate for the Higher Wages Association and the strikers, publishing articles by their leaders, Kinzaburō Makino and Motoyuki Negoro, along with Sōga and Yōkichi Tasaka. Other large newspapers of that time, such as *Hawaii Nichinichi* and *Hawaii Shimpō*, with circulations of 1,200 each, were against the strike. Later, when it was discovered that those newspapers had been bribed by the planters, the *Nippu Jiji* won strong support from the community and its circulation greatly expanded. In 1921, when the Foreign Language School Regulatory Act was passed and the existence of the Japanese language schools was endangered, the *Nippu Jiji* took a more conservative stand against the court appeal. The newspaper continued through World War II to the present, changing its name to *Hawaii Times* in 1942, and becoming a weekly in 1982. When World War II broke out, the *Nippu Jiji* was forced to close during December of 1941; in January 1942, however, it was allowed to resume publication because its importance as a major communications media for the Japanese in Hawai'i was acknowledged by the United States government.

Honolulu Shimbun was first started under Yoshigorō Kimura in 1899 and was then taken over by Dr. Toshiyuki Mitamura and Rev. Takie Okumura. In 1903, it was taken over by Hanzō Tsurushima, who changed its name to *Hawaii Nichinichi Shimbun* and expanded it into one of the major papers. The paper was also called *Aka Shimbun* (Red Paper) because it was printed on pink paper. When the immigration companies were criticized for their abuses in 1905, it joined the *Hawaii Shimpō* in public expression of strong opposition, and, again with the *Hawaii Shimpō*, it stood against the strikers in 1909. This resulted in the demise of the paper in 1916, as it had lost the support of the community.

Hawaii Hōchi was established by Kinzaburō Makino on 7 December 1912. Makino was a drugstore owner prior to becoming one of the major leaders of the 1909 strike. When Makino started the *Hawaii Hōchi*, Motoyuki Negoro, another key leader of the strike, worked for the paper. In 1921, Makino and his paper took a strong stand with the Japanese language schools and continued supporting the cause until the law suits were won in 1927. The paper remains as the major Japanese language paper, with an English section, and recently began publishing the *Hawaii Herald*, an English biweekly paper for the younger generations.

A number of papers were published on the outer islands. *Kona Hankyō* was published by Dr. Saburō Hayashi in 1897 and lasted until June 1940. *Hilo Shimbun* was established by Morito Koga in 1898. After 1900, *Kau Shūhō*, *Ookala Shūhō*, *Hilo Shimpō*, *Kazan*, and *Jiyū Shimbun* were published on the island of Hawai'i. *Maui Shinshi* was the first paper on Maui, started by Rev. Giichi Tanaka in 1901. *Maui Shūkan Shimbun*, *Maui Shimbun*, *Maui Hōchi*, and *Maui Record* followed, but most of these papers did not last long. Sometarō Shiba started the *Kauai Shimpō* in 1904.

The smaller, more specialized, and regional papers provided a wide variety of perspectives on events affecting the Japanese community in Hawai'i, promoted wider intellectual and cultural pursuits, served as employment centers and training grounds for community leaders, and, finally, acted as mobilizing centers for civil rights movements. It was, however, in the dramatic confrontations of the two largest newspapers and their publisher-editors that the essential role of the Japanese press in Hawai'i may best be appreciated. The basic cultural, political, and ideological developments among the *issei* and *nisei* were primarily worked out on the pages of Sōga's *Nippu Jiji* and Makino's *Hawaii Hōchi*. The very identity of the entire ethnic group within Hawaiian society was carved out of their debates over acculturation, civil rights, and labor movements.

Nippu Jiji staff, 25 December 1909 (courtesy of Yoshitami Tasaka).

Front: 4th from left, Yōkichi Tasaka (with cane), Yasutarō Sōga, Motoyuki Negoro.

Subscription rates for *Yamato*, 9 November 1895.

147

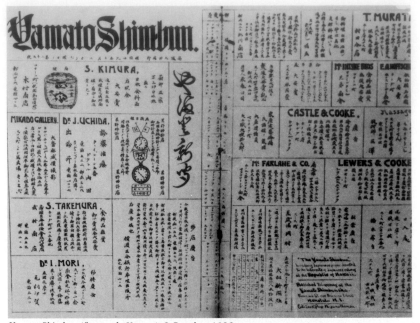

Yamato Shimbun (formerly *Yamato*), 3 October 1896.

The Japanese Press Club of Honolulu, 1917.

From left: front, Fukio Konishi, Kichinosuke Takeuchi (both *Chōhō*); middle, Shōichi Asami (*Nippu*), Masao Sogawa (*Shimpō*), Teisuke Teragaki (*Hōchi*), Saburō Konaha (*Hōchi*), Makoto Hara (*Nippu*), Tadao Yano (*Hōchi*); back, Torakichi Kimura (*Hōchi*), Sei Tsuchiya (*Hōchi*), Kusaka Haga (*Hōchi*), Keitarō Kawamura (*Nippu*), Hijin Misawa (*Nippu*).

Table 14
JAPANESE LANGUAGE NEWSPAPERS IN HAWAI'I, 1892–1920

STARTING DATE	NAME	PUBLISHER	TYPE*	PLACE
1892	*Nippon Shūhō*	Bunichirō Onome	W,M	Honolulu
1892	*Yamato Shinshi*	Yasushi Watanabe	W	Honolulu
1893	*Hawaii Shimbun*	Jūkichi Uchida	W,M	Honolulu
1893	*Nijusseiki*	Hamon Mizuno	SW,L	Honolulu
1893	*Aloha*	Kikujirō Matsuno	W	Honolulu
1894	*Hawaii Shimpō*	Chūzaburō Shiozawa	D,T	Honolulu
1895	*Kazan*	Bunnosuke Shimizu	D	Honolulu
1895	*Yamato*	Shintarō Anno	SW,L	Honolulu
	↓ *Yamato Shimbun* (1896)		SW,L,D,T	
	↓ *Nippu Jiji* (1906)	Yasutaro Soga	D,T	
	↓ *Hawaii Times*** (1942)		D,T	
1895	*Hinode Shimbun*	Hinode Club		Honolulu
	↓ *Shin Nihon* (1897)	Gorō Gunji	W	Honolulu
	↓ *Hawaii Jiyū Shimbun* (1906)	Kusaka Haga	D	Honolulu
1897	*Kona Hankyō*	Dr. Saburō Hayashi	W,M	Kona, Hawai'i
1898	*Hawaii Hilo Shimbun*	Morito Koga	D	Hilo, Hawai'i
1899	*Honolulu Shimbun*	Yoshigorō Kimura	D	Honolulu
	↓ *Hawaii Nichinichi Shimbun* (1903)	Hanzō Tsurushima	D	
1901	*Maui Shinshi*	Rev. Giichi Tanaka	W	Wailuku, Maui
1902	*Maui Shūkan Shimbun*	Tetsuzō Takamura	W	Wailuku, Maui
1902	*Kau Shūhō*	Yuzuru Makino	W	Ka'ū, Hawai'i
1902	*Ookala Shūhō*	Torakichi Kimura	W	'O'ōkala, Hawai'i
1902	*Shin Nihon*	Shintarō Anno	W	Honolulu
1903	*Rōdō Shimbun*	Tōsui Saitō	W	Honolulu
1904	*Kauai Shimpō*	Torajirō Fukunaga	W	Līhu'e, Kaua'i
1906	*Maui Shimbun*	Kinjirō Yokogawa	SW,L	Wailuku, Maui
1906	*Oahu Jihō*	Akira Mitsunaga	W	Waipahu, O'ahu
1909	*Hawaii Shokumin Shimbun*	Kazutami Eguchi	D	Hilo, Hawai'i
	↓ *Hawaii Mainichi* (1914)	Jirō Hayakawa	D	Hilo, Hawai'i
1909	*Hilo Shimpō*	Kōsuke Hagiwara	SW	Hilo, Hawai'i
1909	*Maui Hōchi*	Rev. Shigefusa Kanda	SW	Wailuku, Maui
1912	*Hawaii Hōchi***	Kinzaburō Makino	D	Honolulu
1914	*Kazan*	Kōhachi Yamamura	SW	Hilo, Hawai'i
1914	*Hawaii Times*	Shūji Kubo	W	Hilo, Hawai'i
1915	*Kona Shūhō*	Haruto Saitō	W	Kona, Hawaii
1916	*Taiheiyō Shimbun*	Tsuyoshi Hattori	D	Honolulu
1916	*Hawaii Chōhō*	Rintarō Murakami	D	Honolulu
1917	*Maui Record*	Nagao Ōtsuka	SW	Wailuku, Maui
1917	*Hawaii Asahi Shimbun*	Shirogane Ōshiro	W,SW	Hilo, Hawai'i
1918	*Jiyū Shimbun*	Kinzuchi Terumoto	W	Kona, Hawai'i
1918	*Shin Hawaii*	Kiyoshi Momii	W	Hilo, Hawai'i
1920	*Yōen Jihō*	Hiroshi Suzuki	SW	Līhu'e, Kaua'i

*D=daily; SW=semiweekly; W=weekly; L.=lithographed; M=mimeographed; T=typeset
**Still in operation.

SOURCES: Compiled by K. Sinoto in 1983 from United Japanese Society of Hawaii 1964; *Hawaii Times* 1955; Morita 1915; Kihara 1935; Sōga 1953; Haruhara 1979; Ebara 1936; Fujii 1900.

Yamato, 7 July 1896 (100th celebration issue).

The results of the first All Islands Grand Sumō tournament
are on the lefthand page.

Nippu Jiji (formerly *Yamato Shimbun*), 6 November 1906.

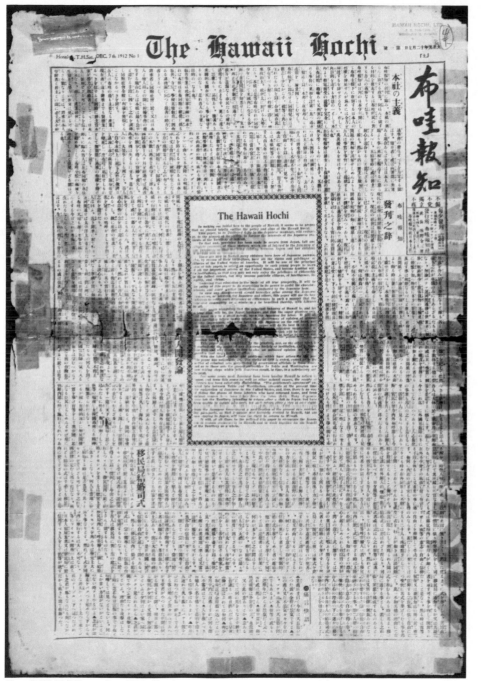

Hawaii Hōchi, 7 December 1912 (first issue).

Japanese barber shop, Honolulu, 1910.
Running a barber shop was a popular profession among Japanese who had completed their contracts and were establishing private businesses. Of the approximately fifty barbershops in Honolulu in 1900, at least forty-five were operated by Japanese.

BUSINESS AND ENTERPRISE

The development of an economically stable Japanese community in Hawai'i was never smooth, proceeding in spurts by overcoming numerous obstacles. In the crucial four decades between arrival in 1885 and exclusion in 1924, the Japanese in Hawai'i responded to a series of challenges in a variety of ways. One basic problem stemmed from the fact that most of the original Japanese immigrants intended to work for the booming sugar industry on a temporary basis, and eventually to return to Japan. Sugar planters worked with the same goal in mind. In point of fact, however, many of the *issei* settled in Hawai'i very early and quickly let it be known that they were unwilling to accept wages that were lower than those paid to workers of other nationalities, or that were insufficient to meet the needs of their families. Most important, they refused to be controlled, and their individual and collective efforts to achieve economic independence and security in the face of considerable opposition did much to shape the economic, cultural, political, and social development of Hawai'i.

With the numerous Japanese camps on the plantations, it was inevitable that demands for many types of services and goods would emerge and grow. Perhaps the earliest such demands came when the first Japanese laborers insisted on the establishment of bathhouses, which would allow washing followed by long immersion in a large tub of hot water, as they had been accustomed to in Japan. Plantations provided the fuel, water, and buildings, while an operator, usually a family unit, charged users a small monthly fee for the maintenance of these *furo*. Other small businesses soon developed to cater to special needs created by plantation conditions. Each camp had one or more families who cooked all the meals for the largely single, male population. Typically, too, some meals were prepared by women whose husbands were plantation workers. Japanese women also contracted to do the laundry for single men, boiling and scrubbing the filthy workclothes and pressing them with charcoal irons. Some managed this business in addition to a full day's work in the field, as well as tending to their own husbands and children.

Some of the early Japanese were provided plots of land at a nominal cost or in exchange for extra labor. Such plots were used for raising vegetables, and the produce was exchanged or sold to others. It was not long before poultry and pigs also became items for small-scale production. By 1915, there were seventy-three Japanese hog farmers on O'ahu, where the industry was concentrated. Most (sixty-nine) were from Yamaguchi, Kumamoto, and Hiroshima, three were from Okinawa, and the last came from Fukuoka. In the 1920s,

153

Kunosuke Isoshima opened the Japanese Bazaar on Fort Street in 1905 (courtesy of Yoshiko Tsukiyama).

By 1900, there were more than a hundred Japanese stores in the Hawaiian Islands. Many of them were started by people using money saved during their contract period, rather than with capital introduced from Japan.

Honolulu was the center of business in the Islands, and Japanese businesses were concentrated here. Large stores in Honolulu imported goods from Japan, and sold merchandise to Japanese stores on the outer islands. The majority of those stores were groceries, which often carried clothing and household materials, and *sake* stores. In 1900, when contract labor was prohibited, more professional business people came as free immigrants. They established import businesses, hotels, *sake* breweries, and so on.

Yamagata Store, Kona, island of Hawai'i, ca. 1908.
Donkeys were an important means of transportation in Kona
and were called "Kona nightingales" because of their braying.

Papaw (papaya) plantation near Honolulu, ca. 1900 (Keystone
stereo postcard).

Okinawans came to predominate, perhaps because Japanese from other prefectures were largely vegetarian and had traditional prejudices against raising and slaughtering animals.

As the community increased in size and complexity with at least some of its members accumulating enough wealth to afford more than subsistence levels of living, a wider range of goods and services became essential. By the turn of the century, professional midwives were delivering the more than one thousand babies being born to the Japanese every year. Tailors and artisans opened up small shops, while barbers and hairdressers were able to earn modest livings. Specialty foods like *tofū* (soybean curd), Japanese fishcake, and noodles were produced and sold. Funeral parlors operated by Japanese replaced the crude practice of burying the dead in plain wooden coffins provided by the plantations. Each plantation camp and urban neighborhood included individuals who, for a fee, would write letters, interpret documents, intervene with management or government officials, or who would teach Japanese music, dance, language, and the games *go* and *shōgi*.

While all but a few Japanese were prevented from entering supervisory or managerial-level occupations on the plantations, many were soon working as skilled laborers, such as carpenters, machine operators, stone masons, and blacksmiths, particularly as the industry continued to intensify efforts to cut costs by expanding its production technology.

Carpentry serves as a good example of the Japanese making their way into the skilled crafts. In 1884, the census of the Hawaiian Kingdom listed 264 carpenters, including 71 Hawaiians, 15 Chinese, and 178 others, most of whom were Europeans or Americans. By 1900, the general economy and the plantation industry had grown so rapidly that there were a total of 1,955 carpenters, including 649 Japanese, who outnumbered any other ethnic or nationality group. The increasing need for carpenters brought more Japanese into the trade and, by 1920, they constituted nearly two-thirds (1,832) of the total 2,890 in the Territory. Many of the farmers arriving from Japan had skills in carpentry and these were readily adaptable to the plantation setting, which required considerable building and maintenance of flumes, mills, housing for increasing numbers of laborers, storage areas, and sheds for animals. Equally important, highly skilled craftsmen were summoned from Japan to build temples and shrines, and their influence extended to the immigrants who stayed in Hawai'i.

It was off the plantation, however, that some of the dramatic improvements were made, with the Japanese entering many segments of the work force. The *Report of the Commissioner of Labor in Hawaii* for 1901 observed that the Japanese seemed to be taking over jobs that had been performed by native Hawaiians. The Japanese had constituted only 7 percent of the fishermen in 1896, but 25 percent in 1900; they were also becoming sailors in the local shipping industry. There was a note of alarm in watching the Japanese "crowding into the stevedore and wharf work to an extent that is causing friction and even influencing local politics in Honolulu." Japanese were also dominating the clothing trades. Given the need for skilled labor in the growing Hawaiian economy, the Japanese had established a vocational school to teach cooking to men and sewing to women. Established by Rev. Takie Okumura, the school opened its doors on 1 September 1896, to accommodate sixty students, most of whom worked during the day and attended classes at night.

Although it was the Chinese who became stereotyped as the shopkeepers and businessmen of Hawai'i, the Japanese were not far behind, in either historical period or the degree of entrepreneurial activity. The first individual Japanese storeowner was Kunizō Suzuki, who arrived in Hawai'i aboard a German whaler in 1867. He first worked on a plantation and later as a servant for a prominent American. In 1886 he opened a small shop in Hilo with savings of $150. He was called "Hilo no Kuni" when the early contract laborers arrived. He sold them Hawaiian fruit and served simple meals. By the 1890s, there were immigrants arriving as independent, if not wealthy, merchants who started out with several hundred dollars in inventory and who peddled these Japanese foodstuffs and incidentals from plantation to plantation.

There was an immediate need for the whole range of Japanese foodstuffs, and the Hawaiian government tried to deal with the issue by assigning the task to Jōji Nakayama, head of the Japanese section with the Bureau of Immigration. Nakayama created a store to import goods from Japan, but the enterprise ended in failure due to problems in distribution and losses suffered because of food spoilage.

Once the Japanese community became large enough to appear attractive as a potential market, however, firms in Japan sent agents to establish branch import businesses, but these invariably failed where the smaller, "local," merchants succeeded because of their detailed knowledge of conditions in Hawai'i. In order to become entrepreneurs, however, the Japanese had to accumulate sufficient capital. Some did this through painstaking self-denial over long years, while saving from their wages. A standard form of lending and borrowing more substantial sums was the traditional Japanese rotating-credit institution, called the *tanomoshi* or *tanomoshikō*. Organized as social and financial groups, these units typically included about ten individuals who contributed a set amount of money each month. That lump sum was distributed to one participant each month, either on a rotating basis or to the person willing to repay the group with the highest rate of interest. An enterprising individual might join or initiate several of these *tanomoshi* simultaneously and accumulate enough capital to invest in a small business. Sometimes, however, the proceeds were not invested but used to repay large debts, cover expenses for weddings or funerals, pay for trips back to Japan, and, occasionally, taken from the group by an unscrupulous individual who simply absconded with the money.

In addition to limited access to banks, another obstacle to capital formation among Japanese immigrants was the need to send money to their families in Japan, which was a basic reason for most immigrants leaving their villages as *dekasegi* laborers. The immigrants who arrived on the *City of Tokio* sent a total of about $4,000 back to families only a few months after they had begun working on the plantations. These remittances were handled by the Japanese Consulate during most of the government contract period, until the Yokohama Specie Bank established a branch in Hawai'i in 1892. An estimated $1 million was sent to Japan annually by government contract laborers. Between 1894 and 1899, some $1.5 million went to Japan each year, and from 1900 to 1907, an average of $2 million was remitted annually. Thereafter, into the 1920s, the figure climbed to $2.5 million. Other calculations suggested that, while the earlier remittances were substantially lower, the totals began to exceed $3 million by 1903. In 1911–1912, the Japanese represented more than 40 percent of the Islands' population. However, during this same period, Japanese savings in Hawai'i banks accounted for only 2 percent of all savings in the Islands.

These remittances were of tremendous importance to the survival and well-being of fami-

Kimura Shōkai in Honolulu, 1912.

The store was established by Saiji Kimura, an 1885 arrival who had worked as a Bureau of Immigration supervisor before he opened a store in 1893 and imported Japanese food and merchandise. The company was incorporated in 1905.

155

Table 15

MEMBERS OF JAPANESE HOTEL ASSOCIATION IN 1893

Chugokuya (Hichizō Fujimoto)→ Komeya
Fukuokaya (Kumatarō Ichikawa)
Hawaii-ya (Unosuke Kobayashi)→ Kobayashi Hotel
Higoya (Yasaburō Kimura)
Hiroshimaya (Naotarō Nishikida)
Kawasaki Hotel (Kiyozō Kawasaki)
Kikuya (Chōshirō Iwamoto)
Kishimoto Ryokan (Toshisuke Kishimoto)
Komatsuya (Kōsuke Satō)
Kumamotoya (Sōgorō Watanabe)
Kyushuya (Jintarō Izuno)
Mizuhaya (Genzaburō Mizuha)
Oshimaya (Shūsuke Nishimura)
Otaya (Yonezō Ōta)
Yoshinoya (Matsutarō Yamashiro)→ Yamashiroya

SOURCE: Nippu Jiji 1935.

Kawasaki Hotel, River Street, Honolulu.

Kiyozō Kawasaki, who came on the first boat from Yamaguchi in 1885, started his hotel business in 1891. The Japanese Hotel Association was organized in 1893. Lodging was 40 cents a day, and meals were 15 cents. The hotels provided accommodations for newly arrived immigrants and helped people in formalities with the Consulate and the immigration companies and in finding jobs. Many people who were returning home or moving to the United States mainland stayed in the hotels, where travel arrangements were made.

lies in Japan and, in some cases — like that of Oshima county in Yamaguchi prefecture — are said to have created wealthy villages where there had been widespread poverty. In Hawai'i, however, such long-term sacrifice for tens of thousands of immigrants resulted in a financial drain and retarded the economic development of the local Japanese community.

In 1895, 10 years after their arrival, Japanese contract laborers could patronize at least thirty-two Japanese merchants in Honolulu and by 1898, at least eighteen in Hilo on the Big Island, including a hotel and a watch repair shop. The general population movement for the Japanese was from plantation camp to the plantation town and, subsequently, to the growing urban areas of Honolulu and Hilo. In Honolulu, the community in 1900 could find 37 Japanese businessmen organized into the Nihon Shōnin Dōshikai (Japanese Merchants Association), which later became the Honoruru Nihonjin Shōkō Kaigisho (Honolulu Japanese Chamber of Commerce), and included 176 separate businesses in the Chinatown area alone, at least before the catastrophic fire that swept that section on 20 January 1900.

Honolulu had been carefully watched because of outbreaks of bubonic plague, and Chinatown itself had been quarantined under military guard since mid-December of 1899. The established procedure was to burn the dwelling of anyone found infected by the plague. Carelessness apparently allowed a gust of wind to carry sparks to the steeple of Kaumakapili Church, from where the fire spread to dozens of blocks in which Japanese, Chinese, and Hawaiians lived. There was no fire insurance and the Chinese and Japanese businessmen turned to the Territorial government for assistance. The official response was most insensitive, requiring the unfortunate victims to pay a $20 filing fee for indemnity claims. Protest from the Chinese and Japanese and support from the *haole* business community persuaded the government to modify its original stand. Ultimately the Japanese submitted claims totalling more than $600,000 and received just over one-half of the sum requested.

The Chinatown fire of 1900 was significant in a number of ways. It demonstrated the extent to which the Japanese had become part of the business and urban world of Hawai'i by the first year of the twentieth century, and it showed that the Japanese could organize joint action with the other ethnic groups. The fire also precipitated major changes within the Japanese community. It destroyed the gangster-controlled prostitution and gambling organizations operated by groups of Japanese in Honolulu. The devastating financial consequences forced the Japanese merchants to adopt innovative methods of shipping, storage, use of credit, and merchandising, which helped build a vigorous commercial base for future growth.

The growth of the pineapple industry in the early 1900s provided more employment, especially for laborers freed from their contracts, and an investment arena for the rapidly developing Japanese community. In 1901, Yasuke Teshima leased several dozen acres to grow pineapple in Wahiawā, O'ahu. In 1913 the total capital investment by Japanese on O'ahu alone amounted to $700,000 in 6,000 acres of pineapple. This amounted to fully one-half of all pineapple cultivation on the entire island. On Maui and Kaua'i, Japanese entrepreneurs formed companies large enough to establish canneries to process pineapple grown by independent farmers, often Japanese as well. In the canneries, Japanese women soon found seasonal jobs preparing the fruit for export.

Not all crops were destined for success. Cotton soon proved to be unsuited to Hawai'i, and coffee had an erratic history in the late nineteenth century. The sudden and steep drop in world coffee prices (from $27 to less than $10 per hundred pounds) in 1900 convinced many *haole* farmers to give up and opened up opportunities for Japanese who were leaving the sugar plantations. Approximately 100 Japanese leased land in 'Ōla'a, just south of Hilo, to cultivate coffee. However, except for a few individuals — such as Bunichirō Onome, who eventually started the first Japanese language newspaper in Hawai'i — the costly investment in money, time, and backbreaking labor proved fruitless because the climate was too wet for coffee. The Japanese who helped develop the industry in Kona on the other side of Hawai'i Island, however, found that some kind of living could be made. As early as 1892, some Japanese began working on coffee farms and the numbers increased as Kona became something of a haven for Japanese who had escaped from sugar plantations and who risked arrest and imprisonment for breaking contracts. Oral tradition insists that a number of Japanese changed their names in order to avoid detection and that close friends often knew families by both "real" and assumed names. Fortunately for these deserters, plantation management found that recapturing them was not cost efficient. As the manager of Paauhau Plantation noted in a letter to the manager of Oahu Sugar Co., dated 10 September 1897:

> I have known for a long time that our deserting Japanese have obtained employment in Kona. I have made no efforts to recover them as we cannot hold them, and the probabilities are that we will lose more or less money through expenses in capturing them. Were there a law to enable us to punish deserters by imprisonment for 2 or 3 years, I would then take steps to stop the deserting of our laborers.

> I am in hopes that the Coffee Planters may have sufficient labor in time so that our men may not be wanted.

The coffee industry experienced many subsequent swings in world prices, but the Japanese maintained their presence so that, by 1914, they were producing about 80 percent of Hawaiian coffee. As in other industries, the ability of the Japanese to move ahead was largely shaped by changes in the larger economic picture — historical shifts in the fortunes of specific economic activities, the rapid growth in the Territory's economy as sugar and pineapple prospered, and the vastly increased need for more and newer forms of goods and services for an expanding population.

The potential for entrepreneurial activity extended quickly to production of Japanese foodstuffs, such as soy sauce and *sake* to accommodate the growing ethnic community's appetite, and to commercial fishing to feed the larger groups being imported to work on the plantations. The particularly large influx of Japanese in 1898–1899 must have generated an extraordinary demand for such foods. In response, Gorokichi Nakasuji from Wakayama prefecture introduced a Japanese tuna fishing boat in 1899 and staffed it with professional fishermen to catch tuna in Hawaiian waters. Similar boats were soon being built by skilled Japanese boatbuilders, most of whom were brought over from Wakayama prefecture. Mechanical and technological improvements followed soon thereafter. Between 1907 and 1914, there were five major fishing companies established by the Japanese. In the 1920s, nearly one thousand Japanese were involved in the fishing industry in Ha-

Advertisement for the Kawasaki Hotel, Honolulu, 1906.

Table 16
Advertisement for new shipment of goods by Takemura Store, King St., Honolulu
Yamato June 30, 1896

soy sauce — grades A, B, C, miso, pickled plums, pickled radish (takuwan), Japanese tea — grades A, B, C, black beans, azuki beans, kidney beans, green peas (dried), baked gluten, dehydrated tofu blocks, somen noodles, buckwheat noodles, Shiratama flour, Katakuri flour, powdered beanpaste, two kinds of seaweed, dried clams, bird feed, fukujinzuke (mixed pickled vegetables in soy sauce), canned Japanese mushrooms, seasoned bamboo shoots, canned boiled bamboo shoots, dried fish for soup stock, canned mackerel, canned seasoned beef, striped material, blue ikat material, designed ikat material, Japanese and western towels, striped shirts, white shirts, collars, handkerchiefs, neckties, sashes, socks, umbrellas, straw hats, felt hats, caps, shoes, slippers, Japanese slippers, legging, yanagigori, bamboo gori, lamps, fishing poles, feather dusters, teacups, shoe polish, toothpaste (a variety), soups, Japanese tobacco, cigarettes, buttons, decorative items, art pieces, new novels, dictionaries, western cookbooks, art books, Japanese music books, diaries, Japanese paper, ink, notebooks, letter-writing paper, pencils, fireworks (for both daytime and nighttime), Japanese-made modern oil stove, miscellaneous food items, notions, accessories, etc.

The above items were delivered by the Tōyō-maru. All are choice quality merchandise carefully selected by the wholesalers. We specially priced those for cash sales and are asking your patronage.

Honolulu Japanese Sake Brewery Co., Ltd., Honolulu, 1908 (courtesy of Honolulu Sake Brewery and Ice Co.).

A branch office of the Japanese bank, Yokohama Shōkin Ginkō, was built in 1910 on Merchant Street in Honolulu.

The bank was first opened in July 1892 on Nuʻuanu Avenue to handle the savings of the immigrants and the money they sent home to Japan. These matters were handled by the Japanese Consulate in Honolulu prior to 1892.

waiʻi. Japanese monopolization of the fishing trades extended into subsidiary activities, including wholesale and retail sales of maritime hardware, boatbuilding and repair, sale of fishing gear and bait, and processing and sale of dried fish.

Sake was available by the late 1880s, but immigrant laborers were already engaged in illegal small-scale brewing and distilling efforts on the plantations. This would hardly be surprising when the original cost of the imported rice wine from Japan was over $3 per gallon (because of the high import tax of $1 per gallon), in a period when men were paid $12 to $15 for 26 days of work per month. Tajirō Sumida established the first *sake* brewery, the Honolulu Sake Brewing Co., in September 1908, but it took years of experiments with new equipment and innovative techniques before he could overcome one major problem. The year-round warm weather in Hawaiʻi prevented successful fermentation in one crucial stage of production. Nevertheless, they marketed their first product in December of the first year. Sumida perfected the process by using refrigeration, and by 1914 he was manufacturing nearly three hundred thousand gallons of *sake*. Along with several competitors, Sumida was providing Hawaiʻi with nearly all it could consume. In the meantime, a sizable illegal operation had developed where beer, *sake*, the Hawaiian distilled liquor ʻōkolehao, and various forms of wine were being made and marketed in the Japanese community.

The combined effect of these economic activities resulted in a Japanese community in Hawaiʻi that was rapidly developing resources of its own. Whereas the 1885 immigrants owned no real property, claimed little in the way of liquid assets, and paid no taxes, the Japanese in 1895 held $56,900 in real property, and $117,309 in liquid assets, although they still were exempted from paying Hawaiʻi taxes. By 1910, the figures were $255,810 for real property, $1,664,402 in liquid assets, and $148,179 paid in taxes. At the end of the immigration period, in 1925, there was unmistakable evidence of enormous growth, with the Japanese then owning $7,159,167 worth of real property, $8,089,862 in liquid assets, and paying $645,062 in taxes. Further, they held more than four and one-half million dollars in savings in the three Japanese banks alone and more in the other banks as well.

As the Japanese community planted its roots firmly in Hawaiian soil with every indication that the immigrants and their children intended to stay, the planter-dominated *haole* elite was hard pressed to find means to accommodate this Asian laboring group, both on and off the plantations, without risking loss of control. The resultant challenges by the Japanese community grew. When banks controlled by the plantation owners would not provide credit for new business venture, capital was generated through the *tanomoshi* or rotating credit associations, from personal loans, and from Japan; when pay scales were too low, both in an absolute sense and relative to other ethnic workers, workers protested and struck, and women contributed more than their share by taking jobs in addition to caring for their families; when sugar plantation labor seemed a limited way to get ahead, the *issei* left, sometimes deserting, for jobs they would carve out of the growing economy. The legacies of this process continue to affect the nature of the Japanese community to this day.

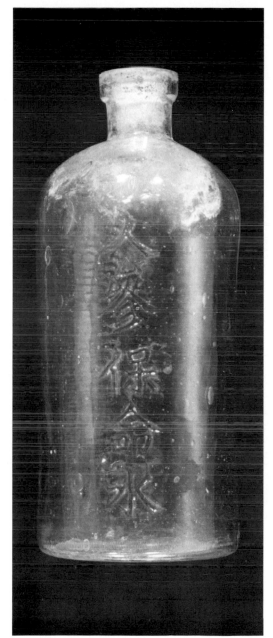

Bottle of *NINJIN HOMEYSUY*.

Store sign for carrot medicine, *NINJIN HOMEYSUY*, from T. Sakamoto Store.

Poster for carrot medicine, from the T. Sakamoto Store, Wailuku, Maui, ca. 1920.

This medicine poster was used at the T. Sakamoto Store in Wailuku. The carrot medicine, *NINJIN HOMEYSUY*, originally made in Hiroshima, Japan, was exclusively distributed by this store.

160

Sakamoto Store, Waikapū, Maui, 1906.

Store owners played multiple roles in early plantation communities — keeping mail and writing letters for people, and working as agents of the Japanese Consulate in Honolulu. Stocked with merchandise imported from Japan, the Japanese store on the plantation was the oasis of the community.

Camp 5 store, Puʻunēnē, Maui, ca. 1915 (courtesy of Alexander and Baldwin Sugar Museum)

The manager was Jirokichi Fujiyoshi. A photograph of the Taishō Emperor and Empress is displayed on the center post.

Hanaoka Hotel, Kahului, Maui, 1914.

A famous guest, Tachiyama, who was with the first *sumō* group to visit Hawai'i in 1914, is shown here.

Kobayashi Hotel, Honolulu.

The hotel was started by Unosuke Kobayashi of Hiroshima in 1892 on Smith Street in Honolulu. The original building was destroyed during the Chinatown fire, and the hotel was reopened in Pālama. In 1903, this building was erected on Beretania Street.

A 1930s broadside of tariffs for the Japanese Hotel Association shows the wide range of services that were offered at these hotels.

During the prohibition period (1918–1932), Honolulu Sake Co., survived by making ice.

Sumida *sake* store on Maunakea Street, Honolulu, ca. 1915
(courtesy of Honolulu Sake Brewery and Ice Co.).

Tajiro Sumida came to Hawai'i from Hiroshima in 1899 at age
16. In 1904 he established the Sumida store, and in 1908 he
started the Honolulu Japanese Sake Brewing Co. Ltd., the
first *sake* brewery abroad. It is the only *sake* brewery still existing in the Islands, in Pauoa Valley, Honolulu.

Celebration of the first *sake* products, brand-named Takara-
jima, Honolulu, December 1908 (courtesy of the Honolulu
Sake Brewery and Ice Co.)

Refrigeration building, constructed ca. 1911 (courtesy of the
Honolulu Sake Brewery and Ice Co.).

Brewing *sake* under refrigeration was an adaptation to the
warm climate of Hawai'i. Subsequently, many *sake* breweries in
Japan adopted this technique so that they could brew *sake* year-
round.

Gold watch belonging to Katsu Gotō, ca. 1885.

Katsu Gotō came to Hawaiʻi on the *City of Tokio* on 8 February 1885 and worked for three years on Soper Wright and Co.'s plantation in ʻOʻōkala, Hawaiʻi. He occasionally helped as an interpreter as he knew English well. In 1888, he took over a Japanese store in Honokaʻa which had been previously owned by Bunichirō Onome, who came to Hawaiʻi as an official interpreter in 1886.

Although Gotō competed with other storeowners and prospered, he continued to represent the rights of Japanese laborers.

Gotō's body was found hanging from an electric pole on 29 October 1889 in Honokaʻa. Investigation revealed that three haoles, a local storeowner, and a Hawaiian were involved in his murder.

Table 17

MAJOR JAPANESE ORGANIZATIONS AND COMMUNITY ESTABLISHMENTS IN HAWAIʻI, 1887 – 1932

1887   Japanese Mutual Aid Assn. Organized among the Japanese Methodist Church members.

1888   Hawaii Japanese Temperence League. Organized under Rev. Kanichi Miyama, a Methodist minister and Tarō Andō, the consul general of Japan in Honolulu. Later reorganized by Rev. Takie Okumura in 1897.

1889   Japanese Women's Benevolent Society, reorganized among the Japanese Methodist Church members under Mrs. Sunamoto, the minister's wife.
Reorganized in 1892 as Japanese Benevolent Society including men.

1893   Japanese Hotel Assn.
Hinode-Gikyo-Isshin United Assn. (Honolulu Japanese Gangs Assn.)
Hilo Japanese League. Organized to recover suffrage rights under Dr. Shin Yamamoto.

1894   Hilo Japanese Mutual Aid Club, Hawaiʻi.

1895   Yamato Club. Organized mainly among immigration company executives.
Honolulu Japanese Merchants Assn.
Japanese Hack Drivers Assn.

1896   Japanese Medical Doctors Assn.
Japanese Cooks Assn.
North Kona Japanese Community Cemetery

1897   Japanese Planters Assn., ʻŌlaʻa Hawaiʻi.
Kona Japanese Agricultural Assn., Kona, Hawaiʻi.
Japanese Library, opened on 8 June in Honolulu with more than three hundred books, sponsored by Japanese Christian churches.
Young Japanese (Christians) Assn. Organized among Japanese church members. Reorganized under Rev. Okumura in 1900 including nonchurch members.

1898   Kona Coffee Growers Assn. Dr. Saburō Hayashi, et al.
Kauai Mutual Assistance League. Organized among Japanese plantation workers.
Kauai Mutual Aid Club.
Buddhist Women's Assn., organized among Honpa Hongwanji members, Honolulu.

1899   Japanese Hospital established on Liliha St. by Dr. S. Kobayashi.
Japanese Benevolent Society was registered with U.S. Government and established their hospital in Kapālama in 1900. Merged with Dr. Kobayashi's hospital in 1901 when the name Japanese Hospital was restored.
Kona Japanese Laborers Union. Later became Kona Japanese Assn.
Hilo Young Japanese Christians Assn. Organized by Rev. Jirō Okabe.

1900   Emergency Japanese Assn. Organized after the Chinatown fire and was renamed Honolulu Merchant's Assn. It became Japanese Chamber of Commerce in 1916.
Honolulu Japanese Barbers Assn.
Young Buddhist Assn. Organized among Hongwanji members under Rev. Yemyō Imamura.
Young Japanese Assn. was organized among young professionals with Kotarō Uyeda as president.

1901   Hawaii Japanese Assn.
The first *Haiku* group was organized in ʻEwa, Oʻahu by Hankurō Ishiguri.

1902   Kendō Assn. Gekken Kai was organized by Dr. Umekichi Asahina. Later it was renamed Kōbu Kai.

1903   Central Japanese Assn. Organized by Consul General Miki Saitō.

1904   Kumamoto Prefectural People's Assn.

1905   Reform Assn. Organized with Motoyuki Negoro as president to protest
       exploitation of immigrants by immigration companies involved in Central
       Japanese Assn.

1906   Honolulu Japanese Carpenters Assn.
       Honolulu Educational Assn.

1907   Prince Fushimi Scholarship Assn.
       Maui Merchants Assn.
       Maui Educational Assn.

1908   Oahu Educational Assn.
       Moiliili Japanese Cemetery.
       Hiroshima Prefectural People's Assn.
       Honolulu Retail Merchants Assn.

1909   Higher Wages Assn. Organized for the first Japanese laborers strike on O'ahu.

1911   Olaa Temperence League. Organized by Jirō Iwasaki, 'Ōla'a 11 miles. Hawai'i.
       Honolulu Japanese Contractors Assn.
       Honolulu Fisherman's Benevolent Assn., Kaka'ako, O'ahu.
       Honolulu Geisha Assn.

1914   Hawaii Japanese Assn. Organized by Consul General Hachirō Arita.
       Maui Japanese Medical Doctors Assn.
       Hawaii Japan-America Assn.

Pre-
1915   Honolulu Japanese Tailors Assn.
       Midwives' Assn.
       Honolulu Japanese Photographers' Assn. It was renamed as Hawaii Japanese
       Photographers League in 1929.

1915   Hawaii Japanese Educational Assn. Organized to unify the Japanese language
       schools and to revise textbooks.
       Kauai Japanese Medical Doctors Assn.

(ca.) Hawaii Naniwabushi Assn. with membership of approximately one hundred.

1916   Honolulu Japanese Women's Society.

1918   Thursday Luncheon Club. Organized under Consul General Rokurō Moroi for
       cultural exchange.
       Japanese Hospital's new building was built on Kuakini St. It was renamed Kuakini
       Hospital in 1942.

1920   Hawaii Federation of Shintō.
       Japanese Assn.
       Hawaii Japanese Federation of Labor. It was renamed Hawaii Laborer's Assn. in the
       same year.

1925   Council of Japanese Christian Churches of Hawaii.

1926   Yamaguchi Prefectural Assn. (Many more prefectural associations were organized
       in the following years for mutual aid and friendship)

1928   The Nippon Orchestra, the first Japanese orchestra playing popular music, was
       formed in Honolulu.

1932   United Japanese Society of Hawaii.

165

Source: Compiled by K. Sinoto in 1984 from Fujii 1900; Morita 1915; *Nippu Jiji* 1921; Washizu 1930;
Watanabe 1935.

Advertisement for Takakuwa Store, Nuʻuanu, Honolulu, 1906.

Yoichi Takakuwa, who came to Hawaiʻi from Tokyo in 1894, opened his store in 1901 on Nuʻuanu Avenue. The advertisement shows the wide range of merchandise carried by the store: refined Japanese rice, canned goods, Japanese tea, *shōyu*, beans and other grain, dried fish and vegetables, dry goods of fine silk, slippers and *geta*, small utensils, umbrellas and parasols, and name-brand medicines (*Hawaii Shimpō*, 1906).

Okazaki tailor, Hotel Street, Honolulu, ca. 1910.

Otoji Okazaki came from Fukushima in 1898. He opened a tailor shop in 1902 after leaving Ewa Plantation in 1899.

Hawaii Shoyu Co. on King Street in Pālama, Honolulu, ca. 1914.

The Japanese in Hawaiʻi depended upon *shōyu* imported from Japan until Nobuyuki Yamashiro started making *shōyu* in 1904. His company was established as Hawaii Shoyu Co. in 1906. American Shoyu Co. was established in Honolulu in 1912.

Ogata watchmaker, River Street, Honolulu, ca. 1914.

Owner Umetarō Ogata came to Hawai'i from Yamaguchi in 1902.

Japanese tailor shop, ca. 1910.

Yamashiroya dry goods store, Waimea, Kaua'i, ca. 1914.

Owner Kanehichi Yamashiroya came to Hawai'i in 1890 from Yamaguchi.

Waimea Pottery Factory, Waimea, Kaua'i, 1915.

The factory was established by Hirobei Tabata, from Yamaguchi in 1915.

Early street scene, Honolulu, ca. 1910 (Edgeworth Collection).

169

Aloha Building Co. and Waikiki Auto Stand. Honolulu, ca. 1918.

Yamamoto photo studio, Hotel street, Honolulu (*Hawaii Shimpō,* 1906).

Yoshio Yamamoto came to Hawai'i from Yamaguchi in 1898 and opened his studio on Smith Street.

Japanese Mercantile Co., Kahului, Maui, ca. 1914.

Japanese and American grocery items and household goods were stocked by owner Umejirō Kinoshita.

Isoshima Store, King Street. Honolulu, ca. 1910.

Kunosuke Isoshima, who came to Hawai'i from Okayama in 1890 at age 23, started this store in 1893, importing Japanese goods. He also had a hat-making business using straw imported from Japan.

Kunosuke Isoshima opened the Japanese Bazaar on Fort Street in 1905 (courtesy of Yoshiko Tsukiyama).

The Japanese Bazaar carried imported arts and crafts and curios, mainly for sale to American customers (courtesy of Yoshiko Tsukiyama).

The Yamato Shim-bun.

LEADING JAPANESE PAPER DEVOTED TO INTERESTS OF THE JAPANESE RESIDENTS
AT REPUBLIC OF HAWAII, PUBLISHED TRIWEEKLY AT THE YAMATO SHIMBUN SHA,
BERETANIA STREET, HONOLULU, H. I.　　　EDITOR AND PROP'R HAMON MIZUNO

NO. 285.　　HONOLULU H.I.　TUESDAY,　JULY 5,　1898　　PRICE FIVE CENTS

Advertisements for various Honolulu businesses in *Yamato Shimbun*, 5 July 1898.

▼新鮮な原料品は毎便日本
より到着致します
▼美味しい物御望みの方は
是非當庵へ御出で下さい

Miyakoan Restaurant, River Street, Honolulu (*Hawaii Shimpō*, 1906).

172

Sato's Fish Market, Lahaina, Maui, ca. 1912 (R.J. Baker photographer).

食料珍物直輸入阿部高店

Abe Store, River Street, Honolulu, ca. 1914.

Wholesaler and retailer for imported Japanese groceries, owner Kamezō Abe was from Niigata, Japan.

Float of Hilo Japanese Merchant Association on 4 July, island of Hawai'i, ca. 1912.

Tomozō Machida from Yamaguchi, owner of Machida Drug Store, is at far left.

Punchbowl-*gumi* (group) was organized by young Okinawans to encourage self-improvement, ca. 1922 (courtesy of United Okinawan Society).

日本人青年倶楽部忘年懇親會
（寫眞は齋藤總領事を中心に今四十三名　小濱健三郎　石川濱　相賀安太郎　磯之九助　大塚靜雄其の他諸氏が九月二十三年九月ヰキキイア日二十九月に）

Members of the newly organized Young Japanese Association at Mochizuku Restaurant in Waikiki, 9 December 1900.

Among those photographed are: Consul General Miki Saitō, Kenji Imanishi, Kenzaburō Ozawa, Tan Ishikawa, Yasutarō Sōga, Kunosuke Isoshima, Shizuo Ōtsuka.

Sanhichi Ozaki's party at Manoa, 1909 (courtesy of Yoshiko Tsukiyama).

Sanhichi Ozaki started as a peddler soon after his arrival in 1891 and became a successful businessman. He is at the head of the table.

Group of Japanese women in Hawaiian dress, ca. 1890 (Hedemann Collection).

Japanese Women's Society of Honolulu, 1939 (courtesy of Yoshiko Tsukiyama).

Japanese women wore predominantly Western dress after the 1920s.

Japanese Women's Society of Honolulu, established in 1916, ca. 1916 (courtesy of Yoshiko Tsukiyama).

The first tour group at a welcoming party, Iwasō Garden, Miyajima, June 1912.

破天荒の大計畫

- ●在留同胞諸君の爲め最も有益にして最も興味深き
- ●母國大觀光團の組織に就き在留同胞諸君に檄す

在布同胞社會の根底ある繁榮策は永住土着主義の實行にあり、然るも眞の永住土着主義は再渡航者を待つて初めて行はるゝ蓋し一度母國に歸りたる者は、日本近時の生活狀態が如何に世智辛く如何に複雜にして窮屈千萬なるかを親しく實見するに引き換へ在留同胞社會の利殖蓄財の上より見るも日常生活の簡易なる點より見て、如何に平安にして如何に呑氣なるやを感ずる切實なるものあるを以てなり、近時再渡航熱の漸次熾なるは在留同胞者の間に唱道せらるゝ利殖蓄財の多くは複雜なる旅券下附の手續に困迷し或は不知案内の土地へ金品を浪費するに至り者しくは蕩盡し途に眼病嫌疑等の故障の爲め豫定の計畫と費用とを...

...官廳より始め母國各地の新聞社及有力なる團体の同情と應援とに困り、一大母國觀光團を組織し經費及時日の節減を計り最も輕便にして有益なる方法を以て帝都を始め京阪五畿の地は素より北は日光の勝に日本の代表的風景を探り、南は嚴杏境に電車に汽車に下り宮嶋詣を試み或は讚州名高き金刀羅神社を參拜し其他各地の都市到る處の名所舊蹟に遊んで諸君が多年異境の都會に散らせる鬱懷を散ずるノ方針を以て誠心誠意在布同胞諸君の利益に資する爲めに...

▲母國觀光團規定

- 一來る五月二十四日ホノルヽ出帆の春洋丸にて出發同七月十六日の同船にて歸布
- 一往復船賃滯在費旅行費一切一人百七十弗
- 一再渡航者渡米手續は總て觀光團幹部にて引受く
- 一規定外同胞滯在希望者は各自の任意とす
- 一東洋滯在中に於て特別優待の約束あり
- 一本年徵兵猶豫願の許可を受けたるものは故障なく歸布する事を得
- 一東洋汽船會社を始め各地に於て歡迎の計畫あり
- 一應募人員三百人限りとす
- 一申込み期間は來る五月五日限り
- 一希望者はホノルヽ日本人旅館を經て豫約金五十弗を添へて申込むべし、尚詳細は主催者父は各旅館の內へ御照會あれば即時御回答す

明治四十五年四月四日

主催者
田阪養吉

賛同者
布哇新報社
布哇日々新聞社
日布時事社

Advertisement announcing the first tour from Hawai'i to visit
Japan, *Nipu Jiji*, 4 April 1912.

Yōkichi Tasaka, organizer of the tour, is wearing formal dress
and a top hat.

175

The Saka family in Kula, Maui, ca. 1900.

From left seated, Chika (wife), Eizō (b. 1883); standing, Raku Saka Morimoto (b. 1889, Hawai'i), Shōhichi, Kura (b. 1886, Hawai'i); missing Yoshitaō (b. 1881).

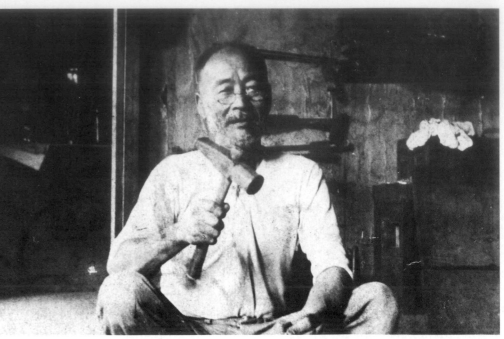

Shōhichi Saka, at his shop on Pauahi Street, Honolulu, ca. 1910.

Shōhichi Saka, a successful brass and coppersmith in Yokohama, came to Hawai'i on the *City of Tokio* in 1885 with his wife and two sons. After he worked on plantations on Kaua'i and Maui, he moved to Honolulu and opened his shop in 1904.

Copper teapot and creamer made by Saka, ca 1910.

Aala Saloon. ʻAʻala Street, Honolulu, ca. 1910.

Table 18
Distribution of Japanese in Hawai'i by Occupation, June 1926 (From Japanese Consulate Records)

	HONOLULU		O'AHU	
TOTAL POPULATION	38,237		22,708	
NUMBER OF FAMILIES	8,370		5,722	
	M	**F**	**M**	**F**
JAPANESE	19,418	16,506	12,463	9,488
KOREAN/JAPANESE	1,593	720	510	247
Agriculture/Dairy owners/manuf.	233		208	8
Laborers	431		3,251	602
Fishing/Salt manuf.	20		3	
Laborers	332		102	
Metal work	132		20	
Cleaners/Dyers	122	81	22	31
Food manuf.	15		6	
Clothing manuf.	130	122	39	30
Contractors	65		18	
Carpenters/Masons/Painters	1,362		171	
Printing/Press	18			
Amusement/Art supplies manuf.	22	8		
Factory Workers	731	141	627	212
Sales	?	48	?	15
Traders	5			
Agents/Brokers	55	3	11	
Rental/Storage	127	27	10	
Businessmen/Office clerks	1,012	312	149	23
Hotels/Restaurants/Theaters	112	4	12	1
Geisha		53		
Barbers/Hairdressers/Bathhouse	136	73	25	12
Others commerce	52	1	17	1
Postal/Telephone	9		7	
Railroad	89		118	
Hack/Taxi drivers	689		218	
Stevedores	147		70	
Government employees	26	2		
Religion	38	2	10	2
Education	37	40	28	15
Doctors/Nurses/Mid-wives	62	45	9	7
Legal work	23		1	
Reporters/Writers	41			
Photographers/Artists/Musicians	21		4	
Other professions	79	24	69	8
Laborers	1,291	619	179	9
Servants	1,068	822	125	128

SOURCE: Sogawa 1927, pp. 82–84.

HAWAI'I 37,107 9,723		MAUI 20,345 5,690		KAUA'I 14,932 4,502		TOTAL 133,329 34,007	
M	**F**	**M**	**F**	**M**	**F**	**M**	**F**
19,178	16,155	11,214	8,423	7,811	6,415	70,084	56,987
1,238	536	474	234	447	259	4,262	1,996
2,282	83	420	3	245	10	3,388	104
3,907	677	2,922	944	2,218	1,415	12,729	3,638
18		5		4		50	
168		67		71		740	
50		31		15		248	
30	40	15	22	28	22	217	196
8						29	
28	32	27	12	18	9	242	205
30		25		12		150	
477		322		165		2,497	
1						19	
						22	8
288	127	321	31	182	28	2,149	539
?	37	?	8	?	20	1,801	128
1						6	
10	10	9		4		89	13
18	5	8		3		166	32
388	62	220	41	171	31	1,940	469
38	3	11	2	10	2	183	12
	5		5				63
47	18	32	7	22	8	262	118
27	2	21		7	2	124	6
8						24	
128		55		59		449	
272	3	195		160		1,534	3
77		50		22		366	
						26	2
20		8		6		82	4
49	33	32	17	23	19	169	124
12	11	7	6	4	7	94	76
4		1				29	
8		5		3		57	
9		3		2		39	
115	112	28	51	35	37	326	232
139	135	279	10	154	10	2,042	783
69	81	99	101	77	88	1,438	1,220

Wai'anae coffee plantation, O'ahu, ca. 1897–1901 (F. Davey, photographer).

Coffee plantation in ʻŌlaʻa, island of Hawaiʻi, ca. 1899 (Okumura Collection).

By 1914, more than 80 percent of the coffee crop was being
produced by the Japanese, with over 3,780 acres planted in
the Hāmākua and Kona districts on the island of Hawaiʻi
(Morita 1915:186).

Coffee pickers at Laupāhoehoe, island of Hawaiʻi.

Waialua pineapple field workers, Oʻahu, ca. 1905.

Maui Pineapple Cannery, Pa'uwela, ca. 1915.

The only Japanese-owned pineapple cannery was started in
1910 by Zenroku Ōnishi.

Pineapple harvesting (R. J. Baker, photographer).

184

Rice fields near Diamond Head, Oʻahu, ca. 1910 (R. J. Baker, photographer).

Although rice was extensively cultivated by the Chinese, the long grain variety did not suit the needs and demands of the Japanese. In 1899, Japanese polished rice was imported by the Hamano Store, and Saiji Kimura established a rice mill in Ka-kaʻako, importing less costly unpolished rice from Japan. Since 1900 the Japanese cultivated their own rice, and their production peaked between 1900–1910 with 7,500 acres of rice fields.

Rice field near Anahola, Kaua'i, 1915 (R. J. Baker photographer).

Aku (bonito) fishing (courtesy of Hawaii State Archives).

Women feeding calf, Pond Ranch, Waialua, O'ahu, ca. 1920.

Japanese fishermen wore *kimono*-style garb made of denim with a small reinforced apron in front to hold the butt of the fishing pole

Sampans in Waiākea River, Hilo, 1900–1910 (A. Gartley, photographer).

186

Funai Boat Builder's Shop in Ala Moana, Oʻahu, ca. 1920 (R. J. Baker, photographer).

Launching of *Hotei Maru*, Honolulu, 1908.

The first Japanese-style bonito fishing boat (sampan) was introduced by Gorokichi Nakasuji in 1899. Soon after, similar boats were constructed locally by skilled boatbuilders brought over from Japan. Sampan fleets became the major method for supplying the fish markets of Hawaiʻi

Nuʻuanu Avenue, Honolulu, ca. 1884.

Urban housing, primarily for Japanese, Honolulu, ca 1910–1915 (Edgeworth Collection).

Housing in Honolulu, ca. 1915.

Chinatown fire. Nuʻuanu Avenue, Honolulu, 1900 (H.R. Hanna, photographer).

The Japanese Doctors' Association, the Japanese Benevolent Society, and an emergency Japanese committee were mobilized to offer well-organized services to the homeless and injured victims of the fire. A total of 7,000 persons were affected, including more than 3,500 Japanese; many of them were merchants and storeowners.

ホノルヽ名妓。お點右上（目出度龍〔左上〕友太郎〔中〕胸龍〔右下〕錦龍〔左下〕

Geisha in Honolulu, from *Saishin Hawaii Annai* (*Latest Guide to Hawai'i*), 1920.

Early *geisha* wore holoku, long Hawaiian dresses, and began wearing *kimono* in the late 1890s.

Women in front of the Susannah Wesley Home, O'ahu, 1908 (Edgeworth Collection).

The Susannah Wesley Home was operated by the River Street Methodist Church Women's Association, with the help of the Board of Missions. Girls from broken families were taken in, or students whose parents lived on faraway plantations. The home also served as a refuge for Japanese women fleeing their husbands or enforced prostitution (Raku Morimoto interview, 1983).

Japanese servant employed at the home of Captain Basil C. Combe, 1813 College Street (presently Poki Street), Honolulu, ca. 1905.

Among the early groups of contract laborers, a certain percentage of immigrants were assigned to work as servants for plantation managers and for private homes.

Japanese *geisha*, ca. 1897–1901 (F. Davey, photographer).

In 1900, there were approximately twenty *geisha* in Honolulu, and their numbers were increasing. They generally entertained at banquets, singing and dancing to musical accompaniment, and were paid $2 each for 2 hours' entertainment. Many *geisha* were second-generation girls who had received training in music and dance.

Phoenix fountain, Kapi'olani Park, Honolulu, 1919 (Okumura Collection).

Completed on 16 March 1919, this phoenix-shaped water fountain was built to commemorate the coronation of the Taishō Emperor. Building funds were accumulated through $1 donations from each Japanese family in Hawai'i. Designed by the Tokyo Art School, the fountain consisted of a bronze phoenix figure and two tiered basins atop a granite pedestal. Local Japanese called it "the chicken in Waikiki," but it was destroyed during World War II because of anti-Japanese sentiment.

194

Cartoon of imprisoned strike leaders, *The Sunday Advertiser,* 20 March 1910.

Leaders of the strike, arrested on 10 June 1909 and imprisoned after the trial from March to July 1910. Honolulu, 1910 (courtesy of Yoshitami Tasaka).

From left: front, Yōkichi Tasaka, Yasutarō Sōga; back Motoyuki Negoro, Kinzaburō Makino.

LABOR MOVEMENTS

The Japanese had been eagerly recruited and heartily welcomed in the mid-1880s. Many Japanese contract laborers returned home or went on to the United States after their contracts expired. Those who stayed in Hawai'i were joined by thousands of fellow immigrants, and many chose to remain in the islands. All but a few continued to work on plantations or in the growing Hawaiian economy servicing the sugar industry. Labor strife was a logical result of their having chosen to make their lives in Hawai'i.

Complaints that planters were failing to honor the contracts soon arose and were directed from workers to their Consul General and to the head of the Japanese section of the Bureau of Immigration. In extreme cases, the protests reached the Japanese government in Tokyo. The language barrier gave rise to frequent misunderstanding and conflict. The most common protests involved physical abuse, unpaid overtime, inadequate facilities, and refusal of managers to comply with contract agreements or promises made to the workers. The long tradition of resistance to both ill-treatment and low wages was a prominent aspect of the early decades of the Japanese in Hawai'i.

In the pre-1900 period, there was little that could be described as "labor movement" activity, although discontent had existed from the earliest days of the sugar industry. As other nationality groups were imported for plantation labor, the Hawaiians were promoted into better positions; they continued to be important in the work force but were far less likely to be involved in labor disturbances. The Norwegians, Portuguese, and Spanish, who were brought to labor in the fields were also active in early labor struggles, but many soon left for the United States mainland for better opportunities or, like the Hawaiians, stayed on to assume positions as *luna* or skilled craftsmen. For the ordinary field or mill workers, dissatisfaction resulted in the discovery of methods to avoid hard labor when possible — hiding from the *luna*, feigning illness, retaliating with violence against abusive *luna*, making collective demands for better wages or treatment, or deserting.

The Japanese reacted like their predecessors in avoiding work or seeking just treatment and better conditions with higher wages. The *ikkaisen,* or first-boat immigrants, soon got into more than their share of conflicts with the managers and *luna.* In the most dramatic incident, in Pā'ia, Maui, only a month after their arrival, the Japanese went on strike to protest plantation refusal to punish a brutal Hawaiian ox-tender. After a vigorous protest, the workers were each assessed fines of $5 and court costs of $1. There were so many com-

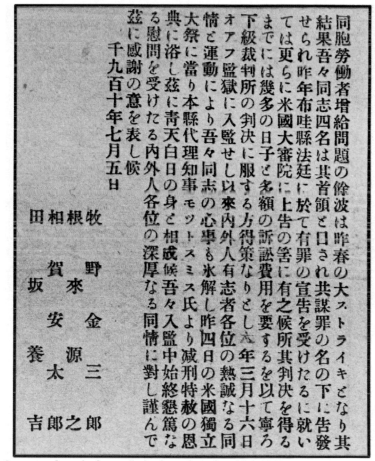

Statement from the four strike leaders released on 4 July 1910, *Nippu Jiji,* 5 July 1910.

195

Motoyuki Negoro, secretary of the Higher Wage Association,
speaking to the strikers in 'Aiea, O'ahu, 1909.

Representatives of strikers from 'Aiea, Kahuku, and Waipahu,
O'ahu, 1909.

plaints from the *ikkaisen* laborers that the Japanese government sent a Special Commissioner, Katsunosuke Inouye, a son of Minister of Foreign Affairs Kaoru Inouye, on the second boat to investigate. Inouye conducted extensive negotiations with the Hawaiian government to improve treatment of the Japanese contract laborers. In response, Walter Murray Gibson, Premier and Minister of Foreign Affairs under King Kalākaua, expressed his willingness to "meet the views and requirements of the Government of Japan on all points." He went on to assure Inouye that all complaints had received careful attention, and explained that

> the number and character of these complaints, coming as they do from a portion of about 720 Japanese people engaged in service here, exceed anything that the Hawaiian Government has had to deal with in the whole course of the immigration into, and employment in this country, of about 30,000 laborers of Chinese, Portuguese and other races.

There were numerous instances of harsh treatment, and observers such as journalist Yasutarō Sōga and plantation physician Iga Mōri compared the treatment of the contract laborers to that received by slaves in the American South, and Dr. Mōri, who had arrived in 1886, recalled in 1921 that

> all Japanese laborers under contract not only worked under oppressive conditions, but their living conditions were as bad as for slaves. There were so many problems between plantations and laborers that the Immigration Bureau was extremely disturbed.

Most of these early disputes were over brutal or unfair treatment, but there were a few that involved wages. In March 1885 the Japanese at Pāpa'ikou struck to protest the plantation's refusal to pay overtime wages, and in 1889–1890, the Hakalau workers walked out to dramatize the unfair use of hours longer than called for in the contract.

On 14 June 1900 the Organic Act went into effect, and Hawai'i officially began operating as a Territory of the United States of America. Two points of American law immediately made a profound impact on plantation labor practices. First, the importation of contract laborers was "rendered illegal by the law of 1885, and all engagements made in advance of landing in this country were declared void." Thus, no further groups of immigrants could be secured under prearranged contract. Second, all previously negotiated contracts were made ineffective by the removal of the penal sanctions against workers. The impact of the Organic Act and its liberation of laborers was immediate and dramatic. After 14 June there were at least twenty-two significant strikes, including one from 22 June through 24 June, in which 188 Japanese and Chinese in the Pūehuehu mill cooperated, and another from 23 November through 3 December, in which 43 Japanese and Portuguese women field workers on the Kilauea Plantation on Kaua'i won their demands for wage increases from $8 to $10 per month.

After 1900, the strikes became longer, better organized, and more violent. In May 1904, for example, nearly 1,400 (of some 2,400) Japanese struck Oahu Sugar Co. in Waipahu to force the firing of head *luna* Patterson, who evidently ran a lottery for which he forced laborers to purchase tickets. Some twenty-seven armed policemen were sent, but the strike was won, and Patterson was fired.

In 1909, the first major sugar strike in Hawai'i was organized by Japanese workers. It lasted from 8 May to 6 August and involved seven thousand workers from five plantations, with extensive plans, negotiations, and support systems. It was the first to incorporate Japanese businessmen and professionals as leaders and spokesmen, with coordinated efforts by the Japanese newspapers to provide current news and to rally support for the strikers.

Press exposure of low wages and poor conditions began with an article written by Gunkichi Shimada, published on 25 August 1908, by the *Hawaii Nichinichi*. For months thereafter, Yasutarō Sōga's *Nippu Jiji* published extensive articles by Yōkichi Tasaka and Motoyuki Negoro attacking the low wages and poor conditions and, in contrast, the considerable plantation profits. These investigations helped to distill the issues so that a clear focus on the demands could emerge: first, eliminate the nationality differentials in the wage scale and provide equal pay for equal work; second, increase wages. After public meetings to discuss the issue, the Japanese leaders formed the Zōkyū Kisei Kai, the Higher Wages Association, at a meeting held in Honolulu on 1 December 1908. It was decided that *Nippu Jiji* would be in charge of communications, and the Association would lead the activities. When the Association solicited membership, several thousand workers responded positively with self-addressed return postcards. The Higher Wages Association instructed all workers to avoid violence, warning that "laborers have the right to strike but violence is a crime."

The officials of the Higher Wages Association were: Kinzaburō Makino, a drugstore owner at that time and later founder of the *Hawaii Hōchi*, president; Negoro, a graduate of the University of California at Berkeley law school, vice-president; and Matsutarō Yamashiro, a hotel owner, treasurer. Sōga and Makino rented an automobile and travelled from plantation to plantation to speak to large crowds of Japanese, generating support for the Association and its objectives. Denounced as agitators by the planters, they met with considerable success in their mission.

In January 1909, the Association submitted its demands to the Hawaiian Sugar Planters' Association (HSPA). The Japanese sought an increase from the base pay of $18.00 to $22.50 per month, which was what Portuguese and Puerto Rican laborers received. In addition, the latter groups were favored with decent cottages and an acre of land to keep animals and grow crops. The Japanese argued that they were at least as efficient as other nationality groups and thus entitled to equal pay. They acknowledged the wage increase provided in 1905 but pointed to the steep rise in the cost of living since that time. Equally important, the Japanese community had grown considerably, and their needs were far greater than in earlier years when single men or young couples could manage on little income and under primitive conditions. In 1908, however, there were 21,000 wives and nearly 29,000 children. They also supported seventy Japanese language schools and fifty-nine temples and churches. The Japanese in Hawai'i, in short, had developed an extensive and vital network of social needs, which marked the emergence of a permanent community. Finally, they appealed to the planters' civic spirit by arguing that higher wages for the Japanese would contribute to the general welfare of Hawai'i by creating a body of responsible and upstanding people who clearly relied on reason and justice to seek their goals.

The HSPA refused to recognize the Higher Wages Association. Specific proposals were

Preparing Japanese sweets for the strikers, who had left plantations and lived in temporary shelters provided for them in Kaka'ako and Mō'ili'ili, Honolulu, 1909.

Strikers lining up with food coupons in front of the cafeteria, Honolulu, 1909.

The Higher Wage Association solicited donations of provisions for the strikers. There was a good response, and volunteers helped in the preparation of food. Prefectural associations got together and offered their support.

Propaganda sheet distributed by the Hawaiian Sugar Planters'
Association, 1920.

Top: Filipino union leaders absconding with contribu-
tions for the strikers.
Middle: Difference in wages received between a laborer and a
striker: monetary wage as opposed to a handful of
rice.
Bottom: Extravagance exhibited by Japanese strike leaders:
"We are the daimyō of Hawaii."
"I hope the strike will last."
"If there wasn't a strike, we could not afford to ride in
a car."
"We are extravagant."
"Our cigars are 50¢ apiece."
Driver: "$10.00 per hour"
Car banner: "Rented by the Central Office of the La-
bor Union"

drafted for submission to each plantation management. The first one was sent to the Oahu Sugar Co. manager on 5 May 1909 and was signed by eighty workers. Before the Waipahu workers could take action, however, 1,500 Honolulu Plantation workers at 'Aiea voted to walk off the job, which they did on 8 May at 9:30 A.M., banging on empty 5-gallon cans. The Waipahu workers, led by young intellectual leader Masao Haneda, followed on 12 May and prepared for their departure by cleaning their plantation homes thoroughly and express-ing gratitude to the manager for the kindness shown them while they had been employed. Then, they filed out of their camps in careful formation to the music of a marching band. Japanese workers on the Kahuku, Waialua, and Ewa Plantations soon joined the strike, but the Waimānalo and Wai'anae workers stayed on their jobs and contributed funds to support the Higher Wages Association.

The Association's strategy was to limit the strike to O'ahu and use the continuing income from workers on other islands to provide moral and financial support until the strike was won. The total number of strikers soon approached seven thousand, all of whom were evicted from their plantation camps. Most went to Honolulu, where the Association orga-nized operations to provide food, shelter, and medical care. In the meantime, the HSPA held a meeting from 24 to 27 May with representatives from sixty plantations. Plantations were instructed to make no concessions to the laborers, and were assured that any losses would be shared by the whole industry.

The strikers received an impressive amount and variety of support from the rest of the Japanese in Hawai'i. Money, provisions, and services were provided by the associations of hotel owners, bathhouse operators, barbers, *shōyu* manufacturers, hardware store owners, and the Japanese physicians who treated ill strikers. In addition to money and services, associations of actors, *tōfu* makers, carpenters, and owners of drugstores and *sake* shops sent letters to the HSPA supporting the strikers' demands. The Hiroshima and Yamaguchi pre-fectural associations provided early support, with Wakayama close behind. These were the prefectures from which many of the immigrants had come and the feeling of solidarity was strong.

Although the Japanese community was largely in support of the 1909 strike, there were important exceptions. The Japanese government was firmly opposed. On 25 May Consul Senichi Uyeno formally announced his regret that the laborers had abandoned more peaceful and conciliatory attitudes. He tried to reassure the public that this was a purely economic matter between planters and workers, and called upon the Japanese to maintain the peace and order of the general community. Rev. Takie Okumura counselled modera-tion and advised strikers to go back to work. The Honolulu Japanese merchants also urged strikers to assume a more cautious position, probably because they supplied plantation stores and wanted to maintain good business relations.

The most divisive arena involved the Japanese press. Sōga was perceived as the chief strike advocate, and several other papers were aligned with his *Nippu Jiji.* Sometarō Shiba, editor of the *Hawaii Shimpō,* was the outspoken leader, along with the *Hawaii Nichinichi,* of the other group of Japanese newspapers that denounced the strike. The English language papers ve-hemently opposed the strike. The strike leaders, in particular, were criticized for antagoniz-ing the planters by encouraging discontent.

The sugar planters agreed to stand together until the strike was broken. Many conceded that a wage increase was reasonable, but that employers should not allow workers to participate in determining how wages should be paid. In particular, the planters insisted on the bonus system, which rewarded reliable and steady work throughout the year, while the Japanese argued that such a system made inhuman demands on workers who could become sick or injured under such conditions.

The planters used a variety of means to break the strike. First, there was a coordinated effort to picture the strike as one led by nonlaborer agitators. Second, planters hired Hawaiian, Chinese, Korean, and Portuguese strikebreakers at $1.50 per day, far more than the strikers were asking. Third, they hired Japanese to monitor the strike activity, and they subsidized the efforts of Shiba and the *Hawaii Shimpō* in trying to convince the Japanese to abandon the strike. Finally, they used the police to arrest and the courts to convict persons active in strike activity. At first, these arrests were limited to acts committed by strikers themselves who had overstepped their bounds, but in June, the leaders themselves began to face serious criminal charges. Sōga, considered the ringleader, was arrested ten times.

The Association hired Joseph Lightfoot as its attorney, and he was kept busy bailing his clients out of jail on a regular basis. After High Sheriff William Henry had led illegal raids on the residences and offices of Makino, Negoro, and Sōga, and confiscated documents and materials from their safes, many of the leaders were charged with being dangerous persons and with conspiracy to impoverish the plantations by intimidating the Japanese and preventing them from performing their work. Shiba was called as a prosecution witness and testified that his life had been threatened.

During the trial, Shiba was seriously wounded by a knife-wielding young delegate of the Higher Wages Association from Maui. This attack doomed the strike. On 6 August, the Higher Wages Association called a meeting to urge strikers to return to work. They also asked representatives from other islands to help find jobs for strikers seeking employment. After 3 months and an estimated loss of $2,000,000 the planters had won. The four leaders, Makino, Sōga, Negoro, and Tasaka, were convicted on 16 March 1910, fined $300 each, and sentenced to 10 months in jail. Rev. Okumura and other community leaders encouraged leniency and started a campaign to secure a pardon, which was granted on 4 July 1910, after the men had served 3 months of their sentence.

The 1909 strike was broken but it was not a total defeat. Within months, plantations throughout the Territory introduced a bonus system that better suited the workers and began improving housing and sanitary facilities. Most important, the HSPA increased the monthly wages of the Japanese to $22 and eliminated the differences according to nationality.

The lessons of the 1909 strike were not lost on either side. Planters continued to rely on paternalism and intimidation to keep the peace. The Japanese were forced back into a decade of relative inactivity, especially during the years of World War I. But it was clear that the issue of race had entered labor negotiations with a vengeance. It had always been there, to be sure, but planters had never been so powerfully challenged by labor, and the simultaneous threat to *haole* domination of the islands was taken very seriously. Between 1910 and 1920, the number of *haole* in Hawai'i increased from 14,867 to 19,708, but the population of Japanese went up by 30,000 (to 42 percent of the total population in 1920) and of Filipinos, by nearly 20,000.

There were few strikes between 1910 and 1920 partly because of World War I and partly

Special issue of *Nippu Jiji*, 26 July 1910, commemorating the release of imprisoned leaders.

Higher Wage Association, Honolulu, 1909.

From left: front, Matsutarō Yamashiro, Yasutarō Sōga, Kinzaburō Makino, Motoyuki Negoro, Yōkichi Tasaka; back, Yasuyuki Imai, Tsurumatsu Okumura, Katsuichi Kawamoto, Hidekichi Takemura, Keitarō Kawamura, Shūichi Ihara.

Table 19
AVERAGE MONTHLY PLANTATION WAGES, 1888–1890

ETHNIC GROUP	CONTRACT LABORERS	FREE LABORERS
Hawaiians	$18.58	$20.64
Portuguese	19.53	22.25
Japanese	15.58	18.84
Chinese	17.61	17.41
South Sea Islanders	15.81	18.56

SOURCE: Report of President of the Board of Immigration cited in United Japanese Society of Hawaii 1971: 172.

because it was exceedingly difficult to overcome the financial, social, and organizational traumas of the 1909 strike. The planters were now much less naive about the capacity of workers to organize and sustain a long strike and had begun to import more Filipino laborers. There was quicker response with more force by the Territorial government and an ominous increase in the level of anti-Japanese hostility in the general community. This was a decade of rapid growth for the Japanese, primarily because of the arrival of young wives — the "picture brides" and other immediate family members allowed under conditions of the 1908 Gentlemen's Agreement. Their arrival and incorporation into the work force brought some additional income into the family unit and probably helped stabilize the labor situation temporarily. More Japanese, especially the most discontented, were also moving off the plantation as the increase in their population created additional demand for provision of goods and services.

Labor activity was not confined to the sugar industry, although it was certainly more difficult to organize workers when employers were relatives or ethnic community leaders. In 1918, however, Japanese fishermen walked off the job from eighty-three boats to protest excessive profits taken by Japanese boat owners.

In the most important example of interethnic labor solidarity to that point, longshoremen of many nationalities went on strike on 18 September 1916 for higher wages and recognition of their union. The strike ended on 10 October with a substantial pay increase, but no recognition. Moreover, the stevedoring firm elected to isolate and blacklist the Japanese workers, refusing to rehire them. About three hundred other longshoremen immediately went back out on strike to protest the discriminatory action. They sponsored a mass meeting and attracted an impressive crowd of fifteen hundred supporters. The company remained firm, however, agreeing only to rehire Japanese when strikebreakers left their positions, and the protest strike ended after 2 weeks.

It is in this period that reference is first made to specific strike activity by Okinawan workers. On 20 March 1912, approximately four hundred Okinawan field hands went on strike in Pāʻia, Maui, to demand the discharge of a particular *luna* and some plantation policemen who had unwisely tried to disperse a "hilarious wedding party." It is not clear whether the demands were met, but the outraged partygoers had already beaten the unwelcome intruders so the point had been made.

The Okinawans developed a reputation as a minority subgroup

especially receptive to labor-organizing efforts. They were already forced into a closely knit ethnic group because of prejudice from *Naichi.* . . . Okinawans felt they had "nothing to lose" in striving to gain the equality and mutual respect that organized labor represented.

The first twenty-six men from Okinawa arrived January 1900 and were sent to Ewa Plantation on Oʻahu, where they met *naichi* prejudice and hard labor. There was enough discontent that some workers even discussed the possibility of killing Kyūzō Tōyama, the Okinawan leader who had succeeded in convincing the Japanese government to allow his people to emigrate to Hawaiʻi.

In 1920 the second major sugar strike shook Hawaiʻi. Japanese and Filipino sugar workers on Oʻahu struck all but two plantations for nearly 6 months, costing the planters about

$12,000,000 and the Japanese community about $300,000. Approximately 5,300 Japanese and 2,800 Filipinos participated in the largest and most impressive of the plantation strikes prior to World War II. Its most distinctive feature was the self-conscious attempt to forge an alliance between the two largest groups of ethnic workers. One measure of the importance of this attempt at working class—rather than ethnic group—organization was the vehemence with which the planters denounced the strike as a Japanese plot to take over the industry and the islands.

The strike was preceded by more than 2 years of discussions involving the rising cost of living and the need to accommodate the growing families of Japanese sugar workers. The sugar industry had substantial earnings during World War I (1917–1918), and the workers were aware of the planters' profits. An Association of Higher Wage Question was formed in October 1917 to discuss the issues and to act on behalf of the laborers by submitting a demand for wage increases. On 20 November the Association sent its proposal to the HSPA calling for adequate wage increases, assurances that bonuses would be paid, and establishment of nurseries for children of workers. The HSPA refused all of these demands, responding with a plan that effectively reduced the workers' bonus. This was necessary, they argued, because World War I had increased plantation expenses. The *Nippu Jiji* and the *Hawaii Hōchi* denounced the HSPA stance, and the issues were widely discussed throughout the Japanese community. The most important discussions took place among young men who assumed major roles in the 1920 labor struggle. On 19 October 1919, representatives from several organizations met at the Hilo Japanese Language School and formed the Young Men's Association on the island of Hawai'i. They issued a declaration urging the promotion of rights of the Japanese in Hawai'i in light of post–World War I trends, especially in politics and industry. They also adopted a resolution calling for an 8-hour day, an increase in wages, and an end to the paternalistic bonus system. On O'ahu, the Waialua Young Men's Buddhist Association met a week later to take similar action and to send appeals to all fraternal associations to follow suit.

In Honolulu, Japanese residents formed the Society of the Supporters of Plantation Laborers to provide general assistance following the 1909 model. During the month of November labor groups were organized by young men on the islands of Maui, Kaua'i, Hawai'i, and O'ahu. These four groups sent fifty-eight delegates to Honolulu where, on 1 December, they formally organized the Japanese Federation of Labor. The conference adopted several resolutions that combined hard data with heavy rhetoric:

> People know Hawaii as the paradise of the Pacific and as a sugar-producing country, but do they know that there are thousands of laborers who are suffering under the heat of the equatorial sun, in field and in factory, and who are weeping under 10 hours of hard labor and with the scanty pay of 77 cents a day?

> Hawaii's sugar! When we look at Hawaii as the country possessing 44 sugar mills, with 230,000 acres of cultivated land area, as a region producing 600,000 tons of sugar annually, we are impressed with the great importance of the position which sugar occupies among the industries of Hawaii.

布哇全島日本人労働者大会各地代表委員

明治四十二年八月ホノルヽ市日本人小学校ニテ紀念撮影

Representatives attending the Hawaii Japanese Laborers' general meeting, Honolulu, August 1909 (courtesy of Yoshitami Tasaka).

增給期成会本部山城旅館前に於ける寄贈品

Donated provisions for strikers at Yamashiro Hotel, the main office for the Higher Wage Association, Honolulu, 1909.

Demonstration march by strikers at Beretania and Nuʻuanu Streets, Honolulu, Oʻahu, 1920.

"My papa's 77 cents a day, my mama's 58 cents a day."

Representatives of Hawaii Japanese labor union with their resolution of strike, Honolulu, Oʻahu, 1920.

The Japanese Federation sent its package of requests to the HSPA on 6 December 1919. The most crucial items included increased minimum daily wages of $1.25 for men and $0.95 for women, an 8-hour day, improved bonus conditions, paid maternity leave, double pay for overtime, and more of a share of the profits for cane-growing contractors. In the meantime, Pablo Manlapit was organizing the Filipino Labor Union, which submitted similar demands. The HSPA flatly rejected both sets of demands and a strike was imminent. While the Japanese awaited HSPA response, Manlapit began the strike on 19 January 1920. The Japanese Federation of Labor asked its members to follow suit on 1 February. The two English language newspapers, the *Honolulu Star Bulletin* and the *Pacific Commercial Advertiser,* immediately attacked the strike as a conspiracy to "Japanize" the islands. One editorial charged that:

> What the alien Japanese priests, editors and educators are aiming at, in our opinion, is general recognition of their claim that they can absolutely control the 25,000 Japanese plantation laborers of this territory. . . . Given the choice, in the last extremity, between destruction of the sugar industry or the Japanizing of this territory, we would prefer destruction.

In the face of this pressure and amidst allegations of bribes from the HSPA, Manlapit called off the Filipino strike on 8 February. Many Filipinos stayed on strike, however, with Puerto Ricans, Portuguese, Spanish, Chinese, and Koreans, so Manlapit was forced to call the strike back on as of 14 February. Workers and their families were evicted from their plantation houses and nearly thirteen thousand men, women, and children were taken care of by friends and in special camps set up in Honolulu. Strikebreakers were again hired and paid $3 or $4 per day. At the end of January, the bonus was pegged at 150 percent of the wage scale, and on 13 February, the *Pacific Commercial Advertiser* announced that it would be 250 percent and that "this is another nail in the seventy-seven cents-a-day-lie spread by the Japanese." Ironically, at least some of these increased bonus payments found their way into the strike support fund through Japanese workers on neighbor island plantations.

It soon became clear that this was a bitter strike, and the entire community was increasingly concerned. Rev. Albert Palmer of Honolulu's Central Union Church called a group of prominent *haole* and Japanese together to formulate a compromise. The "Palmer" plan was submitted to both the HSPA and the Japanese Federation of Labor. It called for the Japanese to cease organizing along nationality lines and asked that plantations allow elected representatives of various races of workers to meet with managers to discuss wages, hours, and living conditions, and that Territory wide meetings be subsidized by the planters. The Japanese accepted the "Palmer" plan on 27 February, but the HSPA rejected it out-of-hand.

Acting-Governor Curtis Iʻaukea urged both sides to adopt the "Palmer" plan and told the Japanese that they simply had to clear themselves of the charge that they were part of a conspiracy to overthrow American control of Hawaiʻi. He went on to add, however, that

> I am inclined to mistrust the Planters. For quite a while there has been much pressure brought to bear upon me to petition the United States Government to use its military forces against the strikers. This was particularly urgent at the time of the cane fires on

Kauai. It is a matter of history that armed forces of the United States were used to overawe the Hawaiians at the time of the overthrow of the monarchy, and there seems to be a desire to repeat this measure of intimidation.

The Japanese tried to blunt criticism of the nationality issue by changing the name of the Federation to "Hawaii Laborers' Association" at a meeting of all unions on 23 April. They also tried to rally support with a parade through downtown Honolulu in the same month. More than three thousand Japanese and Filipino strikers and their families marched with signs and American flags and a large portrait of Abraham Lincoln (who had, they said, freed the slaves; a reference to their own "slavelike" conditions).

In spite of their efforts, the Japanese and the several hundred Filipinos who remained with them announced an end to the strike as of 1 July 1920. As in 1909, the planters proceeded to improve wages and conditions after breaking the strike. The workers again learned the difficulty and the necessity of creating a union that cut across ethnic lines, but this would not happen until the 1940s. Although the fact of unprecedented Filipino and Japanese cooperation is important, the legacy of mistrust and relative labor inactivity among the Japanese in the subsequent two decades indicate that the 1920 strike was a major defeat.

Sumō held near Izumo Taisha for the recreation of the strikers, Honolulu, 1909.

203

Demonstration of women workers, Honolulu, 1920.

Japanese of Ka'ū District who entered the U.S. Army during World War I, island of Hawai'i, ca. 1917.

HUMAN RIGHTS

The Japanese contract laborers in Hawai'i were subjects of a nation that was rapidly developing into a powerful rival of the strongest countries of the Western world. They were acutely conscious of the strides being made by the Meiji government (1868–1912) while they themselves occupied positions of relatively low status. On the United States mainland, the social and political fabric was being rent by extensive turmoil, from the time of the Civil War on into the early twentieth century. Blacks were now freed from slavery, but not yet accorded the rights of other citizens; women were pushing the White male establishment for the right to vote; and the working classes, including immigrant groups from Europe, were fighting for their livelihoods through unionization. The Japanese in Hawai'i were no different than the other immigrant groups elsewhere in exhorting one another to end their inferior status and achieve equality in the islands. The struggle for equal rights became, then, as important as the drive to secure better wages, treatment, and conditions.

The Japanese victories over China in 1894–1895 and Russia in 1904–1905, as well as the annexation of Korea in 1910, occurred during critical periods in the development of the Japanese in Hawai'i and provided considerable psychological and political momentum to their drive for equality. As soon as news of Japan's victory in the Sino-Japanese war arrived in Hawai'i in April 1895, a committee was organized to prepare for a major celebration. On 11 May Japanese immigrants closed their businesses and decorated their homes with flags and lanterns. An estimated $10,000 was spent on that day for the celebration. A ceremony was held at Independence Park on King Street in Honolulu, along with an impressive parade including a full-scale simulated Japanese Imperial Army and Navy. The list of participants included a number of *gannenmono* and first- and second-boat arrivals, as well as prominent doctors and businessmen.

The Japanese victory over Russia in 1905 was a profound event with worldwide impact. For the first time in modern world history, a major European power had been defeated by a nation of non-White peoples. The victory set Japan and the United States on a collision course in the Pacific, and it intensified anti-Japanese feeling in the United States and in Hawai'i. The *issei* drew strength from the surge in national pride to demand more equality at the same time that the heightened racism directed against them led to further assaults on their civil and human rights.

Within a decade after the arrival of the first contract laborers, there were serious efforts to reduce the flow of Japanese immigrants because of widespread fears that there were too

Yamato, ninety-ninth issue, 2 July 1896, commemorating Independence Day.

Japanese reserves embarking at Hilo for the Russo-Japanese War, island of Hawai'i, ca. 1904.

When the contract workers were recruited for immigration in 1885, young men of draft age were excluded; but many young men who were in Hawai'i later were in the reserves for the Japanese army. When the Sino-Japanese (1894–1895) and Russo-Japanese (1904–1905) wars broke out, they were drafted by the Japanese government.

many of them in Hawai'i and that they were moving too rapidly into other types of work after completing the terms of their contract. In 1894, with the establishment of the Provisional Government after the overthrow of the Monarchy, the 1886 Convention fixing the conditions of Japanese immigration to Hawai'i became ineffective. The private emigration companies had begun recruiting laborers in 1894 and this lucrative business provided access to Hawai'i for thousands of Japanese who were not required to have prearranged contracts. In response to this influx, the Hawaiian legislature required all new noncontract or free immigrants to have $50 or the equivalent, ostensibly to protect against the immigration of impoverished newcomers. Immigrants with contracts binding them to "not less than two years" of work on a sugar plantation were still allowed into Hawai'i. There was a simultaneous effort to recruit more Chinese laborers under contract, and their numbers soared from 374 in 1894 to 6,398 in 1897. The legislature passed additional laws restricting Japanese immigration in 1896–1897, and immigration authorities began implementing the new measures at the same time. In 1897, 1,199 Japanese from three boats were rejected because they could produce neither contracts nor the $50.

The official Japanese government response was timely and vigorous. On 5 May, the cruiser *Naniwa* arrived in Honolulu bringing a special commissioner, Masanosuke Akiyama, to seek explanation and redress. There was no progress in the negotiations, however, until sometime in 1898, when it became evident that the United States would annex Hawai'i. When the Newlands Resolution providing for annexation was signed by President William McKinley on 7 July 1898, Washington had already pressured Hawai'i to settle the case with Japan. Then, on 1 August, only days before the 12 August date set for formal transfer of sovereignty to the United States, the Republic of Hawaii—without admitting guilt—approved the expenditure of $75,000 as compensation for shipowners, immigration companies, and the immigrants themselves, who received from $10 to $45 for their troubles.

Attacks on the rights of Japanese to immigrate on the same basis as aliens from other nations wounded their growing sense of national pride, but the Gentlemen's Agreement of 1907–1908 had more direct implications. In 1906, the San Francisco school board had issued a directive segregating Japanese students along with the Chinese. This action provoked angry protest in Japan and the incident threatened to escalate into a major international crisis, forcing the federal government to intervene. Discussions between Tokyo and Washington resulted in the Gentlemen's Agreement, which essentially ended the San Francisco school segregation in exchange for Japan's willingness to restrict passports for those headed for the United States. Thereafter, the only Japanese immigrants allowed into the United States were prior residents, those who owned farms in America, and parents, wives, or children of immigrants. Thus, without enacting humiliating legislation, both governments were able to appease, temporarily, the increasingly powerful forces calling for a complete end to Japanese immigration.

One important result was a law passed by Congress in 1907 prohibiting the movement of Japanese from Hawai'i to the United States mainland. This was partly in response to sugar planters who were watching thousands of Japanese leave plantation work in Hawai'i for better wages on the West Coast. Although this legislation clearly violated Japan's treaty rights guaranteeing equal protection for her subjects, Tokyo made no protest and the immigrants in Hawai'i were given their first clear indication that their government was quite willing to sacrifice immigrant interests to achieve the larger national goal of international respect. The most vulnerable of all immigrants travelling with Japanese passports were the Koreans, whose country had been controlled by Japan since the late 1890s, with formal colonization in 1910.

By the time the American public was clamoring for a complete end to Japanese immigration, the *issei* community was resigned to the fact that they were regarded not so much as *imin* (immigrants) but as *kimin* (abandoned people) by the governments of Tokyo, Washington, and Hawai'i. The Immigration Act of 1924 shut American doors to Japanese immigrants and, in Hawai'i, the Japanese protested as the Act took effect on 1 July 1924. Still, 3 days later, the *issei* came out in force to help celebrate American Independence Day with a grand lantern parade.

It was not until 1952 that Japanese immigrants were permitted to become American citizens, and there was a long history behind the successful elimination of that discriminatory policy. In 1790, the U.S. Congress had limited the right to naturalization to Whites only. This privileged category was extended in 1870 to include those of African birth or descent; however, Asians, or "Mongolians" as they were called at that time, were declared ineligible. Nevertheless, the 1910 United States census showed at least 420 naturalized Japanese because, it appears, there was some flexibility allowed judges in the interpretation of the Constitution, including the determination of Japanese as "white."

Several Japanese became naturalized subjects of the Kingdom of Hawai'i. In October 1844, Governor Kekūanaō'a signed a certificate of naturalization for one "Kanaka Nipona — Kuke Kainoa, a native of Japan," and there were at least two others in the 1840s. After the Bayonet Constitution of 1887 restricted political rights, including suffrage, to Hawaiians, Europeans, and Americans, only two Japanese were naturalized. One was Joe Makino of Ka'ū, born in Yokohama, who was considered eligible for naturalization because his father was British. The second, Tamekichi Abe (Tom Abbey), was given the privilege because he had carried a gun in support of the men who overthrew the Queen in 1893.

In the Bayonet Constitution the Provisional Government maintained voting restrictions based on nationality and race, later explaining the reasoning clearly and publicly:

> It must be distinctly understood that, besides ruling themselves, the whites must create a form of government through which they can rule natives, Chinese, Japanese, and Portuguese, in order to prevent being "snowed under."

The first organized efforts to regain the right to vote took place in Hilo, although Honolulu eventually became headquarters. Shin Yamamoto, a physician, directed activities in Hilo, where the organization included 150 members, while Jukichi Uchida served as president of the general body. The Japanese League of Hilo sent a petition to the Japanese government in October 1893, and the Honolulu group soon followed suit. The Japanese government reacted to the crisis with a formal protest and the dispatching of the *Naniwa*. The battle cruiser arrived in Hawai'i on 23 February 1893 under the command of Heihachirō Tōgō, who was to distinguish himself in the naval triumph over the Russian fleet in the Russo-Japanese war. The *Naniwa* remained anchored in Honolulu for several months,

Participants in the parade were dressed as high-ranking officers of the Japanese army and navy in celebration of the victory in the Sino-Japanese war, Honolulu, 11 May 1895.

ostensibly to protect Japanese lives and property in the unsettled period following the overthrow of Queen Liliʻuokalani, although its real purpose was to serve as a show of force in the international dispute. However, the more serious problems in Korea, eventually leading to war with China in 1894, turned Japan's attention away from the question of immigrant voting rights in Hawaiʻi.

The Japanese struggle to attain equality in Hawaiʻi extended to participation in the military. The United States had maintained an uneasy neutrality during the first years of World War I, but it was clearly a matter of time before Americans would be drawn into the conflict. In Hawaiʻi, for example, the National Guard increased its membership fivefold in the 1-year period after 30 June 1915. The governor of Hawaiʻi, Lucius Pinkham, clung to his belief that the enemy was Japan in the East and not Germany in the West, an assumption that made him a determined foe of the Japanese in Hawaiʻi. Under Pinkham's leadership, the Japanese were not welcomed into the National Guard. The major Japanese newspapers were encouraging their youths to enlist and serve in the American military, however, as a means of demonstrating the community's determination to remain as good, loyal, participating members.

Months before the United States formally entered World War I on 6 April 1917, Kinzaburō Makino noted the severance of diplomatic relations with Germany in the editorial pages of his *Hawaii Hōchi* and exhorted the young men to volunteer when war actually began.

It behooves the local Japanese youths to unhesitatingly volunteer their services in such an event and prove their loyalty to America . . . and protect the honor of Americans, as well as the honor of the Japanese and fulfill our obligations to the country we make our homes in.

After the first group of Hawaiʻi residents enlisted in the army on 2 July 1917, Makino congratulated the thirty-three *nisei* among them and remarked, "It now seems certain that noncitizen Japanese will also be inducted eventually. . . . We believe that enlistees will eventually be granted the privilege of becoming United States citizens."

In 1917–1918, 72,000 young men were registered in the Territory of Hawaiʻi for possible service in the United States Army. Among them were 29,000 *issei* and *nisei.* Eventually, 7,200 men, including 838 Japanese, were actually drafted. Company D of the National Guard became the first all-Japanese military unit in the United States. One *issei,* Kinichi Sasaki, even received a commission as a second lieutenant and Rev. Shigefusa Kanda, through strenuous efforts, became the only foreigner to serve in the American Red Cross units in attending to battle casualties in France.

Unfortunately, the next time Makino heard about the issue of naturalization for the Japanese in the military, it was disturbing news from his brother. Seiichi Tsuchiya, an enlistee at Schofield Barracks, was assigned the task of typing naturalization applications for personnel, and he soon noticed that not one came from the Japanese. He alerted Makino, who immediately contacted Judge Horace Vaughn of the United States District Court. Vaughn agreed that the Japanese should not be excluded from the privilege of naturalization rights that were extended, as of May 1918, to all other aliens who had served in the military. He agreed to help, even making special trips to Schofield to administer citizenship oaths to soldiers who could not easily travel to Honolulu.

Judge Vaughn ultimately granted citizenship to 400 Japanese and 300 other Asians, but the Territorial government refused to recognize them as citizens. In this move, the Hawai'i officials were acknowledging the interpretation held by the United States Naturalization Service, that the special legislation for veterans did not nullify the original principle providing for citizenship only to Whites and those of African descent. This more restrictive interpretation was upheld by the United States Supreme Court, which ruled in 1926 that the World War I Japanese veterans could not be naturalized. As one curious token gesture, Congress passed an act in 1935 that ultimately permitted seventy-nine Japanese, ninety Filipinos, eighteen Koreans, and sixteen Chinese to be naturalized as former World War I military personnel. For the rest of the 321 veterans, and the unknown numbers who might have applied for naturalization, however, the door was firmly closed until Congress removed the restrictions against Asian immigration and naturalization in 1952. As unfortunate as these cases might have been, the worst injustice was directed against women, who lost their citizenship simply by marrying aliens between 1922, when the legislation was passed, and 1931, when the Cable Act restored citizenship to considerable numbers of *nisei* women who had married *issei* men in their communities.

The implementation of some anti-Japanese policies was carried out through the use of these naturalization restrictions. In California, for example, the *issei* were effectively prohibited from owning land by legislation that specifically cited "aliens ineligible for naturalization," thus avoiding the use of ethnic or racial categories. The Hawaiian Rehabilitation Act, passed by Congress in 1921, included Section 109, prohibiting employment on "public work carried on in the Territory of Hawaii, by the government of the United States, whether the work is done by contract or otherwise unless such person is a citizen of the United States or eligible to become such a citizen." In 1925, the Territorial legislature enacted similar legislation. Combined with the powerful prejudice against the Japanese in private business arenas, this public sector racism confined many *issei* and *nisei* to positions below their abilities and expectations.

As a result, the struggle for equality extended quickly into the business world, where the immigrants and their children were allowed to compete only in enterprises where the larger *haole* firms found competition unnecessary or unprofitable. Plantation businesses such as barber shops and bathhouses, or individual family concerns such as laundries or small shops, were good examples of economic activities that complemented rather than competed with more powerful interests. The lack of equal access to land, transportation, insurance, capital, and political power prevented the Japanese business community from developing beyond relatively limited boundaries. Since these barriers were maintained by the structure of the political economy, there was only modest progress to be made, no matter how much effort or energy was expended.

By the time immigration from Japan was completely banned in 1924, the struggle for equality had become deeply embedded in the Japanese community in Hawai'i. These efforts extended into the workplace, living conditions, women's roles, relations within the ethnic community, maintenance of traditional culture and language, and even into military service. By 1924, moreover, the second generation was beginning to make its presence felt,

'Ōla'a 9-mile district men going off to World War I, island of Hawai'i, ca. 1918 (Iwasaki Collection).

and the entire island society was being confronted with a large and growing force of American citizens of Japanese descent who were being educated in the traditions of democracy and equality.

Send off at Olaa Hongwanji for men leaving to fight in World War I, island of Hawai'i, ca. 1918 (Iwasaki Collection).

赤心婦人會發會式

明照

Red Heart Women's Association World War I, 'Ōla'a, island of Hawai'i, ca. 1917 (Iwasaki Collection).

THE IMPERIAL
KOREAN FOREIGN OFFICE

Hereby amkes known that bearer

a native of
Province
Magistracy
District and
Village in the

PASSPORT

No.

Empire fo Korea in accordance wrth treaty rights now is
about to undertake a voyage to

AGE

and back and
requests all those authorities and/or prsons whom this may
coocern to et him travel, trade anb pass unobstructed and
unhindered. with his luggage and belongings oe chis his
voyage.

PRIVATE SEAL

Imperial Korean Foreigu Office.

Seoul, Kwangmu moon day.   Sael

MINISTERE DES AFFAIRES ETRANGERES
DE L'EMPIRE D COREE.

Il est notifie que le porteur du present passeport nonnne
Citoyen de l'Empire de
Coree   et natif de la
Province de
Magistrature
District de
Village de

PASS PORT

No.

mpire de Coree, en vertu des droits comferes par les Traites
desire entreprenre un voyage a destination de
et retour. En consequence les autorites, les fouctionnaires on
personnalites de tous pays que la chose concerne sont pries
de vouloir bien laisser passer librement le susnomme et lui
permettre de circuler sans obstacles et sans obstructions, avec
ees hardes et bagages au cours de son avoyge
Ministere des Affaires Etraingeres

AGE

SCEAU PERONNEL
DU TITULAIRE

Seoul   Kwangmo   hun   jour   Sceau
officiel

Passport issued to a Korean immigrant, Um Si Mun (Shi Mun
Eum), dated 3 December 1904.

TRANSLATION.
THE IMPERIAL JAPANESE GOVERNMENT
PASSPORT.

No.108622

The undersigned, His Imperial Japanese Majesty's Minister of State for
Foreign Affairs, requests all the Authorities concerned, both Civil and Military, to permit the bearer
Kim Sun Yon.
a Japanese subject, proceeding to Hawaii   to pass freely, and
without hindrance, and in case of need to afford her every possible aid and protection.

L.S.   Baron Shimpei Goto.

This 3 Day of the 6 month of the 7 year of Taisho 1918

DESCRIPTION.

Domicile No. 140. Sasento, Suwanfu, Keishonando, Chosen.
Family relation Wife of Oun Si Mun, the master of the house.
Age 16 years 1 months.
Stature 4 feet 11 inches.
Particular features Face: Short. Complexion: Dark. Eyes: Large.
Eyebrows: Thick. Mouth: Large.

Signature of the Bearer

TRADUCTION.
LE GOUVERNEMENT IMPERIAL DU JAPON.
PASSPORT.

No. 108622

Le soussigné, Ministre des Affaires Etrangères de Sa Majesté l'Empereur du Japon,
prie toutes les autorités civiles et militaires compétentes, de laisser passer librement et sans obstacle
M.   sujet Japonais,
allant   , et de lui accorder, en cas
de besoin, toute aide et protection possibles.

L.S.   19

Domicile du porteur
Relation de famille
Age de   ans et   mois.
Taille   pieds   pouces.
Particularités physiques

Signature du porteur

日本帝國海外旅券

第壹〇八六貳號

日本帝國ノ外務大臣ハ夫ノ呼寄ニ依リ米領布哇以下餘白
ニ赴ク前記ノ者ヲシテ沿路故障ナク自由ニ通行セシメ且必要ノ
場合ニ八保護援助ヲ與ヘラレンコトヲ文武官憲ニ請求ス

大正七年六月廿八日

日本帝國外務大臣正三位勲一等男爵後藤新平

所持人自署

金順年

姓名 移民 金 順 年

族籍 朝鮮慶尚南道釜山府佐川洞百四拾番地
縁儀 戸主 嚴時文ノ妻
年齡 拾六年壹ヶ月
身長 四尺九寸五分
特徵 顏九、色薄黑、目大、眉濃、口大、齒揃

慶尚南道警務部十印

HONOLULU, T. H.

admitted AUG 8 1918

Immigrant Inspector

This is to certify that the photograph attached hereto is a likeness of the person to whom this visa is issued. In witness whereof the seal of the American Consulate General at Yokohama, Japan, is impressed upon the photograph.

AMERICAN CONSULATE GENERAL, Yokohama, Japan.

SEEN. No. 6551

Vice Consul of The United States of America.

Dated. JUL 26 1918

Imperial Japanese government passport issued to Japanese subject, Kimn Sun Yon (Soon Yon Kim), dated 28 June 1918.

After the 1910 annexation of Korea by Japan, Koreans immigrated to Hawai'i as Japanese subjects.

Ironwood trees in Kapiʻolani Park, ca. 1903.

Archibald Cleghorn (father of Princess Kaʻiulani), Thomas Cummins, and James Makee were commissioned to develop Kapiolani Park in the late 1870s. These trees, which remain standing along Kalākaua Avenue, are said to have been planted in the 1890s by Japanese of the early government contract period, who were directly supervised by Kintarō Ozawa, one of the *gannenmono*.

EPILOGUE

The United States Congress closed America's doors to Japanese immigration in 1924, exactly four decades after the beginning of the government contract labor period. The following six decades have been as tumultuous and eventful as the first four, and this full century of the Japanese in Hawai'i has been of critical significance to the development of modern Hawaiian society. The current social, political, economic, and racial status of Japanese Americans in Hawai'i is so vastly different from the situation in 1924 that it seems the pendulum has indeed swung from the extreme of poverty and oppression to affluence and power. The realities are more complex, however, and the centennial of contract labor immigration provides a good opportunity to reflect on the struggle and contributions of the past generations as well as to look toward the challenges ahead.

In 1924 the traumatic strike of 1920 remained a vivid memory within the Japanese community, and when Filipinos went on strike in Hanapēpē, Kaua'i, few Japanese were willing to provide active support. The Japanese language school controversy was at its height, and the ethnic community was bitterly divided. Nevertheless, the Japanese community was growing rapidly and becoming increasingly sophisticated. By the 1930s, the Japanese press was publishing enormous amounts of information and literary expression in newspapers, journals, newsletters, and books. Japanese language schools had about forty thousand *nisei* enrolled, and Buddhism continued to flourish as the community religion. The first Japanese language radio broadcast in Hawai'i took place in 1928, and the Japanese began programming with local talent and material imported from Japan. The Japanese influence in Hawai'i could be appreciated in architecture, landscaping, social customs, festivals, and diet.

There was considerable social and cultural interchange between Hawai'i and Japan. Theater troupes, athletic teams, and entertainers routinely travelled from Japan to Hawai'i and organized tours took many Japanese from Hawai'i to Japan. Through the 1930s, some *nisei* were being sent to Japan to be educated. Many of these *kibei* (literally, "returned to America") experienced difficulty being accepted into either Japanese or Japanese-Hawaiian societies, but they became invaluable for their command of the Japanese language. By 1938–1939, at the peak of the *issei* push to educate the *nisei* in Japan, there were about two thousand students in institutions ranging from elementary to professional schools.

The *issei* were still in control of the community's major institutions, but the second generation *nisei* were rapidly assuming greater importance as they grew older through the 1920s and 1930s. The central question for the Big Five elite became the assimilability of this ethnic group which constituted about 40 percent of the islands' total population and had demonstrated consistent ambition and willingness to fight for equality. The *nisei* grew up under enormous pressure, not only because the general society demanded that they discard most of their Japanese heritage and culture—a demand that inevitably meant that many would feel shame and rejection toward their own parents—but also because their parents could not understand the growing tensions. Many of the *issei* parents were convinced that Japan's military victories in Asia were the wave of the future, and they sincerely hoped that the rise in Japan's national fortunes would help the Japanese community in Hawai'i. Others, like Rev. Takie Okumura, were equally convinced that the *nisei* had to conform to demands for complete assimilation.

Many *nisei* were citizens of both Japan and the United States. Japan, recognizing the principle of *jus sanguinis* ("the rule of blood"), would provide citizenship to all children whose parents were Japanese. In addition to *jus sanguinis*, America also recognized the principle of *jus soli* ("the rule of the soil"), in which citizenship was determined by place of birth. Under more relaxed conditions, the fact of dual citizenship might not have assumed such importance. The international rivalries between the United States and Japan were intensifying, however, and local race relations were becoming more precarious.

Two important murder cases and trials compounded the problem. The first occurred in 1928, when Myles Fukunaga was accused of kidnapping and murdering the young son of a *haole* executive. The young man was convicted and hanged in spite of petitions signed by thousands of Japanese mothers pleading for mercy. Several years later, a navy lieutenant's wife, Thalia Massie, accused a group of Hawaiian and *nisei* youths of beating and raping her. The evidence was inconclusive and the case ended in a mistrial. Thalia's husband and her mother, taking matters into their own hands, then kidnapped Joseph Kahāhāwai, and finally shot and killed the young Hawaiian. They were convicted and sentenced to ten years at hard labor, but Governor Lawrence Judd commuted the sentence to one hour spent in his office, after which they were free to leave the Islands. Racial tensions reflected in these pre-War cases were an important part of the environment in which the *nisei* grew to adulthood.

There were indications that some of the *nisei* could do well in spite of the pressures, however, and more of them began to be elected to public office, organize labor unions, teach in public schools, and go on to higher education by the 1930s. The Japanese attack on Pearl Harbor on 7 December 1941 temporarily obliterated the advances and threw the whole nation into turmoil. One result was a wave of anti-Japanese hostility which culminated in some of the worst racial injustices in American history. The Japanese in Hawai'i were spared the wholesale evictions and removal to concentration camps suffered by more than 110,000 Japanese on the West Coast, two-thirds of whom were American citizens. Nevertheless, approximately two thousand people in Hawai'i were directly affected, including some seven hundred *kibei*, and the impact on the community was grave. The selection of Japanese in Hawai'i to be interned conveyed the powerful message that association with Buddhism, Japanese language schools, martial arts, and public expression of pride in Japan was dangerous and suspect. Community leaders, fishermen, and employees of the Japanese consulate were also among the first to be arrested. These official actions convinced most of the Japanese to abandon any attachment to Japanese culture, including their own heritage in Hawai'i.

The military exploits of the *nisei* in World War II emerged out of the confusion and tensions of Hawai'i in the 1930s and early 1940s. The young men who formed the Varsity Victory Volunteers in 1942 did so to offer their services in whatever form the United States military would accept. They and thousands of others joined the 100th Battalion, the 442nd Regimental Combat Team, and the Military Intelligence Service, all primarily *nisei* units that distinguished themselves through uncommon valor and sacrifice on the battlefields of Europe and the Pacific. The Japanese American demonstration of patriotism did much to convince skeptics that they were indeed what they claimed to be — loyal Americans. Equally important, the Japanese Americans themselves had gained considerable confidence and self-respect. The *nisei* returned to Hawai'i having seen how effectively they could compete with Whites from around the nation. The old image of White superiority crumbled in the classrooms, on the playing fields, in the boxing rings, and on the rifle ranges of military training camps. On the United States mainland and in Europe they saw a wide variety of individual, regional, and ethnic differences and class distinctions among Whites. In Hawai'i, these distinctions had been obscured by the fact that being *haole* and being privileged were identical. The veteran *nisei* returned tougher, older, wiser, and much less willing to accept the prejudice and discrimination that marked plantation Hawai'i. They participated wholeheartedly in the post-War G.I. Bill, which paid for higher education for veterans, and emerged with degrees of all kinds. But they also had some help in the form of a society changing rapidly around them and opening up in ways previously thought impossible.

The post-War *nisei* were also able to use more than a decade of intensive labor organizing to produce another power base. Its most visible example was the International Longshoremen's and Warehousemen's Union (ILWU), which successfully brought all nationality groups together. The ILWU organized the dock workers and all areas of sugar and pineapple production before calling major strikes in 1946 and 1949, ending the era of almost total control by plantation management. In these efforts, the *nisei* were among the most effective and energetic organizers.

A final power base forged by the *nisei* was the local Democratic Party, which had been overshadowed by the Big Five-dominated Republican Party for half-a-century. In 1954, the Democrats were led by a coalition including the *nisei* veterans, grassroots ILWU organizers, and a few *haole* leaders like Jack Burns (who eventually became governor) who felt the time was right. Their major goal was to open the doors to political, social, and economic opportunity for more people, including Japanese Americans, who had been denied equality. In the final analysis, however, it was the fundamental change in the political and economic structure that made upward mobility possible for the *nisei*.

The growth of a large military during World War II forced the Big Five to relinquish much of its traditional power. The end of the war consolidated the military presence in Hawai'i, which became the center of United States expansion throughout the Pacific Basin. In the post-War period, sugar began to produce smaller profits, encouraging the expansion of giant American corporations into tourism and resort development. These changes in the structure allowed the *nisei* to move into new areas of business and employment. Both private and public sectors grew rapidly and the energies and talents of the highly trained, underemployed Japanese Americans were drawn into the new economy.

A new and more open political economy, in combination with the released energies of an entire ethnic group that had been repressed on racial grounds, allowed significant upward mobility for the Japanese within a single generation. Hawaiian society witnessed a continuation and expansion of interethnic and intercultural exchange as the Japanese community continued to lose more of its cohesiveness. While some *nisei* were marrying non-Japanese in the pre-War period, the number of mixed marriages increased rapidly thereafter. In the 1980s about half of the Japanese Americans are marrying partners of another ethnic background. Yet this increase in mixed marriages over the decades has not necessarily improved contemporary race relations. The arrival of "new" immigrants from Japan, including the brides of G.I.s who served in Asia during the occupation of Japan, during the Korean War, and the War in Vietnam, has reinvigorated the cultural base of the community in Hawai'i. Further, there are increasing numbers of Japanese nationals, including students and a community of businessmen and their families, living and working in Hawai'i.

In spite of these positive changes, however, there are disquieting signs on the horizon. The Japanese American share of the Hawai'i population is diminishing, as is their influence within electoral politics. Organized labor is also on the defensive. The post-War power sources—ethnic community, a major role in the relatively large Democratic Party, and leadership of a solid organized labor movement—are all in decline.

These new realities are confronting an ethnic group unaccustomed to reflecting on the meaning of past struggles and accomplishments. Previous generations were involved with the need to succeed against great economic, political, and social odds. In the distant past, Japanese contract laborers organized and fought their own government officials and the sugar planters. Today, the children and grandchildren of the plantation workers are in local corporations and government positions. This alone has been an unusual story of immigrant success in the United States, and the Japanese have been congratulated as something of a model for others to follow.

The American dream has included a vision of progress for each generation. Japanese Americans in Hawai'i have held fast to that ideal because it has appeared to work for them, at least in the past few decades. As a result, there is a mythology that purports to explain the upward mobility in terms of cultural values, including an emphasis on education, a willingness to defer gratification, and a mystical attachment to *samurai* tradition. Among the most important elements in the legacy of the contract laborers and their successors through the first forty years, however, is the fact that progress was slow and proceeded through unusual and sometimes desperate efforts. The *issei* quickly understood that they had to do battle with entire systems of thinking and behaving, especially ones that systematically prevented them from being treated with dignity and respect.

Anti-Japanese racism—especially in the wake of Pearl Harbor, which made enemies of things Japanese—in combination with the hope for complete assimilation into White America misled Japanese Americans in Hawai'i into believing that their own history was of no significance. Now that the vision of limitless progress is more obscure, however, there is the opportunity to reevaluate the heritage of the Japanese in Hawai'i. The struggles of the early *issei* contract laborers to create better working and living conditions are at the very heart of the Japanese American experience.

NOTES

Notes have been kept to a minimum. Documentation has been provided for substantially new information or for revisions of traditionally accepted interpretations but avoided where generally accessible in standard histories by Morita and Kihara (in Japanese) or by Wakukawa and the United Japanese Society (in English). In researching this book, extensive use was made of the early Japanese language newspapers in the Bishop Museum collection, e.g., *Yamato, Yamato Shimbun, Nippu Jiji* and *Hawaii Hōchi*, and of the works on the Japanese in Hawai'i published before WWII.

PROLOGUE

"appropriate" marriage partners: When John M. Kapena was appointed "envoy extraordinary and minister plenipotentiary" and sent to Japan in 1882 to help negotiate an agreement to secure immigrant laborers, he hosted a dinner to honor three Japanese princes and various government department heads. At the dinner, he announced that "His Majesty (Kalākaua) believes that the Japanese and Hawaiians spring from one cognate race. . . . Hawaii holds out her loving hand and heart to Japan and desires that Your People may come and cast in their lots with ours and repeople our island Home." Later, at a meeting with Foreign Minister Kaoru Inouye, Kapena read from a prepared statement: "We believe the Japanese and Hawaiians spring from a cognate race and that Japanese children growing up and amalgamating with our population will produce a new and vigorous race." In fact, except for the *gannenmono* immigrants, the Japanese tended to intermarry less than other ethnic groups, probably as a result of more favorable male/female ratios, as well as cultural and national preference (Kuykendall 1967: 159–160).

Kalākaua's proposals to Emperor Meiji (Conroy 1973:75).

RECRUITMENT

Home prefectures of emigrants: The preponderance of southwestern Japanese and Okinawans in Hawai'i does not hold true for other emigrant destinations, including the Japanese colonies in Sakhalin, Korea, Taiwan, Kwantung Province in China, and the South Sea Islands. Immigrants to those areas originated from prefectures scattered throughout Japan.

Causes of Japanese immigration (Wakatsuki 1984:B1–8; Ichioka 1983:2–7).

Irwin to Governor of Tokyo (Doi 1980:8–9).

Convention of 1886 (Conroy 1973:210–221).

Selective screening of emigrants (Doi 1980:40–41).

ARRIVAL

First newspaper account of Japanese arrival (*Daily Pacific Commercial Advertiser*, 9 February 1885).

Japanese Consul report to his government on voyage to Hawai'i (*Nippu Jiji* 1935:17).

Quarantine procedures (*Daily Pacific Commercial Advertiser*, 9 February 1885).

Significance of Japanese arrival (*Daily Pacific Commercial Advertiser*, 10 February 1885).

Sumō attire (*Daily Pacific Commercial Advertiser*, 12 February 1885).

Positive atmosphere surrounding initial Japanese arrival (*Daily Pacific Commercial Advertiser*, 12 February 1885).

Destinations of first-boat immigrants (Hawaii State Archives, Japanese Records).

PLANTATION WORK

Haole: Originally a Hawaiian word meaning "foreigner," soon limited to Whites. For many users and in many situations, it has a negative connotation, largely due to resentment against *haole* domination during the plantation period.

Treatment of contract laborers in Hawai'i vs. elsewhere (Coman 1903).

Holehole bushi (Odo and Urata 1981). Some of these lyrics very likely were created almost as soon as the Japanese arrived, since they refer to people and events of the 1880s. By the publication of the first major history of Japanese in Hawai'i, *Shin Hawaii* (New Hawaii) (Fujii 1900), there was an established tradition of literary production in Hawai'i. Numerous poems exist on the theme of plantation work and life in a collection of *waka, haiku* and *senryū,* in Fujii (pp. 646–649). The *holehole bushi* are popular equivalents of this poetic tradition. The original tune probably was one sung by women in Hiroshima prefecture as they did the tedious and repetitious job of husking rice. Other theories suggest different *motouta* or "base songs" including one traditionally sung by boatmen of the Inland Sea (Tasaka, manuscript).

"any concerted action in case of strikes" (Republic of Hawaii 1895:36).

Number of sugar workers in 1909 (Coman 1903:548).

Kindergarten on Ewa Plantation (Thrum 1922:115).

"The Boy and Girl Scout movement" (Thrum 1922:119).

Number of Japanese laborers in 1899 (Coman 1903:548).

Beating of *hippari* man (Reinecke 1966:3; *Pacific Commercial Advertiser,* 30 December 1893).

"it does not stimulate" (Coman 1903:543).

PLANTATION LIFE

Irwin on the nature of the Japanese immigrants (Hawaiian Kingdom, Board of Immigration 1885:227; *Hawaiian Gazette,* 26 February 1885).

Effect of plantation social structure: A recent treatment explained, "The provision of some respect for their humanity and an opportunity to organize their own supervisory hierarchy would have eliminated many humiliations and resentments, of which some embers still smolder today in those who remember plantation existence, or whose parents and elders relayed stories of misery during those early years in Hawaii" (Rogers and Izutsu 1980:74).

Hawaiian government agrees to retain Japanese doctors (Hawaiian Kingdom, Board of Immigration 1885:231).

Successful recruitment of eight Japanese doctors: Letter from Nakayama to Walter Murray Gibson, Hawaiian Premier and Minister of Foreign Affairs (Hawaii State Archives, n.d. mid-1885).

Travelling peddlers (Archives of Hawaii, Bureau of Immigration).

Vegetables grown by Japanese in Hawai'i (Fujii 1900:337).

1889 inventory (Kubota 1979:146).

Sex ratios: The unbalanced sex ratio for Japanese never approached that for Chinese, Filipinos, or Koreans. For the latter groups, there were long periods when only 10 percent of the group was female (Takaki 1983:120; Reinecke 1979:20–22).

Holehole bushi (Odo and Urata 1981).

"The undersigned went on a field trip" (Morita 1915:543–547; United Japanese Society 1971:122).

"Since the advent of the Japanese" (*Pacific Commercial Advertiser,* 30 January 1896).

Threats to law enforcement agencies: Letter from High Sheriff Brown to E. K. Bull, manager of Oahu Sugar Co., 15 September 1902 (Oahu Sugar Co. Archives). Brown angrily closed by noting that "such threats come with very bad grace from the Manager of Oahu Plantation."

Hongwanji mission established in Hawai'i (Hunter 1971).

"Much trouble has been caused": Letter from Taylor to Consul General Taizō Masaki (Hawaii State Archives, Bureau of Immigration 9 November 1891).

Right to celebrate *tenchōsetsu* (Conroy 1973:222).

Sasakura Ushū poem (Fujii 1900:641) trans. by Kazuko Sinoto.

Rokumei Sanjin poem (Fujii 1900:647) trans. by Franklin Odo.

Contract laborers leaving Hawai'i (Conroy 1973; HIHPC 1984).

Okinawans in Hawai'i (Sakihara 1981:108).

"Related but separate institutions": Rev. Gashū Seikan Higa, for example, became a central figure in the Okinawan community when he arrived as a Methodist minister in 1917. He advocated Christian Buddhist harmony and birth control, praised the peasant rebellions of Tokugawa history, and operated a mission in the Honolulu slums. Higa founded the *Reimei Kyokai,* the "Dawn Association," as a kind of study group, and the *Reimeiryō,* or "Dawn Dormitory," as a place for communal living combined with Christian socialist education. The Hawaiian Sugar Planters' Association considered him dangerous enough to have all his writings translated into English for their use and for transmission to his employers, the Hawaiian Board of Missions (Sakihara 1981:112). Koreans were another group which immigrated to Hawai'i after Japan had assumed control over their homeland. Some 7,000, mostly single males, arrived between 1903 and 1905 with passports issued by the Korean government. After Japan's formal annexation of Korea in 1910, Korean women and children emigrated to Hawai'i to join their husbands, or to become "picture brides"; all travelled under Imperial Japanese Government passports (Nordyke 1977:45).

Japanese marriage statistics (U.S. Dept. of Labor 1901:36).

Japanese arrivals, 1908–1924 (Kihara 1935:164–167).

Number of "picture brides": Most sources on the history of Japanese in Hawai'i use 14,276, a figure compiled from U.S. Immigration Department statistics, but there was a long period from 1917 to 1924, when picture brides were undercounted because the "dockside marriages" had been discontinued (United Japanese Society 1971:165–166).

"If the Japanese government" (Wakukawa 1938:340–341).

"The most important event" (Makino Biography Committee 1965:20–21).

JAPANESE SCHOOLS

"think and feel in sympathy with their parents": Yemyō Imamura of Honpa Hongwanji on opening of first Buddhist-sponsored Japanese language school in 1902 (Hunter 1971:87).

Compulsory education under the Meiji (Passin 1965:272–273).

Literacy rates in Japan (Yamaguchi prefectural government 1972; Dore 1972).

Literacy in Hawai'i (Fujii 1900:40). These are probably the best estimates, although there is an astonishing range of figures regarding literacy among Japanese immigrants in Hawai'i. Reinecke found census reports that suggested that 40 percent of the *issei* was illiterate, while the 1902 U.S. Department of Labor report (p. 102) insisted that only 1.2 percent was illiterate. These figures are clearly too extreme (Reinecke 1979:44).

Enrollment in public schools (Hunter 1971:87).

Farrington at dedication of Hongwanji Mission (Hunter 1971:106).

Court cases for Japanese language teachers (Makino Biography Committee 1965:28–30).

Proposal that teachers be required to pass English examinations (U.S. Department of Interior 1920).

Language schools in support of labor (Kurita 1952:38).

"a legal contest" (Wakukawa 1938:288).

"parts of a deliberate plan" (Wakukawa 1938:297).

"our continued loyalty to America" (Wakukawa 1938:299).

"Americans feel it only proper" (Makino Biography Committee 1965:65–66).

JAPANESE LANGUAGE NEWSPAPERS

Bunichirō Onome (Kawazoe 1960:134).

BUSINESS AND ENTERPRISE

Okinawans and hog industry (Kimura 1981:217–222).

"crowding into the stevedore and wharf work" (Moriyama 1982).

Japanese vocational school (Fujii 1900:158).

Kunizō Suzuki (Fujii 1900: Appendix p. 32).

Remittances to Japan (Kihara 1935:237).

Lower calculations for remittances (Doi 1980:173).

Japanese savings in Hawai'i (Sōga 1953:272).

Japanese merchants in 1895 (Hawaii Nikkeijin Rengō Kyōkai 1964:153).

Japanese women in canneries (Ethnic Studies 1979).

Japanese coffee farmers (Goto 1982).

Coffee farmers in Kona (Ethnic Studies 1981).

"I have known for a long time": Letter, A. Wood to A. Ahrens (Oahu Sugar Co. Archives).

Japanese fishing companies (*Nippu Jiji* 1921:56–59; United Japanese Society 1971:209).

Assets held by Japanese (United Japanese Society 1971:201).

LABOR MOVEMENTS

Early labor disputes: For many Japanese, the first foreign language encountered and learned was not English but Hawaiian. A basic pidgin developed to conduct the most essential transactions. Later the pidgin evolved into a creole that many ethnic groups helped to shape, and which functioned as the common language of the multiethnic and multilingual working class community in the islands.

Incident at Pā'ia, Maui (Kihara 1935:451).

"the number and character of these complaints" (Republic of Hawaii, Bureau of Immigration, Gibson to Inouye 1886:233).

Harsh treatment of contract laborers (Soga 1953:11ff; Mori 1921:244).

Number of Japanese under contract before passage of the Organic Act: Increasing numbers of workers were becoming free or day-wage laborers before 1900, but there were still 20,631 men under contract in 1899, and 12,115 who were free. For the Japanese, the figures were 17,547 and 5,741, respectively (Coman 1903:64). Most of this large number of Japanese under contract had been among the nearly 30,000 Japanese who emigrated in 1898–1899.

Strikes in June 1900 (Reinecke 1966:7–8).

Japanese argue in 1909 for equal pay (Negoro 1915:7–16).

Response of plantation workers to proposals for higher wages (Negoro 1915:189–190).

Motoyuki Negoro contributed a play that depicted the formation of the Higher Wages Association, serving, at the same time, to educate the theater audiences about the issues at hand and to generate support for the effort. The play was well-received, evidently, making the rounds before the strike was on. Unlike the real struggle, however, the play ended on a happy note, with wages being raised to $22.50 without a strike (Negoro 1915:144–153).

Shiba criticized radical advocates of the higher wage movement: "if any encouragement be given to them now, the rule of the black-mailers would be easily reestablished, to the menace of the law-abiding Japanese and the citizens in general. The combination of a newspaper with these elements is deplorable, and should never be allowed" (Wakukawa 1938:175).

Subsidies from the Hawaiian Sugar Planters' Association (HSPA) to *Hawaii Shimpō:* Several years after the strike, a former reporter who had worked with the *Shimpō* revealed that Shiba had been receiving monthly subsidies from the HSPA since 1908, and that nearly $12,000 in special funds had been made available to him and another paper, the *Hawaii Nichinichi,* which had supported the planters (Moriyama 1976:172).

Assessment of 1909 strike: When the Japanese assessed the strike, they noted the lack of adequate financial support; the inability to create a solid, united front of Japanese support and to generate any support from other nationality groups; the lack of any political rights in Hawai'i; and the length of the strike itself. When the federal labor commissioner assessed the strike, he observed that the Japanese government did not support the workers; that the strike was confined to the Japanese; that the leadership came from educated individuals rather than the laborers; that the strike was broken through use of non-Japanese strikebreakers and Japanese financial weakness; and that conditions after the strike improved for the Japanese (Wakukawa 1938:191).

Number of *haole,* Japanese, and Filipinos between 1910 and 1920 (United Japanese Society 1971:277).

Labor strikes by Japanese fishermen (Reinecke 1966:15–16).

Strike activity by Okinawan workers (Reinecke 1966:13).

Prejudices against Okinawans in Hawai'i. The second group went to Honokaa Plantation on the island of Hawai'i where miserable conditions forced them to escape to Hilo and then to O'ahu where they ended up, ironically, on the Ewa Plantation (Hiura and Terada 1981:223).

"People know Hawaii" (Wakukawa 1938:241).

"What the alien Japanese" (Wakukawa 1938:248–249).

"I am inclined to mistrust" (Kurita 1952:46–47).

HUMAN RIGHTS

Numbers of Chinese contract laborers, 1894–1897 (United Japanese Society 1971:137).

Rejection of Japanese laborers in 1897 (Wakukawa 1938:90).

Compensation to ship owners and immigrants (*Yamato Shimbun,* 29 November 1898).

Naturalization of Japanese (Ichioka 1977).

Tamekichi Abe (Jones 1933:66–69; United Japanese Society 1971:242).

"It must be distinctly understood" (Reinecke 1979:4,n.6).

"It now seems certain" and "It behooves the local" (Makino Biography Committee 1965:33–35).

Japanese registration, World War I (Wakukawa 1938:206–207).

Naturalization of World War I military (United Japanese Society 1971:242–243).

Prohibition of public employment of noncitizens (Wakukawa 1938:228–229).

Japanese Benevolent Society of Hawaii (Wakukawa 1938:114).

EPILOGUE

Japanese influence in Hawai'i (De Francis 1973).

Kibei in Japan (Adachi 1977:73).

General histories of the 1920s and 1930s and the entire period covered in this work (Fuchs 1969; Daws 1974).

Japanese military victories seen as wave of the future (Stephan 1984).

Internment of Japanese Americans (Irons 1983).

ILWU (Zalburg 1979).

Post-War economy (Kent 1983).

BIBLIOGRAPHY

ARMSTRONG, WILLIAM
1904   *Around the World with a King*. New York: Frederic A. Stokes.

BEEKMAN, ALAN
1983   "Japanese-Language Press of Hawaii," *Pacific Citizen*, December 23–30. Los Angeles: Japanese American Citizens League.

BRYAN, WILLIAM S., ED.
1899   *Our Islands and Their People as Seen with Camera and Pencil*. St. Louis: N. D. Thompson.

BUSHNELL, ANDREW
1984   "The English Language Press and the 1920 Sugar Strike in Hawaii." Unpublished seminar paper. Univ. of Hawaii Manoa, Honolulu.

COLEMAN, JAMES
1965   *Education and Political Development*. Princeton, N.J.: Princeton Univ. Press.

COMAN, KATHARINE
1903   *The History of Contract Labor in the Hawaiian Islands*. New York: Macmillan.

CONROY, FRANCIS HILARY
1973   *The Japanese Expansion into Hawaii, 1868–1898*. San Francisco: R and E Research Associates.

DAWS, GAVAN
1968   *Shoal of Time: A History of the Hawaiian Islands*. New York: Macmillan.

DEFRANCIS, JOHN
1973   *Things Japanese in Hawaii*. Honolulu: Univ. Press of Hawaii.

DORE, RONALD
1956   *Education in Tokugawa Japan*. Berkeley: Univ. of California Press.

ETHNIC STUDIES ORAL HISTORY PROJECT
1979   *Women Workers in Hawaii's Pineapple Industry, Vols. 1 and 2*. Honolulu: Ethnic Studies Oral History Project.

1981   *A Social History of Kona, Vols. 1 and 2*. Honolulu: Ethnic Studies Oral History Project.

ETHNIC STUDIES ORAL HISTORY PROJECT AND UNITED OKINAWAN ASSOCIATION
1981   *Uchinanchu: A History of Okinawans in Hawaii*. Honolulu: Ethnic Studies Oral History Project and United Okinawan Association.

FEHER, JOSEPH, COMPILER
1969   *Hawaii: A Pictorial History*. Honolulu: B P Bishop Museum.

FUCHS, LAWRENCE
1961   *Hawaii Pono: A Social History*. New York: Harcourt, Brace.

GOTO, Y. BARON
1982   "Ethnic Groups and Coffee," *Hawaiian Journal of History*, Vol. 16, Honolulu: Hawaiian Historical Society.

HAWAIIAN SUGAR PLANTERS' ASSOCIATION
1929   *Story of Sugar in Hawaii*. Honolulu: HSPA.

HAWAIIAN TERRITORIAL MEDICAL SOCIETY
1904   *Transactions of the Thirteenth Annual Meeting*. Honolulu.

HIURA, ARNOLD, AND VINNIE TERADA
1981   "Okinawan Involvement in Hawaii's Labor Movement." In *Uchinanchu: A History of Okinawans in Hawaii*. Honolulu: Ethnic Studies Oral History Project and United Okinawan Association.

HUNTER, LOUISE
1971   *Buddhism in Hawaii: Its Impact on a Yankee Community*. Honolulu: Univ. of Hawaii Press.

ICHIOKA, YUJI
1977   "The Early Japanese Immigrant Quest for Citizenship: The Background of the 1922 Ozawa Case." *Amerasia Journal* 4(2), Los Angeles: UCLA Asian American Studies Center.

1983   "Recent Japanese Scholarship on the Origins and Causes of Japanese Immigration." *The Immigration History Newsletter* 15(2). St. Paul, Minn.: Immigration History Society.

IRONS, PETER
1983   *Justice at War: The Story of the Japanese American Internment Cases*. New York and Oxford: Oxford Univ. Press.

ISHIKAWA, TOMONARI
1981   "Okinawans in Hawaii: An Overview of the Past 80 Years." In *Uchinanchu: A History of Okinawans in Hawaii*. Honolulu: Ethnic Studies Oral History Project and United Okinawan Association.

JONES, MAUDE
1933   "Naturalization of Orientals in Hawaii prior to 1900." *Forty-first Annual Report of the Hawaiian Historical Society for the Year 1932*. Honolulu.

KENT, NOEL
1983   *Hawaii: Islands Under the Influence*. New York: Monthly Review Press.

KIMURA, YUKIKO
1981   "Okinawans and Hog Industry in Hawaii." In *Uchinanchu: A History of Okinawans in Hawaii*. Honolulu: Ethnic Studies Oral History Project and United Okinawan Association.

KURITA, YAYOI
1952   "Labor Movements Among Japanese Plantation Workers in Hawaii." Unpublished seminar paper, Univ. of Hawaii Manoa, Honolulu.

KUYKENDALL, RALPH S.
1953–1967   *The Hawaiian Kingdom*. 3 vols. Honolulu: Univ. of Hawaii Press

KUYKENDALL, RALPH S. AND A. GROVE DAY
1948   *Hawaii: A History*. New York: Prentice-Hall.

LIND, ANDREW
1969   *Hawaii: Last of the Magic Isles*. London: Oxford Univ. Press.

MAKINO BIOGRAPHY COMMITTEE
1965   *Life of Kinzaburo Makino*. Honolulu: Michie Makino.

MORIYAMA, ALAN
1976   "The 1909 and 1920 Strikes of Japanese Sugar Plantation Workers in Hawaii." In *Counterpoint: Perspectives on Asian America*. Emma Gee, ed. Los Angeles: UCLA Asian American Studies Center.

1982   "Imingaisha: Japanese Emigration Companies and Hawaii, 1894–1908." Ph.D. dissertation, UCLA.

Nippu Jiji
1935   "Gojunen Kinenshi." (Golden Jubilee of the Japanese in Hawaii). Honolulu: *Nippu Jiji*.

NORDYKE, ELEANOR
1977   *The Peopling of Hawaii*. Honolulu: East-West Center.

ODO, FRANKLIN, AND HARRY URATA
1981 "Hole Hole Bushi: Songs of Hawaii's Japanese Immigrants." *Mana* 6(1). Hawai'i: Elepaio Press.

OGAWA, DENNIS
1978 *Kodomo no tame ni: For the sake of the children: The Japanese American Experience in Hawaii.* Honolulu: Univ. of Hawaii Press.

PASSIN, HERBERT
1965 "Japan." In *Education and Political Development*, by James Coleman. Princeton, N.J.: Princeton Univ. Press.

REINECKE, JOHN
1966 "Labor Disturbances in Hawaii, 1890–1925: A Summary." Honolulu: privately published.

1979 *Feigned Necessity: Hawaii's Attempt to Obtain Chinese Contract Labor, 1921–1923.* San Francisco: Chinese Materials Center.

REPUBLIC OF HAWAII
1895 *Report of the Labor Commission on Strikes and Arbitration.* Honolulu: R. Grieve.

1878–1898 Report of the President of the Board of Immigration.

ROGERS, TERENCE, AND SATORU IZUTSU
1980 "The Japanese." In *People and Cultures of Hawaii: A Psychocultural Profile*, John F. McDermott, Jr., Wen-Shing Tseng, and Thomas Maretski, eds. Honolulu: Univ. Press of Hawaii.

SAKIHARA, MITSUGU
1981 "Okinawans in Hawaii: An Overview of the Past 80 Years." In *Uchinanchu: A History of Okinawans in Hawaii.* Honolulu: Ethnic Studies Oral History Project and United Okinawan Association.

SPOEHR, ALEXANDER, KAZUKO SINOTO, AND HISAO GOTO
1983 "Craft History and the Merging of Tool Tradition: Carpenters of Japanese Ancestry in Hawaii," *Hawaiian Journal of History* 17. Honolulu: Hawaiian Historical Society.

STEPHAN, JOHN
1984 *Hawaii Under the Rising Sun: Japan's Plans for Conquest after Pearl Harbor.* Honolulu: Univ. of Hawaii Press.

TAKAKI, RONALD
1983 *Pau Hana: Plantation Life and Labor in Hawaii, 1835–1920.* Honolulu: Univ. of Hawaii Press.

TANAKA, CHESTER
1982 *Go For Broke: A Pictorial History of the Japanese American 100th Infantry Battalion and the 442nd Regimental Combat Team.* Richmond, Calif.: Go For Broke, Inc.

TAYLOR, CHARLES M. JR.
1898 *Vacation Days in Hawaii and Japan.* Philadelphia: George W. Jacobs and Co.

THRUM, THOMAS G.
1922 "Plantation Industrial Service." *Thrum's Hawaiian Annual.* Honolulu: Thomas G. Thrum.

TŌYAMA, TETSUO
1971 *Eighty Years in Hawaii.* Honolulu: Sadako Toyama.

UNITED JAPANESE SOCIETY OF HAWAII
1971 *A History of Japanese in Hawaii.* Honolulu: United Japanese Society of Hawaii.

U.S. DEPARTMENT OF THE INTERIOR
1920 *A Survey of Education in Hawaii*, Bulletin No. 16, Washington, D.C.: Government Printing Office.

U.S. DEPARTMENT OF LABOR
1901–1916 *Report of the Commissioner of Labor on Hawaii.* Washington, D.C.: Government Printing Office.

WAKATSUKI, YASUO
1984 "Emigration of Japanese to the United States." In *Pacific Citizen*, Jan. 6–13. Los Angeles.

WAKUKAWA, ERNEST
1938 *A History of the Japanese People in Hawaii.* Honolulu: The Toyo Shoin.

ZALBURG, SANFORD
1979 *A Spark is Struck: Jack Hall and the ILWU in Hawaii.* Honolulu: Univ. Press of Hawaii.

JAPANESE BIBLIOGRAPHY

ADACHI, NOBUHIRO
1977 *Hawaii Nikkeijin shi* (Japanese Americans in Hawaii). Tokyo. Ashi no Ha Shuppan Kai.

DOI, YATARŌ
1980 *Yamaguchi-ken Oshima-gun Hawaii iminshi.* (A history of emigration to Hawaii from Oshima County, Yamaguchi Prefecture.) Tokuyama: Matsuno Shoten.

EBARA, HACHIRŌ
1936 *Kaigai hōji shimbun zasshi shi* (A history of Japanese newspapers and magazines abroad).

FUJII, HIDEGORŌ
1900 *Shin Hawaii* (New Hawaii). Tokyo.

1937 *Dai Nihon kaigai ijumin shi* (A history of Japanese emigration abroad), Vol. 1. Hawaii. Osaka.

GOTŌ, CHINPEI
1940 *Yakyū ippyakunen kinen Hawaii hōjin yakyū shi* (A history of baseball played by Japanese in Hawaii, in commemoration of the 100th anniversary of the game). Hawaii.

HAGA, TAKESHI
1981 *Hawaii imin no shōgen* (Testimonies from Hawaii's immigrants). Tokyo: Senichi Shobo.

HAWAII ANNAI SHA
1920 *Saishin Hawaii annai dainihan* (Latest Hawaiian guide). 2nd ed. Hawaii Annai sha.

HAWAII HONPA HONGWANJI KYŌDAN
1954 *Gomonshu gojunkyō kinen Hawaii Honpa Hongwanji Kyōdan enkaku shi* (A history of the Hawaii Honpa Hongwanji Mission, in commemoration of the visit of the Abbot). Honolulu.

HAWAII NIKKEIJIN RENGŌ KYŌKAI
1964 *Hawaii Nihonjin iminshi* (A history of Japanese Immigrants in Hawaii). Honolulu.

Hawaii Shimpō
1906 *Hawaii Nihonjin nenkan* (Hawaiian-Japanese Annual). Honolulu: Hawaii Shimpō.

Hawaii Times
1955 *Hawaii Times sōkan 60 shūnen kinengo* (The *Hawaii Times* 60th Anniversary, 1895–1955). Honolulu: *Hawaii Times*.

HAYASHI, SABURŌ
1909   *Hawaii jitsugyō annai* (An introduction to business activities in Hawaii). *Kona Hankyō sha.*

HIDARIKATA, IKUKO
1982   *Yomeru nenpyō (7) Meiji Taisho periods* (The readable chronology (7): Meiji Taisho periods). Edited by Tatsuya Naramoto. Tokyo: Jiyu Kokumin sha.

KAIKOKU HYAKUNEN KINEN JIGYŌ KAI, ED.
1955   *Nichibel bunka kōshōshi (5) ijuhen* (A history of cultural relations between Japan and the United States. Vol. 5, Immigration). Tokyo: Yoyo-sha.

KATSUNUMA, TOMIZŌ
1924   *Kibi no shiborikasu [Bagasse]* (Essays about Japanese immigrants from the vantage point of a long time official in Immigration Service). Honolulu.

KAWAMURA, SHIGEHIRO
1935   *Hawaii zaijū Nihonjin gojūnen kinen shashin chō* (A photo album in commemoration of the fiftieth anniversary of Japanese settlement in Hawaii). Honolulu.

KAWAZOE, KENPŪ (Zenichi)
1960   *Ishokuju no hana hiraku* (Transplanted trees in bloom). Honolulu.
1968   *Imin hyahunen no nenrin* (A century of Japanese immigration). Honolulu.

KIHARA, RYŪKICHI
1935   *Hawaii Nihonjin shi* (A history of the Japanese in Hawaii). Tokyo: Bunseisha.

KUBOTA, GAYLORD
1979   "Gotō Katsu rinchi satsujin jiken." *Rekishi Kōron* 38(1).

MORITA, SAKAE
1915   *Hawaii Nihonjin hatten shi* (A history of the development of the Japanese in Hawaii). Waipahu: Shineikan.

MURASAKI, NAMITARŌ, ED.
1920   *Saishin Hawaii annai* (Latest guide to Hawaii). Honolulu: Hawaii Annai sha.

NEGORO, MOTOYUKI
1915   *Meiji 41.42 nen Hawaii hōjin katsuyakushi* (A history of Japanese activities in Hawaii, 1908–1909). Honolulu.

Nippu Jiji-sha
1921   *Hawaii dōho hatten kaiko shi* (Recollections of the development of the Japanese in Hawaii). In *Japanese in Hawaii*, 25th ed. Honolulu: *Nippu Jiji.*
1935   *Kanyaku Nihon Imin Hawaii Tokō Gojūnen kinen shi* (The Golden Jubilee of the Japanese in Hawaii, 1885–1935).

ŌKUMURA, TAKIE
1940–1941   *Rakuen ochiba.* Honolulu.

ONODERA, TOKUJI, ED.
1916   *Hawaii Nihonjin hatten shashin chō* (A photo album of the development of the Japanese in Hawaii). Honolulu: Yonekura Hikogoro.

OZAWA, GIJŌ
1972   *Hawaii Nihongo gakkō kyōikushi.* Honolulu: Hawaii Kyoiku Kai.

SŌGA, YASUTARŌ (Keihō)
1953   *Gojūnenkan no Hawaii kaiko* (Recollections of fifty years in Hawaii). Honolulu.

SOGAWA, MASAO
1927   *Hawaii Nihonjin meikan* (A directory of Japanese in Hawaii). Honolulu.

Sōtōshu
1978   *Sōtōshu Hawaii kaikyō nanajūgonenshi.* Honolulu: Kaikyō sōkanbu.

TASAKA, YOSHITAMI
        Holehole bushi (Plantation songs). Manuscript.

TSUNEMITSU, KŌNEN
1971   *Hawaii Bukkyō shiwa: Nippon Bukkyō No tōzan* (History of Buddhism in Hawaii: The eastward movement of Japanese Buddhism). Bukkyō Dendō Kyōkai.

TSUTSUMI, TAKASHI, ED.
1920   *1920 nendo Hawaii satō kōchi rōdō undōshijō* (An account of the labor movement on sugar plantations in Hawaii in 1920, Vol. 1). Honolulu: Hawaii Rodo Renmei Kai.

WAKATSUKI, YASUO
1972   *Hainichi no rekishi* (A history of anti-Japanese activities). Chuko Shinsho 274. Tokyo: *Chuo Koron sha.*

WASHIZU, SHAKUMA
1930   *Zaibei Nihonjin shikan* (Views on the history of the Japanese in America). Los Angeles: *Rafu Shimpō.*

WATANABE, HICHIRŌ
1935   *Hawaii rekishi* (A history of Hawaii). Tokyo: Kōgakukai Kyōikubu.

YAMAGUCHI KEN KYŌIKU KAI
1972   *Zusetsu Yamaguchi Ken no Kyōiku 100 nen.* Yamaguchi.

Yamato
        Hawaii Times (Yamato Shimbun, Nippu Jiji). Honolulu.

Table 20
A GUIDE TO THE SUGAR PLANTATIONS IN HAWAI'I (Hawaii Shimpo, 1906)

○ 布哇全國砂糖耕地名稱案內

耕地會社名稱	支配人姓名	所轄郵便局
大アフ嶋 OAHU		
Ewa Plantation Co.	G. F. Renton	Ewa
Waianae Co.	Fred Meyer	Waianae
Waialua Agricultural Co.	W. W. Goodale	Waialua
Kahuku Plantation Co.	Andrew Adams	Kahuku
Waimanalo Sugar Co.	G. C. Chalmers	Waimanalo
Oahu Sugar Co.	E. K. Bull	Waipahu
Honolulu Plantation Co.	J. A. Low	Aiea
Apokaa Sugar Co. ○	G. F. Renton	Ewa
Laie Plantation ○	S. E. Wooley	Laie
ハワイ嶋 HAWAII		
Pauhau Sugar Plantation Co.	James Gibb	Hamakua
Hamakua Mill Co.	A. Lidgate	Paauilo
Kukaiau Plantation	Albert Horner	Paauilo
Kukaiau Mill Co. †	E. Modden	Paauilo
Ookala Sugar Co.	W. G. Walker	Ookala
Laupahoehoe Sugar Co.	C. McLennan	Papaaloa
Hakalau Plantation	J. M. Ross	Hakalau
Honomu Sugar Co.	Wm Puller	Honomu
Pepekeo Sugar Co.	Jas. Webster	Pepekeo
Onomea Sugar Co.	J. D. Moir	Papaiko
Hilo Sugar Co.	J. A. Scott	Hilo
Hawaii Mill Co.	W. H. Campbell	Hilo
Waiakea Mill Co.	C. C. Kennedy	Hilo
Hawaii Agricultural Co.	W. G. Ogg	Pahala
Hatchinson S. P. Co.	Carl Walters	Naalehu
Union Mill Co.	H. H. Renton	Kohala
Kohala Plantation	Henry Deacon	Kohala
Pacific Sugar Mill †	D. Forbes	Kukuihaele
Honokaa Sugar Co.	K. S. Gjerdrum	Honokaa
Kailua Sugar Co.	C. J. Hatchins	Pohualoa
Olaa Sugar Co.	John Watt	Olaa
Halawa Plantation	T. S. Key	Kohala
Niulii Sugar Mill & Plantation	Robert Hall	Kohala
Hawi Mill & Plantation	John Hind	Kohala
Puako Plantation	W. L. Vredenburg	Kohala
Puakea Plantatiion ○	H. R. Bryant	Kohala
カワイ嶋 KAUAI		
Kilauea Sugar Plantation	F. Scott.	Kilauea
Gay and Robinson ○	Gay and Kobinson	Makaweli
Makee Sugar Co.	G. H. Fairchild	Kealia
Grove Farm Plantation	Ed. Froadbent	Lihue
Lihue Plantation Co.	F. Weber	Lihue
Koloa Sugar Co.	P. McLane	Koloa
McBryde Sugar Co.	W. Stodard	Eleele
Hawaiian Sugar Co.	B. D. Baldwin	Makaweli
Waimea Sugar Mill Co.	J. Fassoth	Waimea
Kekaha Sugar Co.	H. P. Fay	Kekaha
マウイ嶋 MAUI		
Olowalu Co.	Geo. Gibb	Lahaina
Pioneer Mill Co.	L. Barkhausen	Lahaina
Wailuku Sugar Oo.	C. B. Wells	Wailuku
H. C. & S. Co.	H. P. Baldwin	Puunene
Kaeleku Sugar Co.	J. Chalmers	Hana
Kipahulu Sugar Co.	James Scott	Kipahalu
Kihei Plantation Co.	J. Hanebreg	Kihei
Maui Agricultural Co.	H. A. Baldwin	Haiku

228

Map 5
HAWAIIAN ISLANDS WITH LOCATIONS OF PLANTATIONS, 1915
(Morita, 1915)

布 哇 地 圖

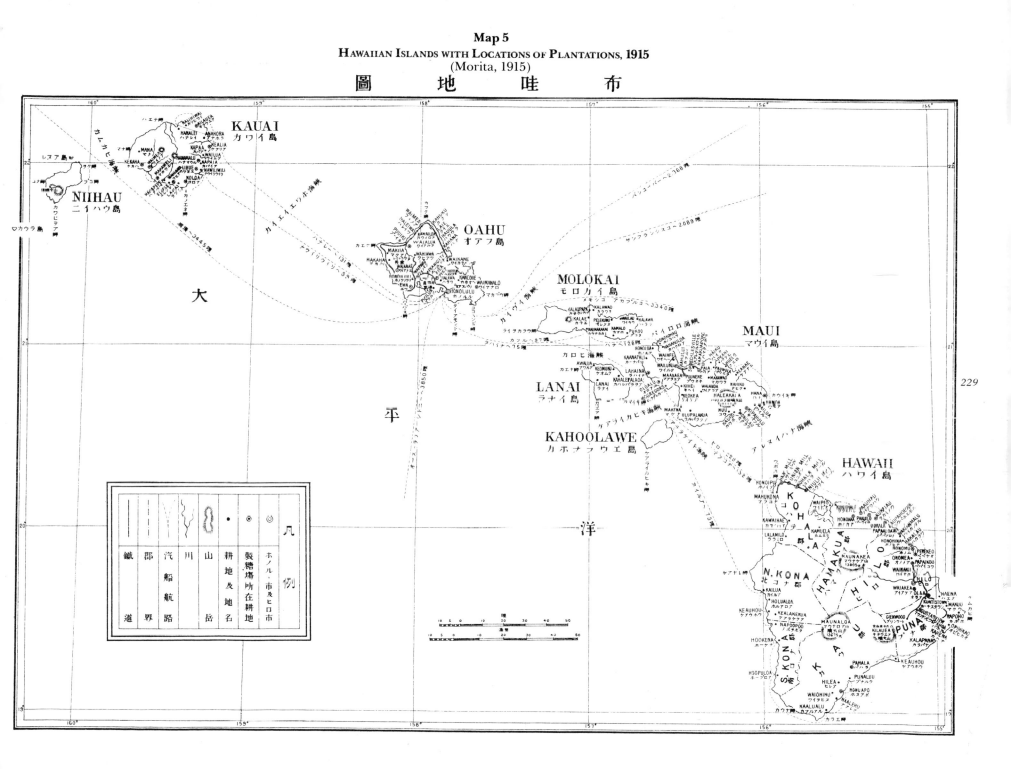